read during Lent, 1992.

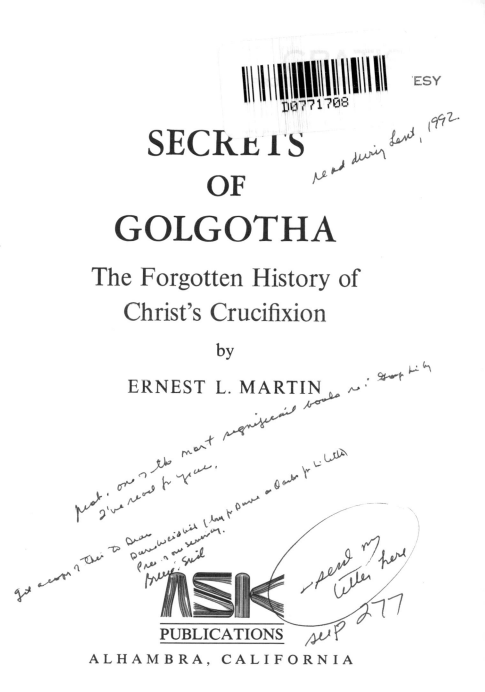

SECRETS OF GOLGOTHA

The Forgotten History of Christ's Crucifixion

by

ERNEST L. MARTIN

Great. one of the most significant books re: [illegible]
I've read for years.

Got a copy of this to Dean [illegible]
Pres. of our seminary.
[illegible]

— send my letter here

sep 277

ASK PUBLICATIONS
ALHAMBRA, CALIFORNIA

From the cowardice that shrinks from new truth,
From the laziness that is content with half-truths,
From the arrogance that thinks it knows all truth,
O God of Truth, deliver us!
— *Ancient Prayer*

A.S.K.
P O BOX 25000
PORTLAND OREGON 97225-5000
P.O. Box 7777, Alhambra, CA 91802

SECRETS OF GOLGOTHA

ISBN 0-945657-77-3
Library of Congress Catalog Card Number 88-070118

TABLE OF CONTENTS

Chapter *Page*

SECRETS OF GOLGOTHA 5
1. The Key to the Crucifixion Site 12
2. A Significant Geographical Indication 20
3. The Altar That No One Can Find 27
4. The Place of Jewish Execution 42
5. The Place of Roman Crucifixion 52
6. Where Was Calvary? 58
7. Christians and the Mount of Olives 65
8. The New Mount Zion for Christians 75
9. Visions, Dreams and Signs 93
10. The Counterfeit Golgotha 110
11. The Site of the Temple of Venus 125
12. Why the Temple of Venus? 138
13. Burial Grounds in Jerusalem 157
14. The Manner of Christ's Crucifixion 169
15. Surprising Cause of Christ's Death 184
16. The Real Jesus of the Bible 203
17. The Temple and the Trial of Jesus 221
18. Temple Rituals and the Crucifixion 236
19. Spiritual Significance of Golgotha 254
20. What Difference Does It Make? 270
EPILOGUE 274

Secrets of Golgotha

Introduction

In this book we will provide new historical and biblical information that will show where the crucifixion of Christ took place and the precise location of his burial and resurrection. Strangely, most of this information has been available for generations but it has been consistently overlooked as a means of identifying one of the most important geographical sites in the biblical revelation. The true locale has great significance in understanding the essentials of the Christian message. Its identity also goes a long way in buttressing the fundamental New Testament concepts regarding the role of Jesus in world history and it greatly illuminates the teaching of salvation as advocated by Christ. This is one of the main reasons why it is important to discover the real place of Christ's crucifixion as well as the whereabouts of the tomb in which he was buried. It is interesting that the actual tomb turns out to be in a far different area than the two popular sites which are being suggested today.

In order to locate the tomb, we must first pay attention to the general teaching of the New Testament regarding the crucifixion site. We are informed that its occurrence was outside a gate of Jerusalem and near a main thoroughfare. The area was of sufficient notoriety that the Gospel writers simply identified it (without elaboration) as "The Place of the Head (or Skull)," which in Hebrew was called *Golgotha* (and which through the Latin has been called *Calvary*). It was in a garden which had to be conspicuously prominent because the crucifixion could be seen from a distance. There was also a rock-hewn tomb near the garden in which Christ was placed after his death.

These are the general points supplied by the New Testament which have been recognized by all individuals endeavoring to identify the place of the crucifixion. The Bible, however, has given us some other significant factors which scholars have not considered and in this book we will relate what those indications are.

The simple fact is, if we knew the exact location of *Golgotha* as demonstrated by reliable historical and/or geographical texts, the matter would have been solved long ago. But herein lies the difficulty. No one is sure (at least up to now) just where "The Place of the Head (or Skull)" was situated in the environs of Jerusalem, nor is it known why the word *Golgotha* was used to identify the place. Three explanations have been suggested: 1) *Golgotha* was so named because skulls were found there; or 2) it may have been a place of execution and the reference to a skull may indicate this; or 3) some topographical features in the area might have resembled some part (or parts) of a human head or skull (either a bald rock outcropping shaped like the top part of a person's head, or perhaps it was a place where two caves gave the appearance of the eye sockets of a skull).

Up to now the majority of scholars have expressed the opinion that the word *Golgotha* probably denotes an area which appeared (or still appears) skull-like. A pair of locations have been proposed which might satisfy this conclusion. One is the present site of the Church of the Holy Sepulchre. It is supposed that there was once in the area a knoll or hillock with a bald outcropping of rock shaped like the top part of a person's head or skull. This and other factors associated with the present Church of the Holy Sepulchre appear to meet some of the requirements of the New Testament description of *Golgotha*.

The other area for consideration is north and east of the present Damascus Gate and is called "Jeremiah's Grotto" (which has no historical connection with the Old Testament prophet). This is a small hill just to the north of the bus station which has two cave-like features within its limestone escarpment. Some people have thought they look like the eye sockets of a human skull. Near the hill was discovered a rock-hewn tomb that was found to be in a garden. The site is now called the Garden Tomb. It also possesses some of the supposed geographical factors associated with the location of the crucifixion mentioned in the New Testament.

These two sites are rivals for the place of Christ's crucifixion. The preponderance of scholarly opinion favors the Church of the Holy Sepulchre as having the best credentials, but there is a vigorous minority who defend the region of the Garden Tomb. There have been other places around Jerusalem which have been suggested over the past hundred years but the two mentioned above are the only ones seriously considered today. The other sites have often had some major inconsistences in the history and/or geography associated with their identification and this has not allowed scholars to give them a favorable appraisal. For example, Dr. Barclay in the nineteenth century suggested the Garden of Gethsemane (where Christ was arrested) as the crucifixion site (*City of the Great King*, p.78*ff*), but M'Clintock and Strong noted that "his arguments are made up of the most uncritical conjectures" (vol.II,p.36). That has been the case with most of the other sites. This has resulted in scholars accepting either the Church of the Holy Sepulchre or the Garden Tomb area as the proper place, yet even here it is normal for all objective historians to admit that no definite evidence has been forthcoming to substantiate either of these locations.

The trouble is, there are numerous problems connected with both sites. As for the Church of the Holy Sepulchre, it required several supernatural experiences to discover the "place" as being that of the crucifixion. People have legitimately wondered why it was necessary in the fourth century to resort to the use of visions, dreams and miracles to vindicate the authenticity of the spot if the sanctity of the site had been consistently recognized by Christians in Jerusalem for the previous three hundred years? Remarkably, the place that was pointed out by the visions happened to be at the Temple of Venus erected by Hadrian not long after A.D.135. Even Eusebius, the church historian (who lived when the emperor Constantine of Rome selected the site), expressed surprise that the place of Christ's crucifixion was discovered at the Temple of Venus. Eusebius said it was "contrary to expectation" (*Life of Constantine* 3:28).

The selection of this Temple of Venus has been accepted by some scholars as a positive factor in establishing the authenticity of the site. This is because it has been imagined that Hadrian hated Christians so much that he erected the licentious shrine in resentment to Christians who supposedly revered the area as the place of Christ's crucifixion. But there is a major problem with this theory. While it is known that Hadrian showed utter contempt for Judaism and Jewish holy places (he built a shrine to Jupiter at the location of the former Temple), yet there is not the slightest historical evidence that Hadrian had *any* quarrel with Christians, even with Jewish Christians, over *any* of their religious convictions. Besides, there are no indications in the New Testament or second century records that there were Christian holy places in Jerusalem to desecrate in the first place. It was not until the start of the third century that we begin to witness an interest by Christians in certain "holy places" and even then there was no special efficaciousness attached to any of the sites for granting "spiritual favors" until well into the fourth century.

This does not mean that early Christians were disinterested in locations associated with the ministry of Christ or the apostles. The pre-fourth century records show that there was, indeed, *one place* in the area of Jerusalem to which Christians displayed attention for special worship [it was a most important locale that we will soon show] but *that place* was not at the site of the Church of the Holy Sepulchre (where the Temple of Venus stood) or in the region of the modern Garden Tomb.

As for the Garden Tomb itself, it has many demerits associated with it. If the skull-like appearance of the hill above the present bus station had the supposed eye socket

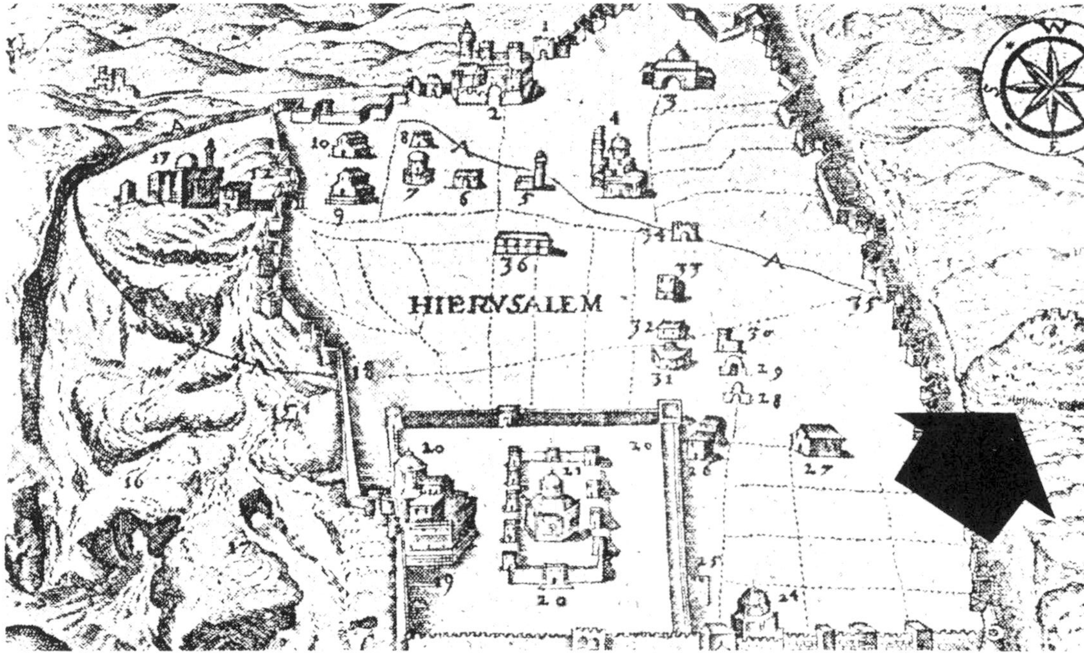

This is the A.D.1610 drawing of Jerusalem by Sandy. The arrow points to the large hill outside the north wall of Jerusalem and not far from the Damascus Gate (numbered 35 by Sandy). As one can observe there is no indication of any skull-like eye sockets (caves) associated with the hill. They were not there in A.D.1610.

features in ancient times, why is there no mention of them in early literature? Why didn't people of the fourth century simply point out the unique configuration and direct Helena to build her Church of the Holy Sepulchre in that location? The fact is, there is evidence that the "eye sockets" which were rather impressive one hundred years ago were not even there in the time of Christ (or at any other period between Christ's time and A.D.1700). When a European traveller by the name of Sandy went to Jerusalem in A.D.1610, he took time to draw a picture of some of the prominent geographical features located within and around the city. Though his drawing displays only the structures and hills which he thought significant (either *over* or *under* exaggerating their dimensions and showing a number of non-existent hills as a background fill-up), Sandy nevertheless emphasized (for some reason) the hill which presently represents the site of "Jeremiah's Grotto." Interestingly, he showed no grottos as having then existed. Had this location contained the two "eye socket" caves that were a rather prominent feature in the hill a hundred years ago, it is strange that Sandy showed nothing of them in A.D.1610. It seems evident that the erosive process that created the unique "eye sockets" only happened between 150 and 250 years ago. As a matter of fact, anyone who has visited Jerusalem over the past twenty years (as I have a score of times) is well aware that the so-called skull-appearance of "Jeremiah's Grotto" has so deteriorated in that short span of time that one can hardly recognize today any skull features at all. The truth is, "skull hill" is a modern creation that has nothing to do with the geography that existed in the time of Christ.

These difficulties have prompted some scholars to attempt new research in their quest to pinpoint the region of Christ's crucifixion. Professor W. S. McBirnie went to Jerusalem and to various academic centers in Europe with what he referred to as a "Task Force" of educated Christians to locate the tomb of Jesus. The result of their research was published in the 1975 book titled "The Search for the Authentic Tomb of Jesus." In the prologue to their book they mentioned that the team of researchers spent thousands of man hours pondering over the geological, topographical, demographical, archaeological and historical data that have been written about the subject since the beginning of the Christian era. After surveying all of this evidence, Professor McBirnie and his "Task Force" concluded that the site of the Garden Tomb had the best credentials for being the actual tomb of Jesus (though he wisely admitted that "the final proof of any location is still absent" p.14).

Though my own opinion concerning the crucifixion site has varied over the past 35 years, I came to feel (with the publication of Professor McBirnie's book) that he made a good case for not accepting the Church of the Holy Sepulchre as the true location, though his suggestion that the Garden Tomb was probably authentic remained for me a shaky conclusion. This is especially true at the present because archaeologists over the past 10 years have identified all the tombs around the Garden Tomb area (including the Garden Tomb itself) as being Iron Age creations. This means that these tombs were actually carved out of the rock about seven to eight hundred years *before* Christ (Barkay and Kloner, *Biblical Archaeology Review*, March/April 1986, pp.22-57). These new discoveries are fatal to the theory that the Garden Tomb could have been that of Christ because the New Testament clearly indicates that Christ was buried in a tomb just recently hewn from the rock.

This book, however, presents new evidence that can show the actual areas for the death, burial and resurrection of Christ. The evidence is so simple to understand that one must express astonishment that no one (as far as I am aware) has previously utilized it to ascertain the location of Christ's crucifixion. By saying this it is not my intention to censure anyone for overlooking some of these key evidences because for the 30 years previous to August, 1983 I failed to recognize them as well. But now, new information has become available that provides some simple (but significant) clues that can solve the geographical mysteries surrounding the crucifixion of Christ. With a reasonable amount of confidence, it is now possible to uncover many of the *real* "Secrets of Golgotha."

1

The Key to the Crucifixion Site

There is an event associated with Christ's death which has not been considered by most people as having any bearing on the identification of the crucifixion site, but had this one fact been recognized the actual location would never have been lost. Strangely, this simple proof has been neglected by scholars and this includes my own research for the first 30 years of my professional career. But once this evidence is realized, a new perspective is made available towards solving the geographical mysteries concerning Christ's crucifixion.

Look first at the scene of the crucifixion as described by Luke. Note carefully his account of the tearing of the Temple curtain. [For clarity's sake, quotes in this book are made directly from the original languages into English.]

> "And darkness occurred over the whole earth until the ninth hour because the sunlight failed, but the curtain of the Holy Place was rent down the middle. And with a loud voice Jesus said: Father, into your hands I entrust my spirit. When he had said this, he died" (Luke 23:44-46).

The Gospel of Matthew reverses the events involving the tearing of the Temple curtain and Christ's death.

> "But again Jesus having cried out with a loud voice, he yielded up the spirit. And, behold, the curtain of the Holy Place was rent in two from top to bottom" (Matt.27:50,51).

It is important to note that Christ's death and the severing of the curtain were regarded by the two Gospel writers as synchronous events. Once this is realized, a significant clue emerges to identify the place of the crucifixion. Pay close attention to what Luke said happened at the exact time of Christ's crucifixion. [I have emphasized certain words.]

"But the centurion *having seen* the thing *having occurred* glorified God, saying: Surely this man was righteous" (Luke 23:47).

In this account Luke lays emphasis on "the thing" that *was seen* by the centurion (note carefully that the evangelist is referring to "one thing" -- a single event -- that prompted the centurion to exclaim that Jesus was truly righteous). What was that single event? It could hardly have been the witnessing of his death because Christ's death was fully expected and represented nothing unusual to anyone. The earthquake that Matthew mentioned could not have been Luke's "one thing" because Luke doesn't even refer to that particular event in his context. The three hours darkness (probably caused by dark clouds and/or smoke, see my "The Location of the Lake of Fire" for proof) could hardly have been "the thing" causing the centurion to glorify God. Note that the darkness did not seem to disturb the other inhabitants of Jerusalem who apparently dismissed it as an event (naturally explainable) which normally occurred in the Jerusalem area at that time of the year. But something caused the centurion to recognize the supernatural origin of one event associated with the death of Jesus. What was "the thing" that the centurion viewed as significant? A careful reading of the context shows it was the tearing in two of the Temple curtain at the precise time of Christ's death.

It is this single fact that allows us to identify the general region of Christ's crucifixion. The truth is, there was only *one place* within the environs of Jerusalem where the centurion could have witnessed the tearing of the Temple curtain (and still be outside a gate of Jerusalem as the Book of Hebrews informs us). This would of necessity have been in an *easterly* direction from the Temple. The reason for this is simple to understand. This is because the Temple curtain, that could be seen from outside the Temple, was the one suspended from a large stone support (or lintel) that covered the *eastern* entrance to the Holy Place (Greek: the *naos*).

This curtain was located directly in front of the *eastern* doors to the Holy Place and only from the *eastern* side of the Temple could this curtain be seen by spectators located outside the walls of Jerusalem. It would have been a physical impossibility for anyone to have seen the curtain from the south, from the north or from the west. This means that anyone near the present area of the Church of the Holy Sepulchre or even around the Garden Tomb would only have been able to see the back walls of the Temple. In no way was it possible to view the Temple curtain hanging in front of the Holy Place from any area around Jerusalem other than from the *east*. Anyone familiar with the Temple and its entrances would recognize this factor instantly.

The Gospel of Matthew gives even more information on this matter that substantiates this conclusion.

"Again Jesus cried out with a loud voice and yielded up his spirit. And, *behold, the curtain of the Holy Place was rent in two from top to bottom,* and the earth quaked and the masses of rocks were split" (Matt.27:50,51).

Matthew then provides some parenthetical details which occurred *after* Christ's resurrection. He said that the tombs were opened and many of the bodies of the saints were resurrected. These saints then entered Jerusalem and showed themselves to individuals who had previously known them. After presenting this added bit of information which happened three days *after* Christ's death, Matthew returns to his account of the crucifixion itself. He mentions that the Temple curtain tore in two at the time of a great earthquake.

"But the centurion and the others with him watching Jesus *having seen* the earthquake *and the things occurring,* became very much afraid, saying: Truly, this was God's son" (Matt.27:54).

It should carefully be noted that not only the centurion but also those standing beside him witnessed the effects of the earthquake as well as "the things" (in Matthew the usage is *plural*, see Greek). What were these particular "things" that Matthew said were happening simultaneously with Christ's death? They were the earthquake, the termination of the sun being obscured, and also the *rending of the Temple curtain*. In fact, Matthew makes an added emphasis concerning the severing of the curtain. He calls attention to its significance by stating: "And, *behold* [that is, *look intently*], the curtain of the Holy Place was rent in two" (Matt.27:51). He wants his readers to pay particular heed to this event -- to "*look intently*" at the tearing of the Temple curtain. This rending of the curtain at the exact time of Christ's death (along with the earthquake and the ending of the sun's obscuration) were prime events of importance to Matthew. Indeed, they would have been to anyone standing amidst the scene of the crucifixion. No wonder that the centurion and the others exclaimed: "Truly, this was God's son."

What is necessary to our present discussion is the realization that these concurrent events can help us to locate the region of Christ's crucifixion. The fact that these occurrences *could be seen* from the site of the crucifixion is one of the things that the Gospel writers were trying to convey. Again this shows (since the Temple curtain could only be seen from the *eastern* side of Jerusalem) that the centurion and the others around the scene of Christ's crucifixion had to be *east* of the Temple. It also means that they had to be at an elevated area higher than the eastern wall of the Temple in order to see the Temple curtain. Thus, they were situated somewhere up the slopes of the Mount of Olives and probably near its summit.

We are provided with more information about this matter in the Gospel of Mark.

> "But Jesus having let out a loud voice died. And the curtain of the Holy Place was rent in two from top to bottom. But the centurion standing alongside and opposite of him *HAVING SEEN that he expired THUSLY* [that is, he died at the exact time the curtain tore in two], said: Truthfully, this man was a Son of God" (Mark 15:37-39).

The adverb "thusly" in the above quote shows that Mark reckoned Christ's death as contemporaneous with the rending of the Temple curtain and that the centurion was able *to see* the two events happening at the same time. It must be understood that it was not simply the death of Christ that caused the centurion to exult (because his death was quite naturally expected), but it was *witnessing* the tearing of the curtain at the time of his death.

One thing we should recognize. Drawing attention to the details of the words found in Luke, Matthew and Mark concerning Christ's crucifixion is not "straining at a gnat" or trying to make a mountain out of a molehill. These are important considerations that have long been overlooked by individuals trying to comprehend the geography of Christ's crucifixion. It is now time to begin paying attention to these details. Once we do, we will then be in a proper position to understand some of the important doctrinal and prophetical teachings of the New Testament that the real site of the crucifixion affords. The fact is, the New Testament makes it clear that the centurion and all the others around the crucifixion site *could see with their own eyes* the Temple curtain being torn in two. This curtain was hanging in front of the *eastern* portal of the inner Temple. This means that the crucifixion had to have taken place near the summit of the Mount of Olives located on the *eastern* side of Jerusalem.

It must be realized that there was no difficulty in witnessing the tearing of the Temple curtain from the Mount of Olives, which was a Sabbath Day's journey of about half a mile away from the Temple mount (Acts 1:12). This outer curtain was 55 cubits high and 16 cubits wide (over 80 feet tall and 24 feet in breadth) (Josephus, *War* V.210-214). This curtain was a magnificent creation of art. Josephus (who was an eyewitness) described it as a wonderfully made tapestry woven with the finest materials (*ibid.*). And how majestic it was! Imagine a curtain about 24 feet wide and as high as a modern eight storey building. It is important to realize how enormous in size this curtain was because one might wonder how people standing about half a mile distant could witness it tear from the top down. But when it is understood how large its dimensions were, all problems of distance vanish away.

It also ought to be mentioned that early Jewish records show that the doors of the Holy Place (in front of which this curtain was suspended) mysteriously opened of their own

This is a general view of the Temple looking directly westward into the Court of Israel, showing the circular steps leading up to the Nicanor Gate and then beyond into the grand area of the Holy Place itself. Between the two Corinthian pilasters on each side of the entrance to the Holy Place was the enormous curtain that was suspended from a stone lintel which was at least thirty feet wide and weighing about thirty tons. This curtain was the one which tore from top to bottom at the time of Christ's death on the Mount of Olives. It was perfectly feasible to view the whole of this gigantic curtain from the top of Olivet. Drawing by Norman Tenedora.

accord in A.D.30 (the year in which Christ was crucified). "Forty years before the Temple was destroyed. . . . the gates of the *Hekel* [the Holy Place] opened by themselves, until R. Yohanan B. Zakkai rebuked them [the gates] saying: *Hekel, Hekel*, why alarmist you us? We know that you are destined to be destroyed. For of you has prophesied Zechariah Ben Iddo (Zech.11:1): Open your doors, O Lebanon [the Temple], and the fire shall eat your cedars" (*Yoma* 39b).

Forty years before the destruction of the Temple in A.D.70 is obviously A.D.30. This is the year in which Christ was crucified (see my "The Date of Christ's Crucifixion" for new information which demonstrates this). Edersheim was of the opinion that the miraculous opening of these Temple doors was in some way associated with the tearing of the curtain since the doors were positioned directly behind the curtain itself (*Life and Times*, vol.II, pp.610,611). This would have to be the case if the tearing of the curtain was to show that the spiritual barriers to the Holy Place were now made redundant by Christ's death. These two doors opened inwardly and the symbolic teaching would have been meaningless had the two doors remained closed. Indeed, for the intended symbol to have any relevance whatever, the two events would have had to occur at the same time.

But how was it possible for the doors to the Holy Place to open? A Jewish Christian work of the early second century called "The Gospel of the Nazaraeans" said that the large stone lintel which supported the curtain (which no doubt had the inner doors attached to it for stability) split in two when the curtain was severed (cf. Hennecke-Schneemelcher, *The New Testament Apocrypha*, vol.I, pp.150,153). Remember that there was a major earthquake at the precise time of Christ's death and this could have been the cause for fracturing the stone lintel. There is no reason to deny the possibility that the collapse of the overhead lintel (which was an enormous stone at least 30 feet long and weighing probably 30 tons) was the "natural cause" of the curtain tearing in two. The fact that the curtain was severed from top to bottom also suggests that it was the force of the falling lintel that caused the curtain to rend. This collapse could also have been the means by which the inner doors next to the curtain were forced open. The crashing down of 30 tons of stone from the height of an eight storey building could surely have opened the two doors that were directly next to the falling stonework. No wonder Jewish people long remembered the event about the opening of the doors to the Holy Place in A.D.30.

The collapse of this lintel at the time of the earthquake (as attested by the "Gospel of the Nazaraeans") is excellent evidence that the curtain did in fact tear in two. It helps to show that the New Testament is giving *literal* information and not *symbolic* teaching alone. But even if some people might believe the biblical accounts are only *symbolic*, the crucifixion would still have to be reckoned as occurring *east* of Jerusalem. This is because anyone living in the first century and aware of the geography of Jerusalem would realize that even such a *symbolic* illustration (if that is what it was) would still demand an *eastern* aspect for the observer if the figure was to have valid geographical parameters. But if the lintel did break in two as shown by the "Gospel of the Nazaraeans," then we have remarkable evidence that the New Testament is giving *literal* teaching when the three Gospels said the curtain was severed from top to bottom.

This means the New Testament is giving eyewitness evidence that the centurion and the other spectators at the scene of Christ's crucifixion were able *to observe* the tearing in two of the Temple curtain. It then follows that the observers were situated in an elevated region that was high enough for them to view the tearing of the curtain over the *eastern* wall of the Temple. Without doubt, this New Testament evidence demonstrates that the crucifixion of Christ occurred *east* of the Temple mount somewhere near the summit of the Mount of Olives. In the next chapter more evidence will be given to show this.

2

A Significant Geographical Indication

There is another piece of evidence from the New Testament which shows that Christ's crucifixion took place on the Mount of Olives. It is interesting that this information (to my knowledge) has never been used in determining the site, yet it has an important bearing in solving the geography of the crucifixion. It concerns a topographical location mentioned in the Gospel of John. He shows that Christ was executed near an area of Jerusalem called "The Place of the City" (John 19:20). The wording of the Greek requires one to render the words as "The Place of the City" (or "The City's Place"), but many translators not realizing that a specific location in Jerusalem was intended by John, usually translate the passage: "For the place where Jesus was crucified was near the city." But this translation is not correct. The text should actually read: "Near was *The Place of the City* where Jesus was crucified" (John 19:20, italics and capitalization mine). The expression in the original has appeared so odd to some scholars in its grammatical construction that many of them have been forced to modify what John wrote. But this "oddity" is the very key to its meaning.

What was "The Place" that the apostle John intended? It can be found if one will transliterate the Greek that John used for the "Place." Utilizing the actual Greek, John said that Christ was crucified near "*The Topos* of the City." It is that "*Topos*" that must be located. And interestingly, that particular *Topos* can easily be found if we pay attention to its use in other contexts of the New Testament!

All Jewish people living in the first century knew what "The *Topos* of the City" represented. It happened to be a well-known description of the Temple at Jerusalem. The usage is found in several texts of the New Testament. Look at Acts 6:13,14 which records the activities of Stephen.

"And they brought forth false witnesses who said: This man does not stop speaking things against *The Topos*, even the Holy [*Topos*], and against the Law. For we have heard him say that Jesus the Nazarene will throw down this *Topos* and change the customs that Moses handed down to us."

In this account "The Topos" clearly signified the Temple in the city of Jerusalem. But there is more. When the apostle Paul was being challanged by the Jews in Jerusalem, they presented some specific accusations against him.

"Men of Israel, help us. This is the man who teaches everywhere against the People, and the Law, and *The Topos*, and what is more, he has brought Greeks into the temple [enclosure] and defiled *The Holy Topos*" (Acts 21:28).

Again, in these New Testament references, it can be seen that the "Topos" signified the Temple. But let us now look at the Gospel of John itself (the Gospel which contains the statement that Christ was crucified near *The Topos* of the City). Recall the conversation of the Samaritan women with Christ. She called the Temple "*The Topos*."

"Our forefathers worshipped in this mountain, but you people say that in Jerusalem is *The Topos* where it is necessary to be worshipping" (John 4:20).

Jews always considered *The Topos* as being in Jerusalem -- and that the Temple could *only* be located in Jerusalem. Christ himself acknowledged this to the Samaritan woman. But even more important to the issue is John 11:47,48. Here we have the authoritative and official pronouncements of the chief priests and Pharisees within the Sanhedrin (the Supreme Court of the Jews). In the clearest of terms they referred to the Temple simply by the name *The Topos*.

"The chief priests and Pharisees gathered together the Sanhedrin and began

> to say: What are we to do, because this man performs many signs? If we let him go his way, they will all put faith in him, and the Romans will come and take away from us both *The Topos* and *The Nation*" (emphases mine).

These scriptures show that the common designation for the Temple and its holy areas was "The Place" (i.e. *The Topos*). There was absolutely nothing strange to the Jews of the first century in using such a name for the Temple. There are a host of references from the Old Testament (both in Hebrew and Greek), and from other Jewish works as well as from Gentile accounts which show that the expression "*The Topos*" meant the Temple in Jerusalem. The phrase was also used to refer to Gentile sanctuaries throughout the world (see Kittel's *Theological Dictionary*, vol.VIII, pp.187-208 for many such references). In the middle of the fourth century, Athanasius simply called the Temple at Jerusalem "the Place" (*The Topos*) without the slightest elaboration.

> "Aliens had invaded the Temple at Jerusalem.... Aliens indeed had held *the Place*, but knew not the Lord of *the Place*.... What profit then is *the Place* to them? For behold they that hold *the Place* are charged by them that love God with making it [the Place] a den of thieves" (*Letter XXIX*, fragment).

Thus, when the apostle John spoke about "*The Place* of the City" (John 19:19,20), this was a clear reference to the Temple complex. The additional part of the phrase ("of the City") was itself a common title in the first century that referred to Jerusalem. This term "the City" was the most used term of Josephus in his abundant references to the capital of the Jews, Jerusalem.

The fact that the phrase "The Place of the City" refers to the Temple is a powerful piece of evidence that (even standing alone) will show us where Christ was crucified. Let us now return to John 19:19,20. When the real meaning of John is understood we will have a significant geographical indication showing the location where Christ died. Note that Pilate made a title and placed it above the head of Christ. John said a great number of people were able to read this title because the site of the crucifixion was near "*The Topos*" ("*The Place*") -- it happened *close to* the Temple!

"Pilate wrote a title: Jesus the Nazarene the king of Jews. Therefore many of the Jews read this title because *it was near The Topos of the City* where Christ was crucified."

John is telling us important information. Being *near* the Temple (but outside its walls) is a clue to the site of the crucifixion. Indeed, John would not have indicated it was *near* the Temple unless he saw some significance to this factor as it related to the Temple and its symbolism. He wanted people to know that Christ was crucified within the environs of His Father's House -- the place where all the sacrifices for sin were offered to God.

John also wanted his readers to understand why there were so many people able to view the crucifixion of Christ. This was because his execution was near an entrance to the Temple. Recall that it was the Passover season and that Christ was being killed while throngs of people were carrying their Passover lambs into the Temple to have them killed.

But how *near* the Temple was Christ? On what side of the Temple was he? One thing for certain, Christ was not crucified *inside* the Temple complex because the Jewish people considered the execution of criminals as in no way appropriate *inside* the sanctuary of God. As a matter of fact, the author of the Book of Hebrews gives us information that not only was Christ crucified "outside the gate" of the city, but more than that, he was crucified even "outside the camp" (Heb.13:12,13). There is not the slightest doubt that Christ's execution took place outside the city walls of Jerusalem, yet it was *near* the environs of the holy Temple. These biblical indications tell us a lot about the location of the crucifixion if we will but pay close attention to the texts.

Let us now use the argument of elimination in locating the proper site. If Christ would have been put to death on the southern flank of the Temple (to satisfy being *near* the Temple as John says), it would violate the statement in the Book of Hebrews that he was crucified outside the city because the whole southern region of Jerusalem abutting to the Temple was *within* the city. This same restriction applies to the entirety of the western area *near* the Temple because it was also *within* the walls of the city. Even if one went further westward to include the present site of the Church of the Holy Sepulchre (which was so far *west* of the Temple mount that it was even located beyond the "Second Wall" of Jerusalem in the time of Christ), this location could not be considered *near* the Temple. This one factor alone prohibits the region of the present Holy Sepulchre Church as being the area of Christ's crucifixion. This also applies to the spot where the present Garden Tomb is situated. Indeed, that site is even further away from the Temple and could in no way fulfill the description of the apostle John that Christ was executed *near* the Temple. Actually, the whole north-western area adjacent to the Temple was occupied by the fortress called the Antonia. It was not possible for Christ to have been crucified inside this fortress, which (by the way) was technically *inside* the city as well.

It might have been possible (in a geographical sense) to be *near* the holy Temple and *within* the northeast sector of Jerusalem which had no walls around it. This region had within it the Pool of Bethzatha (John 5:2) and a little further to the north on a nearby hill was the extension of the city limits called Bezetha. It was quite a populous area. Christ, however, was crucified in a garden (really, an orchard of trees) and in a region where rock-hewn tombs could be built. But both gardens and parks were prohibited in the city limits because of the odor produced by the cut weeds which came from gardens and from the dung used for fertilizer in such areas (*Baba Kamma* 82b). All parts of Jerusalem were thought to be "holy" and this included the areas adjacent to the Temple, including Bezetha. Making new tombs within the city was not allowed for such tombs were considered ritualistically impure. In the time of Christ tombs were only being permitted outside the city (and even outside the "camp") of Jerusalem. [This will be explained more fully in a succeeding chapter.]

The simple fact is, the region of Bezetha on the northeast side of the Temple was an active part of the city of Jerusalem. It was a populated area and it would have been a most unlikely region for any crucifixion. In any event, the

Book of Hebrews precludes Christ's crucifixion *anywhere* within the built-up areas of Jerusalem (whether inside or outside the walls) because the crucifixion occurred even "*outside the camp*" (Heb.13:11). But the area of Bezetha was *within* the camp (as will be demonstrated in the next two chapters). And besides that, it would not have been possible to see the curtain of the Temple from the region of Bezetha (certainly not the whole of the curtain) because the northern exterior and interior walls of the Temple would have prevented it. But, as it has been shown in the first chapter, the centurion and the people at the crucifixion site were able to see the curtain from its top to bottom. Only on the upper slopes of the Mount of Olives was this possible.

But why did the apostle John want his readers to know that Christ was crucified *near "The Topos* [The Place] of the City" which meant the Temple complex itself? Note that he did not simply say "*near* the City" (as almost all mistranslate John today). John was showing, for symbolic reasons, that Christ's sacrifice took place *near* the Temple itself. John wanted to show his readers that the crucifixion was connected with the Temple ceremonies in numerous ways. This allowed Christ to fulfill many typical features indicated in the Old Testament rituals of the Temple. With the crucifixion occurring *near* the Temple complex itself and in connection with the sacred ceremonies, the significance of Christ's sacrifice became more meaningful to the people living in the first century.

What we will discover is the fact that Christ was crucified near an altar that was an eastern extension of the Temple and located on the Mount of Olives. This particular altar of the Temple was the most important one regarding the rites of purification of not only the High Priests and ordinary priests, but this altar was also associated with a significant ritual that even purified the Temple itself. But if one asks scholars today where *that* altar was located and the symbolic role it played in the crucifixion of Christ, many will express surprise that such an altar existed at the time. Yet the Book of Hebrews informs us that it was to *that* very altar on the Mount of Olives that Christians should retreat in

Gal 2:20

order to participate with Christ in his sufferings. And true enough, *this* altar was situated "*outside the camp*" and near where Christ was executed (Heb.13:10-13). This is why it was necessary from the apostle John's point of view to show that Christ was sacrificed "*near* The Topos of the City." And indeed, this is exactly what happened. Christ was crucified not far from an important altar of the Temple (positioned "*outside the camp*") near the summit of the Mount of Olives. In the next chapter we will identify *that* altar.

Ch 1

Crucifixion site had to be where (1) the Centurion could see the torn veil, Lk 23:44f, Mt 27:50f for he saw it happen the moment X expired i.e. at the crucifixion site. Of course, he had also to be outside Jeru. This could only be fr. the East.

p. 13f describes the veil - covered the E. face of Temple suspended fr. stone lintel. 55 80' x 24' - a height ?. as an 8 story bldg. and 30 tons

p 14 on the earthquake. p 18

For this to be seen the centurion had to be on an elevated spot to look down over the Jeru walls: near the Summit of Olivet. This summit was "a Sabbath's day journey" to E.

Jewish records say the doors of Temple (in front of which the veil hung) mysteriously opened on their own. p17-18 "40 yrs before the destruction of Jeru" i.e. 30 AD. The earthquake may have fractured the lintel that fell ripped the veil fr. top to bottom. - earthquake opened the doors

The site of X's of H. Sepulchre; you could not see the rear of the temple.

Ch 2 IV Gosp says cross was at "The Topos" (19:20) - "the place of the city." The Jews living there knew "the place" - well known. Acts 6:13f, 21:28, Jn 4:20. The Topos was in Jeru, another name for Temple area. Jn 11:47-8 Same term used by Gentiles of their temples. - Where was "the Topos of the crucifixion"? where people trafficked Jn 19:19f, but close to the Temple and where people would be going & coming. John mentions that because X's death would be ... Also near the Cattle house where sin sacrifice was made. "outside the gate." Heb 13, outside the walls i.e. but close by. The ch of H. Sepul. was not "near" the Temple; so too w/ Garden Tomb. To the No. was tower of Antonia - also he was Tomb. Crucified in a garden (orchard of trees) i.e. a place that allowed for rock hewn tombs. - Both prohibited in the city

3

The Altar That No One Can Find

The Book of Hebrews has geographical information about the place where Christ was crucified yet there is hardly anyone who recognizes the significance today. This evidence should be looked at afresh because of the symbolic interest shown by the author of Hebrews relative to the site of the crucifixion. He simply states without elaboration (which indicates that all his readers were well aware of the truth of his illustration) that the offerings for sin were burnt on an altar outside a gate of Jerusalem and they were typical of Christ at his crucifixion. This is one of the principal sections of the New Testament which proves that Christ was executed outside the walls of Jerusalem. But *where* outside? Where was that altar that the Book of Hebrews has reference to? If that altar can be found, then the general site of the crucifixion can also be identified.

> "We have AN ALTAR, whereof they have no right to eat which serve the tabernacle. For the bodies of those beasts, whose blood is brought into the sanctuary by the high priest for sin, are burned *without the camp*. Wherefore Jesus also, that he might sanctify the people with his own blood, *suffered without the gate*. Let us go forth unto him *without the camp*, bearing his reproach" (Heb.13:10-13 capitals and italics mine).

The first thing that must be recognized is that a *literal* altar is being discussed by the author of Hebrews. It has been abundantly proved by Helmut Koester ("Outside the Camp," *Harvard Theological Review,* 1962 (55), pp.299-315) that the "altar" cannot be a symbol for the Lord's Supper nor is it a figure of speech for the "cross" of Christ. After all, the "bodies of those beasts" were *literal*, the "blood brought into the sanctuary" was *literal*, the "high priest" was *literal*, the sin offerings that were "burned outside the camp" were *literal*, and the fact that the priests "had no right to eat" of those particular sin offerings was also *literal*, so why shouldn't "the altar" itself be *literal*? The truth is, the altar being discussed in the Book of Hebrews was a well-known holy place to the inhabitants of Jerusalem in the time of Christ. It was a specific altar located outside the camp of Jerusalem where certain sin offerings were burnt to ashes. It will pay us to rehearse what these sin offerings were because the Book of Hebrews singles them out as symbolically referring to Christ when he became the great sin offering for the whole world at the time of his crucifixion.

There were three types of sin offerings that were killed within the precincts of the Temple, that had their blood sprinkled before the inner curtain of the Temple and then had their bodies carried out of the camp to be burned to ashes. The first category were those sacrificed for any of the priests who had sinned unwittingly (Lev.4:2-12). The second category were those for "the whole congregation of Israel" if they also had unknowingly committed sin (Lev.4:13-21). The third category (and certainly the category that the Book of Hebrews was particularly interested in) were the important sin offerings sacrificed on the Day of Atonement (Lev.16:27). The main symbolic emphasis of the Book of Hebrews to the rituals of the Old Covenant deals with Christ's fulfillment of the Day of Atonement sacrifices for sins. "But into the second [the second compartment of the Temple, that is, into the Holy of Holies] went the high priest alone once every year, not without blood, which he offered for himself, and for the errors of the people" (Heb.9:7). This happened on the Day of Atonement. The symbolic theme of this holy day continues through chapters nine and ten and is finally concluded with Hebrews 13:10-13 -- the verses we have been concerned with. Recall that priests could not eat from the altar mentioned in Hebrews. "Whereof they have no right to eat which serve the tabernacle" (Heb.13:10). Indeed, none of the sacrifices offered on the Day of Atonement could be eaten (which day, by the way, was a *fast day* in which no food of any kind could be consumed). The bodies of the animals offered for sin on that day were burnt to ashes on the altar located outside the camp. It was this outside altar that became the important altar for Christians to which they were expected to retreat to have the forgiveness of sins. Why this particular altar? Because the sacrifices on *this* altar were the prime ones which dealt with the sins of Israel and they prefigured precisely what Christ would be doing for mankind at his crucifixion.

"Wherefore Jesus also, that he might sanctify the people with his own blood, suffered *without the gate*. Let us go forth therefore unto him *without the camp*, bearing his reproach" (Heb.13:12,13).

The location for burning these sin offerings was to be "in a clean place" (Lev.4:12). Note that Moses commanded "a clean place" (singular), *not* clean places (plural). There was only one place outside the camp of Israel in the wilderness, and only one place outside Jerusalem in the time of Christ, where these holocausts were burnt to ashes. The Jewish authorities have maintained records which show the location of this "clean place" within which the altar was situated mentioned by the Book of Hebrews. They show that it was *east* of the sanctuary.

In the time of Moses the holiest region within the encampment of Israel was in front of the entrance to the sanctuary (on its *east* side). This was the area of the camp within which Moses, Aaron, and his sons pitched their tents (Num.3:38). The eastern region was also the side of the sanctuary governed by the tribe of Judah, out of whom came King David who was to give rise to the Messiah of Israel (Num.2:3). As a matter of fact, the author of the Book of Hebrews consistently used the theme of the tabernacle of the wilderness as his standard and model in showing how Christ fulfilled the Mosaic rituals. This is significant in our present discussion because there was only one entrance for people to enter the tabernacle and that was on its *east* side. Indeed, the entrances to all three compartments of the tabernacle were on their *east* sides. There was no way of entering (or exiting) any area of the tabernacle on the south, the west or on its north sides. Since the author of Hebrews exclusively used the tabernacle in the wilderness as his standard for illustration, it follows that the bodies of the animals taken outside *the* gate (note the text says *THE* gate) has to refer to the *eastern* gate of the Temple through which the priests took the sin offerings to be burnt. Dr. Hutchinson in the last century believed that this indication alone gave weight to Christ's crucifixion being *east* of the Temple (*Palestine Exploration Fund Quarterly*, 1873, p.115).

Indeed, it was the region *east* of the Temple and up the slopes of the Mount of Olives that was reckoned the holiest part of the Jerusalem area surrounding the Temple (*Berakoth* 9:5). One of the main reasons for this was because the sin offering known as the Red Heifer was killed and burnt to ashes in this area *outside the camp* (Num.19:1-22, see especially verse 9 where the Red Heifer is called a sin offering). We will show evidence in a moment that proves the place where the Red Heifer was sacrificed was exactly the same "clean place" where the bodies of the offerings referred to by the author of Hebrews were also burned "*outside the camp*."

The Red Heifer was considered one of the holiest of Israel's offerings. Its ashes were saved and periodically part of the ashes was mixed with pure water in a large container. The sprinkling of this water purified a person for a number of important ceremonial functions associated with the Temple and the camp of Israel (Num.19). It was also the means for purifying the Levites so that they could perform their functions in the Temple (Num.8:7). In order to sacrifice the Red Heifer, the selected animal was taken from the Temple through the *eastern* gate ("*without the gate*") and then led further *east* ("*without the camp*") to the "clean place" where it was killed and burnt to ashes. The early rabbis noted that the Red Heifer was taken through the *eastern* gate of the outer walls surrounding the Temple.

"There were five gates to the Temple mount: the two Huldah Gates on the south, that served for coming in and going out; the Kiponus Gate on the west, that served for coming in and going out; the Tadi Gate on the north

JERUSALEM LOOKING WEST JUST AFTER THE TIME OF CHRIST

The Temple Mount is seen with its entrances on the east. The black stripe indicates the position of a double tiered bridge (described on pages 32 and 34) which connected the Temple with the Miphkad Altar on the Mount of Olives. The Temple complex was called "The Topos of the City" and included the altar on Olivet.

that was not used at all; *the Eastern Gate* on which was portrayed the Palace of Shushan. *Through THIS [Gate]* the High Priest that burned the [Red] Heifer, and the heifer, and all that aided him *went forth to the Mount of Olives*" (*Middoth* 1:3 capitals and italics mine).

This reference shows that in the time of Christ the place for burning the Red Heifer was located *east* of the Temple *on the Mount of Olives*. This is also attested in another part of the early Jewish records (*Parah* 3:6,7). This latter section of the Mishnah also gives us further details about the roadway that led from the Temple up to the summit of the Mount of Olives. It shows that from the east gate of the sanctuary the priests constructed a causeway for pedestrians that went *eastward* from the Temple mount to a bridge which crossed the Kidron Valley onto the western slopes of the Mount of Olives. This was an arched bridge. It had pillars on the bedrock of the valley floor which went upwards to form several arches for the first tier. On top of the crowns of those arches another tier of pillars went upwards to form a second group of arches. The causeway was then built on top. The bridge was constructed in this fashion because of ritual interpretation. According to the rabbis this type of bridge prevented anyone coming in contact with bones or other contamination that might have been in the valley below and it would allow people to enter the Temple in a purified way.

The two tiered arched bridge must have been an imposing sight for it allowed pedestrians to walk *eastwards* apparently from the level of the Temple mount straight across the Kidron Valley (which was quite precipitous in this area) to intersect with the western slopes of the Mount of Olives. The arched bridge made it unneedful for worshippers to descend into the depths of the valley and then climb up a portion of the mountain on the east to reach the summit of Olivet. Conversely, people walking westward from the Mount of Olives into the Temple enclosure were afforded the same convenience. This roadway on the slopes of Olivet which led *westward* into the Temple had a special name and it is mentioned in the New Testament. It was called "The Descent of the Mount of Olives" (Luke 19:37).

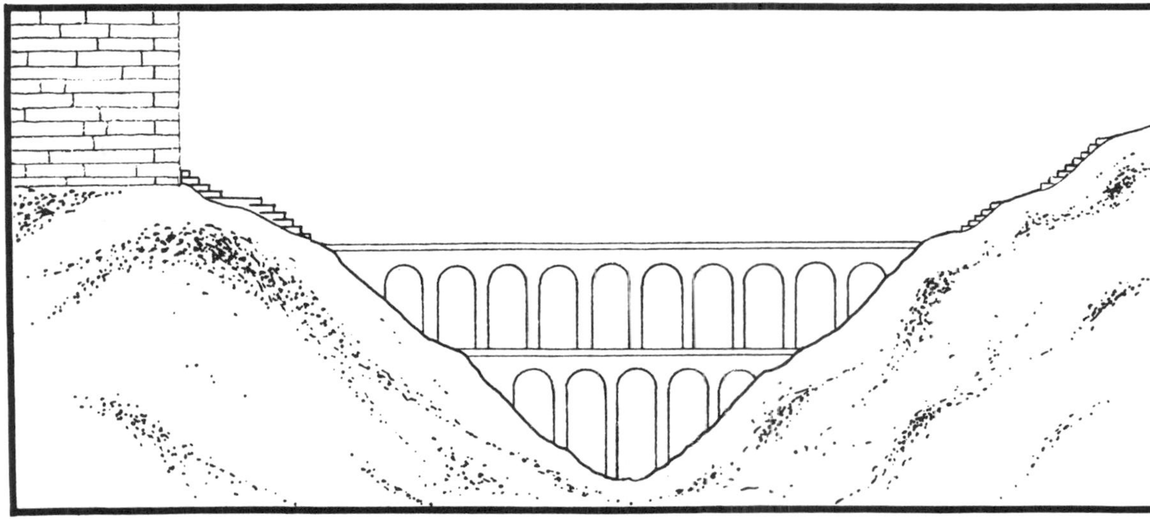

This drawing is a reasonable facsimile of the bridge across the Kidron Valley. It was two tiered with the upper pillars located over the lower crowns of the arches in order to prevent any physical contact with a bone, grave, or tomb in the valley below. The bridge connected the temple mount with the "Broadway" known as the Descent of the Mount of Olives.

Jesus must have thus approached Jerusalem on Palm Sun.

This was the holiest roadway into the Temple. Indeed, the whole area of the Mount of Olives in front of the *eastern* part of the Temple was considered the most sacred region outside the walls of Jerusalem because it faced the Holy of Holies (*Berakoth* 9:5). The holiness was further enhanced because at the top of the Mount of Olives was the "clean place" where the Red Heifer was burnt to ashes and (as we will see in a moment) where the bodies of the sin offerings mentioned by the author of the Book of Hebrews were burnt to ashes. From this summit area of the Mount of Olives one could look westward over the eastern wall of the Temple directly into the sanctuary itself. The eastern wall of the Temple enclosure was made lower than the other walls surrounding the Temple in order to allow a full view of the sanctuary interior including the curtain that was hanging in front of the Holy Place.

"All the [Temple] walls were high, save only the *eastern wall*, because the [High] Priest that burns the [Red] Heifer and stands *on the top of the Mount of Olives* should be able to look directly into the entrance of the Sanctuary when the blood is sprinkled" (*Middoth* 2:4).

This area from the "clean place" on top of the Mount of Olives westward into the Temple itself was reckoned to be of special religious significance. And while the southern and western entrances to the Temple allowed worshippers access into the unrestricted regions of the Temple enclosure, the purifying waters from the ashes of the Red Heifer could only be obtained in Jerusalem at the *eastern* entrance to the Temple and at the "clean place" on top of the Mount of Olives (*Parah* 3:11 *cf.* 3:3). Since the Red Heifer was burnt to ashes at this location on Olivet, it follows that it represented the site of origin for the main purification rituals for the people of Israel. This was understood by all Jews of the time. And indeed, this is why it was essential that Christ was crucified (to purify not only the earth but even heaven itself) near the spot where the purifications for Israel were ordained to take place -- on top of the Mount of Olives.

With this in mind, it can be better understood ~~why *this*~~

region on Olivet has great symbolic significance in relation to Christ's crucifixion. Not only was it the area of origin for the purification rituals of Israel and where the sin offerings were burnt "*outside the camp*," but it was in this general area where the greatest of all sin offerings (Christ) was sacrificed to God. [As a matter of contrast, however, the present site of the Church of the Holy Sepulchre and the Garden Tomb area *have nothing* to do with *any* Old Covenant ritual.] This site of purification is why the author of the Book of Hebrews was so interested in associating the altar outside the Temple with the crucifixion of Christ. This is because both the altar for burning the sin offerings and the location of Christ's crucifixion were near each other on the Mount of Olives.

It is important to recognize that the site of the altar for burning the sin offerings situated "*outside the camp*" was at the same place at which the Red Heifer was burnt to ashes. That the two rituals were performed *at the same place* can be shown from a discussion that took place among the rabbis just after the destruction of the Temple in A.D.70. The inquiry was in relation to this very matter. In analyzing scriptural verses that discussed the subject, Rabbi Eliezer (who had seen the Temple before its destruction) was certain that the place located "*outside the camp*" in Leviticus 4:12 (speaking about the burning of the sin offerings) was identical to the place "*outside the camp*" mentioned in Numbers 19:3 (speaking about the burning of the Red Heifer).

> "It is said here [in Leviticus 4:12]: *Without the camp,* and it is said there [in Numbers 19:3]: *Without the camp.* Just as here [in Leviticus] it means outside the three camps [of the priests, of the Levites, and of the Israelites], so does it mean there [in Numbers] outside the three camps; *and just as there* [Num.19:3] *it means TO THE EAST OF JERUSALEM, so does it here* [Lev.4:12] *TO THE EAST OF JERUSALEM*" (*Yoma* 68a, see also *Zebahim* 105b, capitals, brackets and italics mine).

This is rabbinic proof (from an eyewitness to the Temple and its rituals) that the place "*outside the camp*" for burning the Red Heifer was identical with that for burning the sin offerings mentioned by the author of the Book of Hebrews. And what is highly significant is the fact that Rabbi Eliezer (just like the author of the Book of Hebrews) applied rituals pertaining to the Tabernacle of Moses with those which governed the Temple in Christ's time.

This means that the Old Testament legislation concerning the Tabernacle was applicable to the later Temple. It was thus necessary for the priest performing the sacrifice of the Red Heifer to be *east* of the Temple so that he could face *directly west* in order "to sprinkle the blood seven times towards the Holy of Holies" (*Parah* 3:9). The priest had to be able to see the full curtain that was hanging in front of the *east* entrance to the Holy Place. This is one of the main reasons that the *eastern* wall of the Temple was lower in height than the other walls. Recall again what *Middoth* 2:4 says about this matter.

> "All the [Temple] walls were high, save only the *eastern wall*, because the priest that burns the [Red] Heifer and *stands on the top of the Mount of Olives* should be able to look directly into the entrance to the Sanctuary when the blood is sprinkled (italics mine)."

There is a further reference in the Mishnah about what the High Priest did on the Day of Atonement at this same place "*outside the camp*." It shows that the altar for burning the sin offerings was far enough away from the Temple that the High Priest standing near the entrance to the Holy Place could not distinctly make out the features of the priests who were getting ready to set the torch to the sin offering at the summit of the Mount of Olives. What must be understood in this account is the fact that it was *distance* between the High Priest in the Temple and those on the Mount of Olives which made both parties obscure to one another. I will explain why this matter is important in a moment. Note the account.

> "He that can see the High Priest when he reads [in the Temple] cannot see the bullock and the he-goat that are being burnt; and he that can see the bullock and the he-goat that are being burnt cannot see the High Priest when he reads: not that it was not permitted, but because the *distance apart* was great and both acts were performed at the same time" (*Yoma* 7:2).

This reference tells us very much. It shows that the High

Priest could not be seen distinctly because of the *distance* between the simultaneous ceremonies. The summit of the Mount of Olives is a little over half a mile from the place where the High Priest was standing. From the Mount of Olives I have tried to distinguish friends of mine among a crowd of people standing around the Dome of the Rock on the Temple mount, and though my friends could be seen, it was not possible to identify them individually. And so it was with the priests on top of the Mount of Olives. The High Priest was just a little too far away to distinguish him clearly.

Now why is it important to recognize that the early Jewish records show the altar for burning the sin offerings on the Day of Atonement was *directly east* of the Temple? The reason is because of an opinion among some Jews in the fifth century of our era that the "clean place" for burning the sin offerings was located *north* of the Temple (see *Yoma* 68b and Tosefta *Kippurim* 3:17). But this opinion could in no way be correct because it contradicts the eyewitness account of Rabbi Eliezer that in Temple times the place was *east* of Jerusalem (*Yoma* 68a; *Zebahim* 105b). The Mishnah also shows that the priests *"outside the camp"* were able to look *directly west* and see the High Priest in the interior of the Temple (*Yoma* 7:2) and this would have been impossible if the priests were situated north of the Temple. Besides that, the outer northern wall of the Temple was higher than the eastern wall and this would have prevented anyone north of the Temple from observing much of the activities even in the outer part of the Temple. But fatal to the theory that the sin offerings were burnt north of the Temple is the fact that the Temple's north wall itself totally obscured the ground level of the courts inside the Temple where the High Priest had to perform his rituals. The reason some rabbis of the fifth century began to say the "clean place" was in the north (erroneously so) will be explained in chapter twelve.

There can actually be no doubt that the "clean place" for burning the sin offerings on the Day of Atonement as well as the Red Heifer sacrifice was located *directly east* of the Temple. It was a permanent site called the *Beth ha-Deshen* (the House of the Ashes) where also the "ashes are poured out" from the animals consumed on the altar of burnt offering in the Temple (Lev.4:12). Some of the later rabbis understood that it was apparently situated on the slope of a hill (*Yoma* 68b). Since Rabbi Eliezer said that in Temple times this area was *east* of the Temple, it must have been on a slope of the Mount of Olives and being on a slope it may mean that it was located just to the west of the summit itself.

In this place was the altar for burning the sin offerings which the Book of Hebrews said was "*outside the camp*." It had a special name attached to it. As far back as the sixth century B.C. the prophet Ezekiel, in describing his ideal Temple, called this altar outside the Temple by the title *Miphkad*. Note Ezekiel 43:21.

"Take the bullock of the sin offering, and it shall be burnt at the *Miphkad* belonging to the house [a building] *outside* the sacred area."

Note that Ezekiel located this altar *outside* the actual Temple. It was positioned inside "the house" (Hebrew: *ha-Beth* and in the Talmud it was called *Beth ha-Deshen*, the House of the Ashes). The name *Miphkad* associated with this altar tells us that it was a place of "the Muster" (Numbering or Census). The word *Miphkad* is sometimes mistakenly rendered "appointed place," but it is the untranslated word that should be retained in Ezekiel. The actual meaning of the word is "Numbering Place" or "the Place of the Muster."

The location of the *Miphkad* (and the altar for burning the sin offerings which was in "the house") is most important regarding the matter of the crucifixion because the Book of Hebrews identifies it as the area of the altar associated with Christ's death. Strangely, the majority of biblical scholars seldom mention that such an altar existed in the time of Christ or that it had a major part to play in the Temple worship at Jerusalem. But the altar at the *Miphkad* was as holy and significant as was the Altar of Burnt Offering in the outer court of the Temple and the Golden Incense Altar within the Holy Place. The author of the Book of Hebrews, however, said that this *altar* had real Christian symbolism attached to it and that it was the one located "*outside the gate*" and "*outside the camp.*" He advised all Christians allegorically to go out to Christ at that altar. What is important to realize is that the Book of Hebrews is referring to a *literal* altar which was well known to the people of Jerusalem in the time of Christ. And where was it located? Without doubt, that altar for burning the sin offerings to ashes was situated on the Mount of Olives. It was the altar at the *Miphkad* mentioned in Ezekiel 43:21.

This *Miphkad* area was directly *east* of the *eastern* entrance to the Temple. There is further evidence to prove this. In the time of Nehemiah there was an *eastern* gate of Jerusalem known as "the Miphkad Gate" (Neh.3:31). Prof. Mazar in his excellent book *The Mountain of the Lord* shows that the Miphkad Gate was no doubt a part of the Temple (p.199). It was positioned within the eastern wall just south of what Nehemiah called the "going up (ascent) of the corner" (Neh.3:31). Nehemiah's "corner" of the wall was most likely the northeast angle of the Temple enclosure. Thus, the Miphkad Gate had a roadway through it which led up to the top of the Mount of Olives where the sin offerings were burnt. This can easily be shown. It was common in Jerusalem to refer to the various gates of the city by the names of areas toward which the roads were leading. The Damascus Gate, for example, was the northern gate of Jerusalem through which passed the road that led to Damascus. The Jaffa Gate led to the port city of Jaffa. The Dung Gate led to the area for dumping refuse, etc. Thus, the Miphkad Gate mentioned by Nehemiah was so named because it led to the *Miphkad Altar* on the summit of Olivet.

It should be recalled that there was a roadway that left the Temple mount *eastwards* across the Kidron Valley (via the two-tiered arched bridge) and then it led up the slopes to the summit of the Mount of Olives. This is where the building (the house) containing the *Miphkad Altar* was located. Thus, the fact that Nehemiah called this *eastern* portal "the Miphkad Gate" is a prime indication that the roadway through it led to "the Miphkad Altar."

Let us remember that the New Testament tells us of only one *eastern* gate which it called "the Gate Beautiful"

(Acts 3:2). This was probably the Miphkad Gate of Nehemiah which simply had the descriptive name "Beautiful" in the time of the apostles. If one transliterates the New Testament name of the gate, it becomes "the Gate Horaia" -- signifying (besides "Beautiful") the Gate of the Seasons. In Greek literature it can refer to the gathering of fruits in due season, to render sacred offerings in the proper seasons (fruits and/or animals). Since the Gate Horaia was associated with the *eastern* side of the Temple, it makes perfectly good sense that it was so named because it was the main gate used by the people to present their proper (and seasonable) offerings to God in the Temple. The Old Testament made it plain that certain types of sin offerings had to be taken out via this *eastern* gate to the *Miphkad Altar* for burning, while other offerings were brought into the Temple through this gate.

Another name for this *eastern* portal was the Shushan Gate because of the decorations that Nehemiah placed on the outside of the gate, and it is so named in the early Jewish records (*Middoth* 1:3). Nehemiah was so thankful that the Persian king had allowed him to rebuild the walls around the city of Jerusalem that he decorated this *eastern* entrance with a motif resembling aspects of the capital city of the Persians. To the *east* of this gate was the market for sheep, cattle and other offerings (Alfred, *New Testament for English Readers*, p.667). Just further to the east were the shops belonging to the sellers of necessary things for the sacrifices of purification at the Temple (Jeremias, *Jerusalem*, p.48; see also Midrash Rabbah, *Lamentations* II.2.4). This is the very region where Nehemiah said the Temple servants and merchants lived (Neh.3:31).

It is perfectly reasonable that the Seasonal Gate was also the Miphkad Gate of Nehemiah (which he designed with Persian decorations). What is important to our discussion is the fact that the Mishnah (in *Middoth* 1:3) states that this was the *eastern* gate through which the sin offering of the Red Heifer was taken from the Temple up to the summit of Olivet in order to be burnt to ashes. It certainly has to be the same gate that the author of the Book of Hebrews referred to. As the bodies of the sin offerings were carried through this gate, he reminded Christians that Christ in similar fashion "suffered *without the gate*" (Heb.13:12) and that all Christians should symbolically retrace his steps and "go forth unto him *without the camp*, bearing his reproach" (Heb.13:13). To do this, Christians symbolically had to go *eastward* from the physical Temple at Jerusalem, pass through the *eastern* gate, go over the two-tiered arched bridge, and proceed on to the summit of the Mount of Olives for the forgiveness of their sins. Why to Olivet? Because not far from the *Miphkad Altar* (the altar where purification for sins were dealt with) was where the greatest sin offering of all time was sacrificed to purify all people in the world.

In concluding this chapter, it should be mentioned that the *Miphkad Altar* and the sin offerings which were sacrificed on it was really a cardinal part of the Temple complex that existed in the time of Christ. This altar was not one with a ramp leading up to a square elevated area, but it is described in the Mishnah as a pit in which animals could be burnt to ashes (*Parah* 4:2). The *Miphkad Altar* was located *outside* the walls of the Temple (as Ezekiel 43:21 states), but the roadway leading up to the altar (and including the altar itself) were part of the ritualistic furniture associated with the Temple services. This is important to realize because the apostle John said that Christ was crucified "near *The Topos* [the Temple] of the City" (John 19:20), and indeed, Christ was crucified near the *Miphkad Altar* (which was a part of the Temple furniture associated with the ceremonial rituals at Jerusalem). He was executed in a locale where the Temple curtain on the *east* side of the Holy Place could be seen by all people at the scene. Thus, we find that Christ was crucified in the holiest area surrounding the city of Jerusalem (*Berakoth* 9:5). It happened on the *east* side of the city near the summit of the Mount of Olives.

4

The Place of Jewish Execution

One of the principal teachings of the Book of Hebrews concerning the crucifixion of Christ is to make it clear that he was executed "*without the gate*" and even "*without the camp*" (Heb.13:10-13). This fact is fundamental to the whole issue of trying to discover the site of the crucifixion because Moses made it clear that those deserving the death penalty had to be killed "*without the camp*" of Israel (Num.15:35,36). In the time of Christ, the Jewish authorities had determined the limits of the camp surrounding the city of Jerusalem. These outer boundaries of what were considered the city limits of Jerusalem were known by the Jews who lived at that period. If we can determine what those outer limits of the camp were when Christ was crucified, then it will help us in finding the place of the crucifixion. This is because it is certain that Christ could not have been executed *within* the boundaries of the camp. This is what the Book of Hebrews tells us. Somewhere *outside* those limits of what the Jewish authorities considered the "encampment" at Jerusalem was the place of the crucifixion.

The early Jewish records show that there were *three* camps surrounding the Temple and the city of Jerusalem. The first camp was that of the priests which was located within the inner Temple. This corresponded to the area of the Altar of Burnt Offering and the Holy Place of the Temple which included the Holy of Holies. The second camp was that of the Levites and it comprised the entire area of the Temple mount and it included all of the Temple itself outside the inner courts which belonged to the priests. The third camp was the region around Jerusalem in which ordinary Israelites from the other twelve tribes could have their residences. This camp of the Israelites was located on all four sides of the Temple mount surrounding the sacred enclosure itself. It will pay us to read what the early Jewish records in the Talmud have to say about the positioning of these *three* camps.

"Just as there were *three* camps in the wilderness, so there was a camp in Jerusalem. From Jerusalem to the Temple mount was the camp of the Israelites; from the Temple mount to the Gate of Nicanor [the east gate of the inner Temple court] was the Levitical camp; beyond that was the camp of the *Shechinah*, and that corresponded to [the place within] the curtains in the wilderness" (*Zebahim* 116b brackets and italics mine).

Now note this point carefully. On the *east* side of the Temple mount [that is, directly *east* of the Levitical camp] there were no walls encompassing the city of Jerusalem. The third camp of the Israelites on the *east* side of the Temple mount extended *eastward* over the Kidron Valley and up the slopes of the Mount of Olives to a boundary almost near the summit of Olivet. There were no walls on the Mount of Olives which enclosed this *eastern* section of the camp of the Israelites in the city of Jerusalem. The reason for this is simple. Since the slopes of the Mount of Olives facing the Temple mount were considered the holiest region surrounding Jerusalem because this area faced the Temple itself (*Berakoth* 9:5), it was not permitted in the time of Christ for ordinary residences of the Jews to be built in this quarter. This region was reserved only for the necessary activities associated with the ritualistic functions of the Temple.

And now to an important point. When the early Jewish scholars wrote about the limits of the camp of the Israelites surrounding the Temple mount in the time of Christ, they said there were "gates" into the camp of Israel. Jews had to pass through these "gates" before a person would reach the Temple mount (the camp of the Levites) (Midrash Rabbah, *Numbers* VII.8). True enough, there were "gates" on the *east* side of the Temple mount into the camp of Israel but these "gates" were not found in walls made of stone because there were no walls near the summit of Olivet enclosing the camp of the Israelites. These "gates" were the same type of "gates" that existed in the outer boundaries of the camp of Israel when they were in the wilderness in the time of Moses (Exo.32:26,27). Yes, there were "gates" into the camp of Israel but as in the time of Moses these were not "gates" like those found in stone walls. There were no walls of any kind surrounding the camp of Israel when the Israelites were encamped in the wilderness. The "gates" mentioned in the Midrash of the Book of Numbers were simply designated "entrance" ports into the area in which the tribes of Israel pitched their tents. And so it was in the time of Christ. Near the summit of the Mount of Olives (and slightly down the western slope of the mount) was what was called the *eastern* "gate" into the camp of Israel. This entry point commenced the *eastern* city limits of Jerusalem. From this boundary one could walk down "The Descent of the Mount of Olives" (Luke 19:37) and then over the two-tiered arched bridge directly through the *eastern* gate of the Temple into the region called "the camp of the Levites." Thus, the area from the *eastern* wall of the Temple mount up to near the summit of Olivet represented the *eastern* part of the camp of the Israelites. And situated just *east* of this *eastern* boundary of the camp was the "clean place" called the *Miphkad* in which was the altar on which the sin offerings and the Red Heifer were burnt to ashes. The reason it was located here is because Moses had commanded that this spot had to be "*without the camp*" (Lev.4:12).

How far *east* of the sanctuary was the "clean place" called the *Miphkad*? It was just beyond 2000 cubits. What was the length of a cubit? This question has been much disputed and no one can be certain of its exact length in any given circumstance. But there is an eighth century B.C. inscription which King Hezekiah placed at the terminus of a tunnel he had his engineers dig underneath the city of Jerusalem. It states that the length of the tunnel was 1200 cubits. By modern measurement this works out to 17.49 inches for each cubit and this length should be considered close to the normal reckoning. This means that a span of 2000 cubits answers to just under 3000 of our feet today.

But why 2000 cubits? It was determined that the

"place" of a person's residence could extend outward 2000 cubits from his central "place" of abode. If, for example, one lived in a tent in the desert, one could consider his "place" as extending 2000 cubits from the tent itself. If one lived in a town with walls around it, then his "place" was reckoned as being 2000 cubits from the walls because the whole of the town was looked on as a corporate "place." This reckoning was arrived at by noting that there were about 2000 cubits between the Ark of the Covenant [where God symbolically resided] and the rest of the Israelites while they were on their march toward the holyland (Josh.3:4). From this it was determined that God considered his own "place" (or residence) as having an extension of 2000 cubits from the Holy of Holies wherein was supposed to be the Ark of the Covenant. Similarly, each of the Levitical towns was allowed 2000 cubits surrounding its walls as being their "city limits" (Num.35:5,6).

A derivative of this allowance was called a "Sabbath day's journey." In this case, it was permitted to walk up to 2000 cubits on the Sabbath (either from one's tent if in the desert or from one's city walls if in a town). In the case of a "Sabbath day's journey," the rabbis agreed that 2000 cubits should be marked off from the east wall and the same for the other three cardinal directions. Later rabbis thought that a perpendicular line could then be drawn both to the left and right of this 2000 cubit marker to intersect with the lines from the other three directions thus making a square area around each town within which people could walk on the Sabbath (taking advantage of the corners which, of course, would have been slightly more than 2000 cubits from the city walls) (*Erubin* 4:8; 5:1). But the limits of the "encampment" were accounted by the Sanhedrin differently. The 2000 cubits were reckoned as a radius encircling the court of the Sanhedrin (*Rosh ha-Shanah* 2:5, see also *Sanhedrin* 1:5 and *Shebuoth* 2:2 for the authority of this Jewish Supreme Court to set these limits of the camp). In chapter 17 we will show that the Sanhedrin was located on the Temple mount in Christ's time.

Though the "Sabbath days' journey" was a similar reckoning of 2000 cubits, its designation was from the walls of

Jerusalem and the perimeter was in the shape of a square (not a circle) in order for people to take advantage of the corners. But in the measurements of the "camp," there were 2000 cubits as a radius encircling the Sanhedrin on the Temple mount, so the outer limits of the "camp" were just shy of the summit of the Mount of Olives. And that is the exact spot where the Jewish authorities located the "clean place" (the *Miphkad Altar*) at which the sin offerings and the Red Heifer were burnt to ashes. It was necessary that this area for burning the sin offerings be positioned *directly east* of the sanctuary and "*without the camp*." This was also close to the "Sabbath days' journey" boundary because the Book of Acts tells us that the Mount of Olives was a "Sabbath days' journey" away from Jerusalem (Acts 1:12). This is just a further indication that the summit of Olivet was just over 2000 cubits (about 3000 feet) from the Sanhedrin on the Temple mount.

But what has all of this to do with the official Jewish place of execution? It has very much to do with it because the regulations of the Mosaic law demanded that all executions of criminals take place "*without the camp*" (Num.15:35,36). The early Jewish records within the Mishnah indicate that in the time of Christ there was "the place" for execution (and in the Old Testament legislation this was the place of stoning). This "place" was well known because the records speak of judicial matters that occurred at designated distances away from "*the* place" (*Sanhedrin* 6:1-4). Where was this "place" of execution?

One thing for certain, the Jewish place of execution had to be "*without the camp*" (at least 2000 cubits away from the sanctuary) and this absolutely prohibits the present Church of the Holy Sepulchre or the Garden Tomb area from being the location of Christ's crucifixion, because both of those sites were *within* the 2000 cubits' zone. They were *not* outside the camp! The region where this *one* place of execution was located is not difficult to determine. What we must do is pay attention to the biblical and historical records about Jewish affairs regarding such matters. It will be easy to discover the general area for Jewish executions for those who had committed capital crimes.

Let us note an important ritualistic principle that dominated Jewish thought in the time when the Temple was in existence. It was that all *unclean* things associated with the Temple, with Jerusalem or with the people of Israel (whether of animals or human beings) had to be disposed of *east* of sacred areas. Recall that the sin offerings killed in the Temple had to be taken *east* to the *Miphkad Altar* for burning to ashes (Lev.4:1-21). The bullock and the goat (both sin offerings) which were sacrificed on the Day of Atonement had to be taken *east* to the same altar and burnt into ashes (Lev.16:27). Even the live goat (the scapegoat) was led by a fit man into the wilderness *east* of Jerusalem (Lev.16:20-22). The sin offering called the Red Heifer was also burnt to ashes at the *Miphkad Altar* which, of course, was *east* of the Temple and Jerusalem. Even the ashes of all the sacrifices offered at the Altar of Burnt Offering in the Temple itself had to be taken *east* to the same "clean place" at the *Miphkad Altar* (Lev.4:12). Ashes to the early Jews were a symbol of sorrow and repentance and these had to be deposited *east* of Jerusalem in the area where the main animals bearing the sins of Israel were also burnt to ashes.

There was a definite reason why these things representing "sin" and "sorrow" had to be taken *east.* That is because all things reckoned to be "unclean" were placed *east* of the holy city. In the recently discovered "Temple Scroll" found in the Dead Sea area there was a general reference that "unclean" persons who lived near the ideal city of God had to live at designated places *east* of the city.

"And you shall make three places *to the EAST* of the city, separated one from another, into which shall come the lepers and the people who have discharge and the men who have had a nocturnal emission" (Yadin, *The Temple Scroll*, p.173).

These "unclean" persons had to live "*without the camp*" and on its *east* side (*ibid.*,p.174). Indeed, Josephus (who was a priest who lived while the Temple existed) said that "persons afflicted with gonorrhoea or leprosy were excluded from the entire city [of Jerusalem]" (*War* 5:227). And in *Antiquities* 3:261 he said that Moses "banished from the city alike those afflicted with leprosy and those with gonorrhoea." And in the "Temple Scroll" it states that lepers must be kept out of the Temple city. It was necessary for them to reside "*east* of the city" (Column 46:16,17).

There was a special reason why such "unclean" persons had to be kept *east* of the Temple. Professor Yadin provides the answer. "There can be no doubt that the stress that lepers were to be isolated in a separate place *east* of the Temple city was prompted by the belief that this disease was contagious and was carried by the wind. Since the prevailing winds in Jerusalem are westerly, the areas *east* of the city, particularly the eastern slopes of the Mount of Olives facing the Dead Sea, would have been considered least likely to endanger the people in the Temple and city of Jerusalem" (*The Temple Scroll*, p.177). Yadin gave proof of this from an early Jewish commentary on the Scripture. In the Midrash, Leviticus Rabba 16 it says:

> "Rabbi Yohanan said: One is not permitted to pass within four cubits *to the east* of a leper. Rabbi Simon ben Lakhish said: Within a hundred cubits. There is no contradiction. The one who said within four cubits meant when there is no wind blowing; and the one who said within a hundred cubits meant when there is a wind blowing."

Yadin reports that in the Baba Batra 3:9;13 of the Palestinian Talmud more evidence of this principle is found: "Rabbi Mana would walk with people afflicted with boils. Rabbi Abbaya said to him: Do not walk *east* of him, but rather to the west of him."

Yadin's observations on this matter are very interesting because he also calls attention to the New Testament reference that Jesus two days before the Passover stopped off at the village of Bethany on the *eastern* side of Jerusalem at the home of a leper: "And while he was at Bethany in the house of Simon the leper, as he sat at table..." (Mark 14:3). Yadin makes the point that this account is important to the matter at hand because the village of Bethany was situated on the *eastern* side of Jerusalem and even on the *eastern* slope of the Mount of Olives. According to Yadin, this is clear proof that lepers lived *east* of Jerusalem in the time of Christ. This New Testament indication fits the pattern of placing "unclean" things *east* of the Temple and the city of Jerusalem.

But what does this factor have to do with the crucifixion of Christ? Very much indeed! It means that the place of execution for murderers and blasphemers had to be "*outside the camp*" but in an area that would not affect the sacredness and purity of the Holy City of Jerusalem. All "unclean" things (including the major sin offerings ordained of God) were sent out *eastward* of the Holy City and the Temple itself. In actual fact, in the theological thinking of the Jewish authorities in the first century, it was determined that each person who committed a capital crime and was executed for his criminal act was reckoned as being a *sin offering* to himself. It was believed that no animal could take the place of such a heinous person but that he (or she) had to be a *sin offering* himself (or herself) for the sins that had been committed. "May my death be an atonement for all my sins," said the one being executed (Cohen, *Everyman's Talmud*, p.317). In simple terms this meant that no animal sacrifice for sin could act as a substitute for the person but that the individual had to be *his own* sin offering to atone for the terrible sins that had been done. The animals that were burnt "*outside the camp*" as sin offerings provided the example for a human who was also executed as his own sin offering "*outside the camp*" (See *Sanhedrin* 42b and especially 52a). The two "offerings" were considered analogous.

The reason this point is important to our present discussion is the fact that all animal sin offerings that were consumed "*outside the camp*" were offered to God *east* of the Temple near the summit of the Mount of Olives. And since all judicial executions were considered the judgment and wrath of God upon the wrongdoer, such executions were accomplished in the "presence" of God, that is, on the side of the Temple that God faced (its *east* side) when his people were brought before him to be judged. It is important to realize that each time in the scripture that the phrase "*before the Lord*" is used in connection with the Tabernacle or the Temple it means that the people or the occasion were always located on the *east* side of the holy sanctuary. Since the sanctuary was considered the house (or palace) of God on earth and the mercy seat in the Holy of Holies was reckoned as the throne of God, he was always depicted as sitting on his throne facing *eastward* where all the entrances of the Tabernacle were situated.

When Israelites approached God for worship and even for judgment, they were always coming before him on the *east* side of the Holy of Holies (never on the south, west or north of the Holy of Holies because there were no entrances to the inner sanctum on those sides). This is why the three main courts of the Tabernacle only had entrances on their *east* side. And in the time of Christ the three main judicial courts of Israel to dispense the judgments of God to the people were located within the Temple on its *east* side (Cohen, *Everyman's Talmud*, pp.300-302; Mishnah *Sanhedrin* 11: 2 and *Middoth* 5:4). This allowed all judgments to be given "*before the Lord*" (that is, in the presence of "God's face"). And indeed, even the sentences of those judgments were also expected to be carried out "in the presence of the Lord." This principle is even found in judgments recorded in the New Testament: "he shall be tormented with fire and brimstone *in the presence* of the holy angels, and *in the presence* of the Lamb" (Rev.14:10). It was common to expect judicial decisions by the courts to be given by God as people came *before* him, that is, on the *east* side of the Temple. Women who were accused of adultery were brought "*before the Lord*" (to the *east* entrance to the sanctuary) for judgment (Num. 5:16-31). When the two sons of Aaron were judged for offering strange fire "*before the Lord*" they were judged and punished on the *east* side of the sanctuary (Lev.10:1-7). When Korah and his Levites were punished it was on the *east* side of the Tabernacle (Num.16:41-50).

Even when it comes time for God to judge the world from Jerusalem, those to be judged will come "*before the*

Lord" which means on the *east* side of God's throne (Psa. 96:13; 98:9). In a literal sense this means those being judged will have to position themselves on the slopes of the Mount of Olives facing the Temple in which God will then be sitting. In actual fact, the great judgment in the Valley of Jehoshaphat mentioned in Joel 3:2,12 was acclaimed by people in the first century as referring to the Kidron Valley which separated the Mount of Olives from the Temple mount. Since the word "Jehoshaphat" means "*God judges*" it became common to believe that the final judgment for people in the world will occur on the *eastern* side of the Temple and up the slopes of the Mount of Olives. Many Jews and Moslems over the last few centuries have wanted to be buried in this region so that they might be the first of the righteous to be given their rewards when God comes to judge the world.

But what has this to do with the crucifixion of Christ? It is highly significant to it! Since the New Testament makes it abundantly clear that Christ bore all the judgments for sin and that he endured the wrath of God in place of the whole world (II Cor.5:14-21), it was necessary that Christ bear his judicial punishment in the area where "all the world" is destined to be judged. For Christ to be executed "*in the presence of God*" for the sins of the world, he had to bear those sins in the region designed by God for that purpose. This is why the sin offerings that were sacrificed by the priests were carried "*outside the camp*" to the top of the Mount of Olives in order to be burnt into ashes. This is also why the holiest of sin offerings (called the Red Heifer) was killed and burnt to ashes "*outside the camp*" at the summit of Olivet directly *east* of the Temple. It was also in this same region (but somewhat to the south, as we will see) where criminals deserving the death penalty were taken "*outside the camp*" to become a sin offering for themselves. Thus, in Christ's time, we find that the official Jewish place for execution was near the southern summit of Olivet but facing the eastern entrances to the Temple so that the evildoers would be executed "*in the presence of God*." Only an area *east* of the Temple (and Jerusalem) will fit all the requirements regarding the judicial execution of criminals.

5

The Place of Roman Crucifixion

There is a major point to help us identify the site of Christ's crucifixion that has not been applied until recently (at least to my knowledge). It concerns the Roman legal requirements for crucifying criminals. It appears that Pilate may have been legally obliged to crucify Jesus at the place of his arrest or at the place where his crime was considered to have occurred. The evidence is quite interesting and it could well have a bearing on locating the spot where Christ was crucified. The research on this matter appeared in a 1980 book *The Enigma of Jesus the Galilaean* (pp.301-305) by Nicholas Kokkinos. Mr. Kokkinos and I were speakers at a conference on the nativity of Christ which was conducted by Mississippi State University in December, 1983. The Cobb Archaeological Institute of MSU had asked Mr. Kokkinos to come from London, England (his present home) to be a panel speaker for the conference and this is where we became acquainted. Though we have similiar interests in trying to determine the time of Christ's nativity, I was especially fortunate to find that Mr. Kokkinos had done research on the site of the crucifixion. The following information from Roman and Greek sources is largely from the research provided in Mr. Kokkinos' book and from personal letters from him. Again, the evidence shows that Christ was crucified on the Mount of Olives.

What is important to the issue is the fact that Roman jurists held that convicts sentenced to crucifixion, particularly pirates or enemies of the state, must be crucified at the scene of their misdeed (*Digest* 48:9.19.28.15; cf. *Collectio Legum Nosaicarum et Romanarum*, I.6). This was the manner of crucifixion prescribed by tradition and law that had been followed through the years and it can be seen in various examples. Note some of them. "...he crucified the soldiers in the spot where they had committed their crimes" (*Scriptores Historiae Augustae* 6, Vulcacius Gallicanus, *Avidius Cassius*, 4.1*f*). Also, the proconsul of Africa punished the priests of Saturn "by crucifying them *on the very trees* of their temple, in the shadow of which they had committed their crimes" (Tertullian, *Apologeticus*, 9:2). Additionally, there is Chariton, *Chaereas and Callirhoe*, 3:4.18 which says: "A great proportion of the crowd followed Theron as he was led away, and in front of Callirhoe's tomb he was crucified upon the cross, and from the cross gazed out upon the sea *over which he had carried capitive* the daughters of Heromcrates." This shows that Theron's crucifixion was at the site of his criminal abduction. These are examples to show that it was common to crucify people where their crimes had been committed (cf. Justinus, *Epitome*, 22.7.8).

There was yet another method for selecting a spot for crucifixion. If it were not possible to return the criminal to the site of his crime, then the place where the person was arrested was viewed as proper. We find the following in the *Acts of Pilate*, IX.5: "According to the law of the pious emperors. . .hanged on the cross in the garden in which you were seized" (cf. Ps.Cypr., *De Montibus Sina et Zion*, 3; Cyril, *Catechetical Lecture XIV*, 5; *Toldoth Jeshu*, IV.20-25; also cf. *Song of Solomon* 6:11).

If, however, the crucifixion of a malefactor was not feasible at the scene of the crime or place of arrest, it was also common to select an area of *high ground* and/or *crossroads* for the execution. This was done to attract the attention of a large number of people to provide a visible deterrent to others not to commit such crimes. Since crucifixion represented the utmost form of humiliation for the criminal, his naked body had to be on public display at a prominent place. In Quintilian we read: "The crowded roads are chosen. . .penalties relate not so much to retribution as to their exemplary effect" (*Declamationes*, 274). See also *Scriptores Historiae Augustae*, 18, Aelius Lamridius. In *Alexander*

Severus, 23:8 we read: "As a deterrent to others he had them crucified on the street that his slaves used most frequently."

What is interesting in the above examples is the fact that Christ fulfilled *all* the factors for a normal Roman crucifixion. Notice first the place where Christ was arrested. This was at the Garden of Gethsemane. Just where was this garden located? Prof. J.A.Thompson has this to say:

"The site of Gethsemane is not known with certainty, although it was across the Kidron valley on the side of the Mount of Olives. There are today several rival sites for the place. The confused visitor will be shown the scene by the Roman Catholics, the Greeks, the Armenians, and the Russians. The oldest tradition places the scene [of Christ's praying] on the ground now occupied by the Tomb of the Virgin. But the fact is that we have no clear information, archaeological or historical, which will allow precise identification" (*The Bible and Archaeology*, 3rd ed. (1982), pp.359,360).

The truth is, no one knows exactly where the Garden of Gethsemane was located yet it is clear that it was somewhere east of the Kidron Valley and on the slopes of the Mount of Olives. This is made certain in the Gospels. We are told that Christ had been in the city of Jerusalem for the Last Supper (Luke 22:10). After that event he and his disciples left the city and went "across the Kidron" (John 18:1) and "onto the Mount of Olives" (Mark 14:26). They then came to the place which had been Christ's habitual rendezvous area for teaching his disciples (Luke 22:39). Or, as the apostle John put it, where "Jesus had many times met there with his disciples" (John 18:2). This place was, of course, the Garden of Gethsemane and we should note that it was certainly on the Mount of Olives (Luke 22:39).

But where on the Mount of Olives was the Garden of Gethsemane? No scholar today has the slightest idea where it was! We only have traditional beliefs available which were determined in later centuries and no one can be certain if any of them is reliable. As a matter of fact, Peter the Deacon's description of the holy places puts it near the summit of Olivet and not far from the burial site of Stephen (Wilkinson, *Egeria*, p.185). This reference makes the arrest of Christ to be higher up the mount than most think today.

Whatever the case, the New Testament shows that Christ was taken into custody on the Mount of Olives and one of the customs of the Roman government was to crucify a criminal at the place of his arrest. Gethsemane was even the scene of a "crime." Christ always forbad the carrying of weapons by his disciples (Luke 22:36), but at the time of his arrest he specifically commanded that his disciples have at least two swords in their possession (Luke 22:38). The reason for this was to make Christ appear as though he were indeed a "criminal" (Luke 22:37). Thus, the Garden of Gethsemane became "the scene of a crime" -- a crime of sedition against the constituted authorities.

If Pilate followed one of the Roman rules for crucifixion, he would have executed him near the area of arrest. We are told by the Gospel accounts that Christ was killed near (or in) a *garden* (John 19:41). Was this the same *garden* as the Garden of Gethsemane because the identical Greek word was used for the place of his arrest as well as that of his crucifixion? This is one of the reasons that Dr. Hutchinson in the *Palestine Exploration Fund Quarterly* (1870, pp.379-381) thought the Garden of Gethsemane could be a candidate for the crucifixion site. Kokkinos in his book called attention to the third century work *The Acts of Pilate* (IX.5) that Christ was crucified in the garden where he was seized because this was the law of the Romans. This evidence deserves serious consideration but to me the case remains doubtful. The evangelists tell us the crucifixion was at the "Place of the Head (Skull)." Why did they use this designation instead of "Gethsemane" if the two sites were identical? Also the Temple curtain could be observed from the scene of the crucifixion and this means that Christ was executed high enough up the Mount of Olives to view that Temple curtain. From this evidence alone, Gethsemane cannot be considered unless further historical or archaeological evidence is discovered to show that it was located near the top of the Mount of Olives.

There was, however, a much higher charge than sedition against Christ for having two swords among his disciples. His more serious "crime" was allowing the people to proclaim him as a king -- not just an ordinary king but the prophesied messianic king who was destined to rule over all nations on earth (including Rome). It was against Roman law for anyone to be proclaimed a king without the express permission and approbation of the emperor of Rome. And while Christ forbad the multitudes to make him a king early in his ministry (John 6:15), a few days before he was crucified, Christ did allow many of the people at Jerusalem to call him the king of Israel, and he approved of it. Notice *when* and *where* this proclamation of Christ's kingship took place.

At the time of his triumphal entry into the city of Jerusalem on what is called today "Palm Sunday," the Gospel of Mark said that as he drew near "to Jerusalem, to Bethphage and Bethany, *at the Mount of Olives*," he let the people proclaim him as the king of Israel and the world (Mark 11:1). The actual place where the triumphal procession began was at Bethphage where he mounted the donkey, and this was precisely at the southern summit of the Mount of Olives (Wilkinson, *The Jerusalem Jesus Knew*, pp.113-116). From that spot Jesus rode the animal down the slopes of Olivet along the roadway called by Luke "The Descent of the Mount of Olives" (Luke 19:37). Nearby the village of Bethphage was the *Beth ha-Deshen* (the House of the Ashes) which contained the *Miphkad Altar* (the altar where the sin offerings were burnt *outside* the regular Temple).

This means that Christ committed the "crime of treason" against Rome and the emperor by having himself proclaimed a king (indeed, the intimation of the people was that he represented the king of kings) from near the crest of the Mount of Olives until he reached the city of Jerusalem. Could *this* have been the "crime" that caused Pilate to crucify him? (Luke 23:2; John 18:37; 19:12,14,15). Since we have shown in this chapter that the Romans customarily crucified criminals where their infringements took place (or at the place of arrest), and if possible on high ground and/or at crossroads, *all these factors* were applicable for Christ on the *east* side of Jerusalem. This is just another possible reason why Pilate may have felt obliged by Roman law or custom to crucify Christ on the Mount of Olives. There would have been no reason whatever for the Romans to select a spot on the south, west or north of the city to crucify Christ. All of the activities of Christ outside the city and the Temple mount (two pro- hibited areas for crucifixions) were on the Mount of Olives. Christ actually *lived* on that mount while in the environs of Jerusalem. "By day he was teaching in the Temple, but by night he would go out and lodge on the Mount of Olives" (Luke 21:37). It was his "habitual" place for meeting with his disciples (Luke 22:39), or (as John stated) "where he many times met there with his disciples" (John 18:2). Even the village of Bethany where he sometimes resided was on the eastern slopes of Olivet (Mark 11:1).

As a closing thought to this chapter, one might wonder if the Roman rules for execution also applied to the two thieves who were crucified with Christ? No one, of course, can know for sure. It may be that they committed their crimes in different areas of the country and were brought to the capital for crucifixion. But one thing is certain. The thieves were in Jerusalem and apparently they were Jews (it was against imperial law to crucify Roman citizens). And in Jerusalem (as we have shown in the last chapter) there was only one general area in which Jewish criminals could be executed so as to be "in the presence" of God at the time of their judgment. That place was on the *eastside* of the Temple and *outside the camp*. Only at some area near the summit of Olivet could these Jewish requirements fit in a perfect manner. But we will see in chapter 17 that Christ was actually executed according to Jewish law, not Roman! Though it is interesting that even Roman requirements for execution were also met in Christ's crucifixion, we will see in chapter 17 that it was the Law of Moses that caused him to be killed.

Still, all of this shows that the crucifixion of Christ and the two robbers could justifiably have occurred near the summit of the Mount of Olives, whether by Jewish or Roman law. In the next chapter more information will be given to corroborate this fact.

6

Where Was Calvary?

In order to identify the geographical location of "Calvary" we must first realize what the word itself signifies. It is a Latin derivative of the Greek word *cranion* which means "skull." It is familiar to English readers because from it we obtain our modern word "cranium." In the New Testament we are told that Christ was crucified at a spot called "The Place of a Skull" or for short "Skull Place" (Matt.27:33; Mark 15:22; John 19:17). But whether one uses the Latin derived "Calvary" or the Greek "Skull Place," both are translations of the Hebrew "Golgotha" which can mean "head" or "skull." The word *Golgotha* is used in the Old Testament and it signifies a "skull" in two places (Jud.9:53; II Kings 9:35), the human "head" once (I Chron.10:10) and nine times it denotes "poll," that is, a *head-count* which is like our *poll* in "polling booth" (Exo.16:16; 38:26; Num.1:2,18,20,22; 3:47; I Chron.23:3,24).

If one used the word *Golgotha* as referring to a "head-count" (or, "poll"), then a geographical area by that name could mean "Polling Place." But this is not the meaning that the New Testament writers placed on *Golgotha*. They made it clear that it referred to a "skull" and that's why they called the location of Christ's crucifixion as the "Skull Place."

No one knows for certain why the designation "Skull Place" was chosen by the people of Jerusalem, but it must have been a well-known geographical area since none of the apostles thought it necessary to explain exactly where it was. Scholars have wondered over the centuries just why the place was called by this unique name. As mentioned in the introduction to this book, three general suggestions have been made: 1) *Golgotha* was so named because skulls were found there; or 2) it may have been a place of execution and this reference to the skull might indicate this; or 3) some topographical features in the area might have resembled some part (or parts) of a human head or skull (either a rounded outcropping of earth shaped like the top part of a person's head, or perhaps it was a region where two caves presented the appearance of the eye sockets of a skull).

The preponderance of scholarly opinion believes that "Skull Place" was shaped like the top part of a human skull. This means that it represented a rounded outcropping of earth which could be called a knoll or a hillock. The belief that it was some kind of hill is strengthened by the fact that Christ's crucifixion was eminently situated and could be seen "from afar" (Matt.27:55).

In this book we have been showing that Christ was crucified on the Mount of Olives far enough *east* of Jerusalem to be *"outside the camp"* yet high enough up the mountain to be able to view the Temple curtain from the site. This latter indication makes it certain that the crucifixion could not have been too far *east* (that is, over the ridge of the mountain itself) because this would have prevented the spectators from seeing the Temple curtain. The evidence makes it pretty clear that "Skull Place" must have been near the summit of Olivet and facing the Temple and Jerusalem which could be seen to the west.

Interesting enough, there is (or rather *was*) a small knoll or hillock located at the exact southern summit of the Mount of Olives and it is described by a Christian pilgrim who visited the site in A.D.333. He is known in history as the Bordeaux Pilgrim and he wrote an itinerary of his trip from Europe to the Holyland and to Jerusalem itself. He gives us valuable information about some of the important geographical areas in and around Jerusalem before major building programs were constructed by later Christians which in some cases altered the previous features of the land quite drastically. His description of the southern summit of Olivet is most instructive and it will go a long way in helping to identify the exact spot of "Skull Place" -- the site of Christ's crucifixion.

The Bordeaux Pilgrim tells us that on top of the Mount of Olives there was a *monticulus* which in Latin means "little hill" or "hillock." In his words he called it "a little hill on top of the mountain." And what is most important to the matter of the crucifixion site, is the fact that the Pilgrim also called the "Golgotha" discovered by Helena, the mother of Constantine, on the *west* side of the city (found only seven years before) as a *monticulus*. He used the same word to describe *both* sites! But note this. The Pilgrim was able to see that a great deal of building activity was progressing around and upon the *monticulus* discovered by Helena, but in contrast, the *monticulus* on top of the Mount of Olives was apparently in its natural state and free of buildings. Even modern archaeological investigations have been made on and around the "little hill" on the summit of Olivet and it was found that the site was uninhabited at the time of Christ (Hoade, *Guide to the Holy Land*, p.260). This is important to realize because Christ was crucified near a garden area (not in a built-up region) and this indicates that the spot was apparently free of buildings.

Be this as it may, what does this *monticulus* have to do with the site of Christ's crucifixion? It could have very much to do with it because the Bordeaux Pilgrim had more to tell us about this location. The Pilgrim said, to the puzzlement of scholars over the centuries, that on this "little hill" the transfiguration of Christ took place! This was a blatant geographical mistake because it is clear from the Gospels that the actual transfiguration occurred in the region of Galilee many miles north of Jerusalem. And even the Christian authorities in Jerusalem a short twenty years after the Pilgrim reported this information were assured that the transfiguration happened in Galilee and not on the Mount of Olives (Cyril, *Catech*.xii.16). Admittedly, however, some of the common people were still making the mistake of thinking the transfiguration was on Olivet as late as the time of Jerome (*Comm.Matt.*5:1).

But why the confusion? The fact is, there were several different words used in Latin to denote the crucifixion of a person. One of them was *transfigere* which meant to transfix a person with nails or some other sharp instruments. And remarkably, this word which meant "transfixiation" was one which was very close phonetically to that which meant "transfiguration." The word for "transfiguration" was *transfigurare*. For a comparison of both Latin words and how similar they are, see the Oxford Latin Dictionary, ed.1982, p.1964; also the unabridged Oxford English Dictionary, vol.XI, pp.258,259; and Merriam-Webster (3rd ed.), p.2427.

In spoken Latin (and with various Latin accents found among the pilgrims and residents of Jerusalem when the Pilgrim was there) the words *transfigere* and *transfigurare* could well have sounded similar to the Bordeaux Pilgrim. And since he probably composed his final work long after he left Palestine and without the means to apply any critical apparatus to the understanding of Palestinian geography, he could well have confused the site of the Christ's transfiguration (*transfigurare*) with that of Christ's transfixiation (*transfigere*). But even the Latin people in Jerusalem at the time of the Pilgrim were also making the mistake of thinking the transfiguration occurred on Olivet. The truth is, however, the "little hill" (*monticulus*) on top of the Mount of Olives was not the place of the transfiguration. It was the place of the *transfixiation* (the crucifixion) of Christ

There is even another historical incident that could help to show this. The Old Testament tells us that when King David was fleeing Jerusalem at a crucial time in his life, he ascended the Mount of Olives and went to a designated site on the mountain in order to worship God (II Sam.15:30). This location was at the very top of Olivet and he went to the same *monticulus* that the Bordeaux Pilgrim had reference to. In the Septuagint Version of the Old Testament, the translators called this spot "The Place of the Ros (Head)." It meant that it was the *chief* spot, or the *head* region, of the Mount of Olives. It was there that King David worshipped God. Calling this prominent spot by the word "head" has interesting ramifications. This is because the meaning of "head" is also found in the word "Golgotha." It means either a "head" or a "skull." The use of this word also signifies that this "little hill on top of the mountain" was the southern summit (the *head*) of the Mount of Olives. In the Hebrew language this highest summit of Olivet was known as the

"Bamah." It was the "high place" on the Mount of Olives and this is where King David went to worship God overlooking the city of Jerusalem to the west. It also answers to the same *monticulus* that the Bordeaux Pilgrim talked about. Indeed, this highest point on the southern summit of Olivet became known as the *Imbomon* (which comes from the Greek "*en bommo*" which means "high place" or "altar"). It is this name which has been attached to this *monticulus* on Olivet for the past 1600 years. At the present there is a small Moslem shrine built over the site.

This place was significant in the crucifixion of Christ. It was at the very top of the Mount of Olives. Would not Pilate have wanted to crucify him at the highest point of eminence in order to *heighten* his degradation in the eyes of the people? Since Christ claimed to be the King of kings, the messianic offspring of King David himself, then it would have seemed sensible to exacerbate his debasement by crucifying him at the exact spot where his father David once worshipped God when he was turned out of Jerusalem by his family and friends. It would mean that Christ was crucified stark naked "*outside the camp*" of Israel at the highest point of Olivet. There would have been no greater humiliation!

When the Bordeaux Pilgrim went to the summit of the Mount of Olives to see this "little hill on top of the mountain," he was able to observe it without any buildings covering the area. But about 50 years later, a noble woman by the name of Poemenia had a church constructed on this "little hill." She did this because she thought this was probably the area of the ascension of Christ back to heaven. Little did she realize that this was instead the very spot of the original "Golgotha" where Christ was crucified.

Remarkably, on top of Poemenia's church there was placed a great glistening cross which became the standard landmark for all people to see in the Jerusalem area (Jerome, *Comm.Soph.*,i.15). This gigantic cross was so magnificent to behold that it came to dominate all the area around Jerusalem for several decades afterwards. It could be seen for many miles by people approaching Jerusalem and it was a wonder to behold.

There is further significance to this "little hill" on the top of Olivet. It was from this region that fires were lit by the Jewish authorities in early times to signal Jews throughout the world (via a network of fire signals from mountain top to mountain top) to show when Jews should begin their yearly festivities to Yahweh. Because of this, the Mount of Olives became known as the Mountain of Light. When Brother Felix Fabri went to this very spot in the year A.D.1484 he said it was significant because King David worshipped here when he was turned out of Jerusalem. It was also the place where Christ said to his apostles to "go into all the world and preach the Gospel to every creature."

Brother Felix gave seven reasons why Olivet was called "The Mountain of Light." First, it was because its summit was the first to catch the rays of the sun each day, even before the Temple itself received the light. Secondly, it was the Mountain of Light because the lamps of the Temple always lit up the whole of its western side. Thirdly, this was the mountain where the great fire was lit by the priests for burning the Red Heifer sacrifice. Fourthly, because the church at the summit was always lit with many lights. Fifthly, the olive trees of the mountain provided the oil for the lamps in the Temple. Sixthly, a man at the top of Olivet could with the light of his eyes see the world far and wide. And seventhly, it was the Mountain of Light because it was the most delightful area to behold in all Jerusalem and gladdened the eyes of mankind (*Palestine Pilgrim Texts*, vol.VII,pp.495-499). Brother Felix could also have added, had he known this was the place of Christ's crucifixion, that this was the very spot where "the Light of the world" (John 1:9) was sacrificed to atone for the sins of all mankind.

It was on this "little hill" on top of the Mount of Olives that the Church of the Ascension was built by Poemenia with its bright and glistening cross atop. Burchard of Mount Sion (about A.D.1232) said that the site was made more appropriate for the ascension when a stone bearing the supposed footprints of our Lord as he left for heaven was transported to the spot (*Palestine Pilgrim Texts*,vol.XII,p.83). That stone can be seen today under the small Moslem shrine

Yet in IV Gosp. X [illegible] did ascend his throne: gain heaven at the cross

ascension near Bethany

which now occupies the site. Of course, the area of this "little hill" was not the actual region from which Christ ascended to heaven because that was much further to the east near the village of Bethany (Luke 24:50).

Yet this "little hill on top of the mountain" that the Bordeaux Pilgrim described was important, because it was on (or near) this very spot where the crucifixion of Christ took place. And even though the Pilgrim used the same word *monticulus* to denote the newly "discovered" Golgotha on the west side of Jerusalem (which had only come to light some seven years before), the real *monticulus* of the Gospels was on the Mount of Olives.

Once it is realized that the actual "Golgotha" was located at the southern summit of Olivet, it makes it easier to discover the *actual tomb* in which Christ was placed because we are told in the Gospels that it was not far from Golgotha. In the next chapter we will show some new and reliable information that will locate *the very tomb* in which Christ was placed and from which he was resurrected from the dead.

See p74 - for review of Ch 6

Ch 7 review. So that the place Constantine chose was "unknown": 64

Xians revered only one "Holy Place" in Jer. after 70, 135 A.D.; Olivet. (not Holy Sepul. area) and the only site Chr. pilgrims visited. The latter surprised Eusebius.. Actually the vision of a non Xian Jew convinced Helena, that no sacred knowledge was expected at that time. p64 But historical records of Xians show otherwise; a cave on Olivet where Jesus had taught his disciples.. That cave: the Bethlehem one is where Chr. pilgrims came to visit; not the site of Venus. Yet on the site of Cave Helena built the Eleona Church on site of ascension. 69

How that site came to be associated w/ ascension. See 69

The cave is where Jesus stayed, and taught when in Jeru, Lk 22:39, 21:37, Jn 18:2, his home away from home, Olivet was called "Mt of Anointing" - appropriately where the Anointed One (X) spoke. Also sacred to Xians as where he was crucified, raised, & ascended — Indeed it was believed the Shekinah removed to Olivet after 70 AD 66 [illegible]

Tho the NT does not mention the "cave" X does the "tomb" -- The cave was the tomb. But Roman occupation — 10th Legion - on the site would have changed the topography 71 - thus the monument of Joseph was kept a cave, cf late Gosp. of Nazareans, 72 - 2nd cent knew it only as a "cave". The tomb had deteriorated into a mere "cave" by then, But it was to that cave that early Chr pilgrims came to worship. Near the cave early

7

Christian Beliefs and the Mount of Olives

One of the main reasons why scholars today are willing to allow the possibility that the Church of the Holy Sepulchre located on the west side of Jerusalem could be the site of the crucifixion is because it seems sensible that a succession of traditions about its location would have been continually available among the Christian population of Jerusalem. Would not Christians have wanted to remember where the site was and have retained its memory in Constantine's time?

While this supposition appears reasonable, it must be recalled that Jerusalem and its surroundings underwent two devastating destructions (A.D.70 & A.D.135) which drastically altered its geographical features. There were also major political upheavals within that two and a half centuries. Indeed, there is almost nothing known about the Christian bishops of Jerusalem for a hundred years after the emperor Hadrian destroyed the city in A.D.135 nor are Christian activities precisely documented for the Jerusalem area during that time. In spite of these "unknowns," most scholars feel the Church of the Holy Sepulchre is "probably" the proper site for Christ's crucifixion. But when the biblical and historical data given in this book are considered, the Mount of Olives has far better credentials.

This is supported by a further fact. During those two and a half centuries of obscurity, there is only *one tradition* of any "holy place" which Christians esteemed in the Jerusalem area. And that place was located on the Mount of Olives. (The references to this will soon be pointed out.)

Interestingly, when it was finally determined in the time of Constantine (A.D.326) that the sepulchre of Christ was situated under the Shrine of Venus, Eusebius (the great historian who lived in Palestine and one who was well acquainted with the early traditions of the Christians) expressed surprise that Christ's tomb was found at the pagan shrine. In his *Life of Constantine* he candidly admitted that the discovery at that site was "contrary to expectation" (3:28). That's right, neither Eusebius nor others of which we have records expected the tomb to be found there. Even Constantine when he was exulting over the discovery wrote the governors of the eastern provinces that the site had "remained *unknown* for so many cycles of years" (*ibid.* 3:30).

Such statements as these coming from the top authorities of the time do not give the impression that Christians in Jerusalem (or anywhere else) thought that Christ's tomb was located at the site of the Venus Shrine. In fact, they show that it was *unexpected* to find it in that area of Jerusalem.

Actually, the "discovery" came about through the intervention of a miracle, visionary experiences and information supplied by a non-Christian man that convinced Helena, the mother of Constantine, that the Shrine of Venus was the precise spot to find Christ's tomb. Constantine himself acknowledged that the discovery was prompted "by divine direction -- through a *wonder*" (*ibid.*). To people of the fourth century miraculous events were of profound importance in revealing the "authentic" locations of Christian holy places. In the vast majority of circumstances this was the medium through which the early sites associated with Christ, the apostles and prophets were determined. Indeed, the historian Sozomen, writing about a hundred years after the "discovery" of the so-called tomb of Christ, said:

> "The place was discovered ... *by means of signs and dreams; for I do not think that human information is required* when God thinks it best to make manifest the same" (*Hist.*II.1 italics mine).

About 25 years after Helena supposedly rediscovered the new "Golgotha" at the Venus Shrine, Cyril (the bishop of Jerusalem) reminded Constantine's son that it was by "divine grace" (*not* by historical or archaeological data) that Christians were able to locate "*the long hidden holy places*" (*Letter to Constantius* 3 italics and underlining mine). In fact, when Cyril tried to convince some of his doubting parishioners as to the truthfulness of the Church of the Holy Sepulchre being the correct site for Christ's tomb, all that Cyril could provide them for proof was a discourse on the Song of Solomon which he said had the mystical clue as to the whereabouts of Christ's crucifixion and burial (see Parrot's *Golgotha and the Church of the Holy Sepulchre*, pp.56,57 for more information on this interesting point).

As far as real traditional and historical records go (written at least 100 years before the "discoveries" and reconfirmed by Eusebius about 25 years before Helena came to Jerusalem), there was only *one spot* in the Jerusalem region which Christians held in esteem as a "holy place." And that *one spot*, of all things, was a *cave* on the Mount of Olives. Dr. Wilkinson has some excellent comments about this significant site.

"Since before the early third century, when it is mentioned in the apocryphal Acts of John, *one particular cave on the Mount of Olives* had been regarded by Christians as the place where Jesus imparted his teaching to his inner group" (*The Jerusalem Jesus Knew*, p.119).

There is another reference about this *cave* on the Mount of Olives before Constantine began to build the Church of the Holy Sepulchre west of the Temple mount. This is from Eusebius himself in his *Demonstratio Evangelica* (*Proof of the Gospel*) written in A.D.303. Eusebius gave a powerful confirmation that there was *only one site* at Jerusalem [at least he mentioned no other] to which Christians from around the world came to visit and it was to the *cave* on the summit of the Mount of Olives.

"And *this Mount of Olives* is said to be over against Jerusalem, instead of the old earthly Jerusalem and its worship. For as Scripture has said with reference to Jerusalem: The city shall be taken, and the nations that are her enemies and foes shall be gathered together against her, and her spoils shall be divided, it could not say that the feet of the Lord should stand upon Jerusalem. How could that be, once it was destroyed? But it says that they will stand with them that depart from it, to the mount opposite the city called *the Mount of Olives*...since *believers in Christ all congregate from all parts of the world*, not of old time because of the glory of Jerusalem, but they *rest there* [*on the Mount of Olives*] that they may learn both about the city being taken and devastated as the prophets foretold, and that they *may worship at the Mount of Olives* opposite to the city...*TO THE CAVE* that is shown there" (Bk. VI, ch.18 all emphases mine).

It is interesting that Eusebius tells us (about 25 years before "signs and dreams" supposedly discovered the "lost" tomb of Jesus by Helena) that Christians were coming to Jerusalem from all over the world to congregate at a *cave* near the summit of the Mount of Olives. There was no other area in the region of Jerusalem that Christian pilgrims were coming to see or at which they wanted to worship God. And note this point. Eusebius in this early period said nothing about Christians coming to Jerusalem to give homage to God at the Shrine of Venus on the west side of the city. This oversight is most conspicuous. Only two places in Palestine were important to people who came from around the world. Eusebius said in this early work that one place was the *cave* on the Mount of Olives and the other was where Christ was born.

"Bethlehem the place of his birth, which is today so famous *that men still hasten from the ends of the earth to see it*" (Bk. I, ch.1).

In actual fact, the place of the Venus Shrine (which after the time of Constantine became the most revered spot in all Christendom) was not even remotely discussed as important by Eusebius in his early work called the *Demonstratio Evangelica*. This helps to show that the "Golgotha" of Constantine was of no significance whatever to Eusebius.

But all of a sudden (after "dreams and visions" finally selected the Venus Shrine as the place of the crucifixion and burial of Christ), it was the *western* side of Jerusalem that became all important to Christians around the world. The location of the *cave* on the Mount of Olives, however, had been so ingrained as significant to Christians at Jerusalem that Helena was forced to erect a church over the Olivet *cave*. She called it the Eleona Church which indicated that it was situated on the Mount of Olives. As soon as the church was built, people in Jerusalem then began to associate it with the site of Christ's ascension to heaven.

The actual ascension, on the other hand, took place near Bethany about a mile *east* of the cave (Luke 24:50). On this Dr. Wilkinson comments:

> "Where did the Apostles experience this final parting? Though Luke says at the end of his Gospel that it was at Bethany no later pilgrims or Jerusalem Christians ever seemed to remember it there. Nor indeed was it in the place where the Jerusalemites first commemorated it, for this was none other than the Eleona Cave, and Acts 1:10 demands that the place of the Ascension should be in some open place from which it was possible to look up into the sky. The unsuitability of *the cave* as a 'scene' for the Ascension no doubt led to plans to build a sanctuary for the Ascension elsewhere" (*ibid.*, p.173 italics mine).

The fact is, the cave on the Mount of Olives in the early references was not connected with the Ascension. However, near the end of the fourth century, the *monticulus* [the Imbomon] mentioned by the Bordeaux Pilgrim was erroneously selected as the Ascension site though it was actually much farther *east* near Bethany (Luke 24:50). The *cave*, however, finally came to be called *the Cave of Christ's Teaching*. It was considered a spot where Christ did a considerable amount of speaking to his disciples when he was in the area of Jerusalem. What is not usually recognized is the fact that the area of the Mount of Olives was where Christ actually *lived* when he was in the vicinity of Jerusalem. Not only was the region his "habitual" place for meeting with his apostles (Luke 22:39), and "where he many times met there with his disciples" (John 18:2), but "by day he was teaching in the Temple, but by night he would go out and lodge on the Mount of Olives" (Luke 21:37). Even the village of Bethany where he sometimes resided was on the eastern slopes of this same Mount of Olives (Mark 11:1).

It could be rightly said that the district of the Mount of Olives was the "home" of Christ when he was in Jerusalem.

Other than the time he taught in the Temple or the occasion of the Last Supper (which took place within the city of Jerusalem), *all* the other teachings of Christ near Jerusalem were conducted on the Mount of Olives.

And what a fit place for the expected Messiah (the Anointed One) to teach. It was customary in Jewish circles to call the Mount of Olives by the name "the Mount of the Anointing" (*Parah* 3:6). It was the holiest area around Jerusalem other than the Temple itself. The Mount of Olives also had its special sanctification because it housed the *Miphkad Altar* (where the Red Heifer and the other sin offerings were burnt *outside* the camp). But to Christians it had even a greater anointing. More significant than anything else, it was the area where Christ was crucified, buried and resurrected from the dead. It was also near the place of Christ's ascension, and the site to which he will return from heaven (Acts 1:9-11; Zech.14:1). Besides this, Christians saw another importance to the Mount of Olives. Rabbi Jonathan (a few years after the fall of Jerusalem in A.D.70) reported that the Shekinah glory of God left the inner Temple in A.D.66 and for three and a half years he said the Shekinah . . .

> "abode on the Mount of Olives hoping that Israel would repent, but they did not; while a *Bet Kol* [a supernatural voice from heaven] issued forth announcing, *Return, O backsliding children* [Jer.3:14]. *Return unto Me, and I will return unto you* [Mal.3:7], when they did not repent, it said, *I will return to my place* [Hos.5:15]" (Midrash *Rabbah*, Lamentations 2:11).

Early Christians would no doubt have seen in this miraculous event much more significance than may meet the eye today. And indeed they did! Eusebius mentioned the importance of this removal of the Shekinah glory in his *Proof of the Gospel* (Bk. VI, ch.18). It was a sign that God had departed from the Temple on the western hill and had retreated to the Mount of Olives on the *east* as the *new* place of his divine residence. This event of the Shekinah glory leaving the Temple and abiding on the Mount of Olives became highly significant to Christians because this was the mountain where Christ did most of his teachings in Jerusalem (and telling the Jews to repent in his day). It was also understood by Christians that this will be the exact area to which Christ returns to earth at his second advent. These matters alone show how symbolically important the Mount of Olives was to Christians in the first century.

In the period before Constantine it is not difficult to see why Christians from around the world would pay attention to the Mount of Olives as a place of special holiness. What may be surprising to some of us is the fact that they paid particular attention to the *cave* very near the summit of Olivet and located about a hundred yards to the south and a little west of the *monticulus* ("the little hill on the mountain" that the Bordeaux Pilgrim described). But why a *cave*? This may at first seem puzzling because there is not the slightest mention of such a *cave* in the Gospels nor in any place in the New Testament. That's right, there is no attention attached to any *cave*, but there is considerable importance shown to a *TOMB* -- the *tomb* of Jesus from whence he came forth from the dead!

Could the *cave* on the Mount of Olives have been the *tomb* of Jesus? There is every reason to believe that it was! Look at it this way. We are told by Josephus that the Tenth Legion of the Romans occupied the whole area of Olivet for the 3 and 1/2 years' war with the Jews (*War* V.70,135). The legion bivouacked in all areas of the mountain and this would have decimated most of the buildings, gardens and grave-areas in the region. This was especially so in the last stages of the war when the Romans stripped the whole landscape of trees (for almost a 10 miles' radius from Jerusalem) in order to build armaments and bulwarks against the Jews. Listen to Josephus' lament about the countryside surrounding Jerusalem at the end of the war.

"The Romans though struggling terribly in collecting the timber...stripped the whole area around the town to a distance of 90 stadia [about 10 miles]. The countryside like the city was a pitiful sight, for where once there had been a multitude of trees and parks, there was now an utter wilderness stripped bare of timber; and no stranger who had seen the old Judaea and the glorious suburbs of her capital, and now beheld utter desolation, could refrain from tears or suppress a groan at so terrible a change. The war had blotted out every trace of beauty, and no one who had known it in the past and came upon it suddenly would have recognized the place, for though he was already there, he would still be looking for the city" (*War* VI.5-8 Cornfeld trans.).

This eyewitness description tells us much about the awful condition of Olivet after the war was over. It was left in sheer desolation! What was no doubt a beautifully decorated tomb made by Joseph of Arimathea in which Christ was buried would certainly have been left in shambles (as well as all other buildings, tombs, etc. on Olivet) at the conclusion of the war in A.D.70. Stripped of its ornaments and interior decorations and serving as a shelter for Roman troops of the Tenth Legion for 3 and 1/2 years would have left the *tomb* looking more like a natural *cave* rather than a resplendent *tomb* of a rich man. Indeed, when the *tomb* of Christ is described by Jewish Christians in the early second century, they were then calling it a *cave*.

In the work called "The Gospel of the Nazaraeans" (written in the second century) it was said that a guard of armed soldiers sent to the tomb of Christ were set *"over against THE CAVE"* (Hennecke-Schneemelcher, *The New Testament Apocrypha*, vol.I,p.150). And in the late second or early third century work called "The Acts of Pilate," Christ's burial place was called both a *tomb* and a *cave* in the same context. That work has Joseph of Arimathea saying: "See, I have placed it [the body of Jesus] in my *NEW TOMB*, having wrapped it in clean linen, and I rolled a stone before the door *OF THE CAVE*" (*Acts of Pilate*, Bk.XII). This reference is no doubt speaking of the *tomb* as it appeared in the early third century. It then had the appearance of a *cave*. There is a further reference in "The Acts of Pilate" to the *tomb* of Christ being a *cave*. "And we saw an angel descend from heaven, and he rolled away the stone from the mouth of *THE CAVE*" (*ibid.* Bk.XIII).

Since it is clear in the Gospel records that the *tomb* of Christ was a recently hewn tomb for the rich man called Joseph of Arimathea (Luke 23:53), in no way could the Gospel writers have called the *tomb* a *cave* -- and they didn't!

They consistently called it a *tomb*. But by the time the Jewish Christians wrote "The Gospel of the Nazaraeans" and when "The Acts of Pilate" was written, the *tomb* no longer resembled a *tomb*. It then had the appearance of a *cave*, and this is how it is always described in later literature.

This means that the *tomb* of Joseph of Arimathea (from the early second century to the early third century) had deteriorated into nothing more than a *cave*, and that is how it was described. Remarkably, another work called the "Acts of John" referred to earlier by Dr. Wilkinson (and probably written in the late second century) has Christ talking to the apostle John at *this CAVE on the Mount of Olives* at the exact time of the crucifixion -- and even with the *real* crucifixion of Christ as occurring on the Mount of Olives. As stated by Hennecke-Schneemelcher in their work *The New Testament Apocrypha*, we find that Christ gave to the apostle John some last minute instructions: "Jesus said to John on the Mount of Olives at the moment of the crucifixion: 'John, someone must hear this from me; for I have need of one who will hear it'" (Vol.I, p.301). And what is interesting is the fact that this gnostic work actually places the apostle John (whom the New Testament puts in eyeshot of Christ's crucifixion) standing opposite the *cave* on the Mount of Olives at the exact time Christ was crucified. This gnostic account describing the apostle John being on Olivet when Christ was crucified can only be considered a further indication that Christ was executed on the Mount of Olives.

But this is not all the important information about this *cave* on the Mount of Olives. It should be recalled that the church historian Eusebius (who was himself a native Palestinian and well versed in the history of Jerusalem as well as an astute observer of what was happening in Christian circles at the end of the third century) said that Christians were coming to Jerusalem from all over the world to assemble at the *cave* on the Mount of Olives in order to worship God.

"Believers in Christ all congregate from all parts of the world...that they may worship at the Mount of Olives opposite the city...*TO THE CAVE* that is shown there" (*Proof of the Gospel*, Bk. VI, ch.18).

What we find from this historical information is that there are good credentials that the *cave/tomb* on the Mount of Olives is indeed the very *tomb* of Joseph of Arimathea in which Christ was placed after his crucifixion. There is not *any other place than this CAVE in the Jerusalem area* that the historical records reveal Christians as accepting as a "holy place" before the time of Constantine. Even Eusebius is completely silent about any other site, and especially he says *nothing* about the region of the Temple of Venus on the west side of Jerusalem as having the slightest significance.

In closing this chapter, it would be profitable to get the summation of Dr. Wilkinson on this matter of the *cave* before the time of Constantine. He says:

> "Besides the places where events mentioned in the New Testament had actually taken place there were evidently places set aside for prayer. *Such was THE CAVE on the Mount of Olives*, which is first mentioned about a century before Constantine erected a church over it.... Perhaps there were other places being used before Christianity finally came out in the open under Constantine. If there were, we have no firm evidence about them" (*ibid.*, p.177 emphases mine).

This means that the *only place* recognized in history as being "holy" to the Christians around Jerusalem before A.D.326 was the *cave/tomb* on the Mount of Olives. Remarkably, it was somewhere near this *cave* that the bishops of Jerusalem were buried and there is a newer tomb built in the second century directly adjacent to the *cave* with spaces for five bodies. Dr. Wilkinson does not think that this newer tomb was built for some of the bishops because it is too crudely constructed (*ibid.*, p.122), yet they were certainly buried not far away. It was normal for high ecclesiastical authorities to be entombed in prominent burial grounds and this *cave/tomb* must have been reckoned important to the Jerusalem bishops. Did they not want to be buried near the place where their Lord was buried and resurrected from the dead? From what has been shown in this book, this may be the reason the bishops chose this *cave/tomb* region.

The next chapter has an abundance of *new* evidence which helps to substantiate this proposition.

8

The New Mount Zion for Christians

From the historical records, the only Christian area of significance in Jerusalem before the time of Constantine was the Mount of Olives. But suddenly, when churches began to be built (and *rebuilt*) in Jerusalem after A.D.325, the most important areas for Christian attention became the former site of the Temple of Venus in the western part of Jerusalem and also the hill located just to the south of the Venus Shrine. Granted, Constantine had a church erected over the cave on the Mount of Olives, but the other two *western* regions took on a more significant role than the Mount of Olives. In fact, the area of the Venus Shrine became known as the "New Jerusalem" and the hill to the south (the large southwest hill of Jerusalem) began to be called "Mount Zion."

This transfer of attention from the *eastern* region abutting to Jerusalem over to the *western* section of the city was accomplished primarily through the application of visions, dreams and miracles. The "signs and wonders" were instrumental in establishing the supposed site of *Golgotha* (the place where Christ was crucified) as being at the Shrine of Venus. It was also determined at the same time that the southwest hill was the place where Christ held his Last Supper with his disciples as well as the area where (on Pentecost day after Christ's resurrection) the Holy Spirit descended upon the first Christians (Acts 2). Because of this it became common after the time of Constantine to call the southwest hill "Mount Zion" (usually spelled in Christian circles "Mount Sion").

But before A.D.325 a very different attitude prevailed among Christians at Jerusalem. In no way was the region of the Venus Shrine called "New Jerusalem" nor was the southwest hill reckoned as "Mount Sion." It may come as a surprise to many people but the "Mount Sion" for Christians prior to the time of Constantine was none other than *the Mount of Olives!* We have absolute evidence that this was the case from no less than Eusebius (the first Christian historian and an eyewitness to what was happening in Palestine in the early fourth century). At this early time, Eusebius was consistent in stating that Christians acknowledged the Mount of Olives as *the new* Mount Sion. This did not mean that the original "Mount Sion" of the Bible was lost sight of. There was never any doubt where the *real* Mount Sion was. It was on the south*east* hill of Jerusalem and by figurative extension it reached north to include the Temple mount.

These historical facts are found in one of Eusebius' early works (written several years before A.D.325). It is called the *Demonstratio Evangelica* (or in English, *Proof of the Gospel*). In this work, Eusebius records that after the destruction of Jerusalem in A.D.70, the "spiritual" headquarters of the Church of God [the name Eusebius used for the Christian Church] came to be established on the Mount of Olives. A church building was constructed on this mount and it was called the "Mother Church" (the foundational church) for all Christendom. The information concerning these matters comes directly from Eusebius in this pre-Constantine work. It is surprising that scholars over the centuries (as far as I am able to determine) have *not* referred to these important early opinions of Eusebius.

In simple terms, Eusebius in this early work shows that a church building existed on the Christian Mount Sion (the Mount of Olives) and that it had been there from shortly after A.D.70. This church was founded to take the place of the old Jerusalem and it became the *new* and *spiritual* Mount Sion for Christians. He called it no less than the "House of God" for Christians (using the phrase that Jews called the Temple) and that this church on Olivet was the "Mother Church" for those of the Christian faith.

Let us now look at the information that Eusebius provides in his early work called the *Proof of the Gospel*. The first thing that we should note is the fact that Eusebius was well aware of the actual site of the original Mount Sion. His primary identification was the Temple mount. Notice how Eusebius shows this.

"*The hill called Sion and Jerusalem*, the buildings there, *that is to say, the Temple, the Holy of Holies, the Altar*, and whatever else was there dedicated to the glory of God, has been utterly removed or shaken in fulfillment of the Word.... Therefore for your sake *the land of Sion* shall be ploughed, and Jerusalem shall be a quarry of stones, for being inhabited by men of foreign race it is even now like a quarry, all the inhabitants of the city choosing stones from its ruins as they will, for private as well as public buildings. And it is sad for the eyes to see stones *from the Temple itself*, and from the sanctuary and holy place, used for building of idol temples, and of theatres for the populace. These things that are open for the eyes to see" (VIII,3).

"Their once famous *Mount Sion*...is a Roman farm like the rest of the country, yea, *with my own eyes* I have seen the bulls ploughing there, and *the sacred site* sown with seed. And Jerusalem itself is become but a storehouse of its fruit of old days now destroyed, or better, as the Hebrew has it, a stonequarry" (*ibid.*).

"*Mount Sion* was burned and left utterly desolate, and the *Mount of the House of God* became as a grove of wood. If our own observation has any value, we have seen in our own time *Sion* once so famous ploughed with yokes of oxen by the Romans and utterly devastated, and Jerusalem, as the oracle says, deserted like a lodge" (VI,13).

There can be no doubt that at this pre-Constantine period, Eusebius essentially reckoned the original Sion to be the Temple mount. And the Temple with the old city area of Jerusalem on the south (the early City of David) were then in ruins. Pagans for the most part were occupying Jerusalem when Eusebius saw these activities going on. They were building idol temples in which to worship false gods and for entertainment the general populace were resorting to the theatres. To Eusebius, with the Temple in ruins and the people in the city of Jerusalem performing their sacrilegious deeds, such things were not pleasant to behold. It is no wonder that the Christian pilgrims who came to Jerusalem retreated to the Mount of Olives *east* of Jerusalem for their worship services and left the city to the "theatre-goers."

Be this as it may, the point we wish to make in our present context is that Eusebius knew full well that the actual *Sion* was primarily the Temple mount. At no time in this early work did he even remotely suggest that the south*west* hill was the *real* Sion or that it was even the *spiritual* Sion of Christians.

A hundred years before Eusebius, the great scholar Origen went to Jerusalem and viewed the region. In his writings he always identified "Sion" with the Temple mount and *not* the south*west* hill (*In John* IV.19,20; and see *ISBE* (1929), Vol.V, p.3151). Even about a hundred years after the time of Eusebius, we find Jerome pointing out the City of David as real *Sion* and that it extended to the Temple mount (*In Isa.*, i.21; ii,3; xxii.1,2; xxxvi; xli.25; *In Zech.* ix.9,10; xiii. 1,2; xiv.5). Jerome also made the correct identification in his New Testament commentary (*Matt.* x.28). But from the time of Constantine onward, it became common to transfer *Sion* from its actual location in the eastern side of the city to the *southwest* hill, and in Jerome's translation of Eusebius' *Onomasticon* (one of the latest works of Eusebius) he allows for the *new* interpretation (*Palestine Pilgrim Text*, Vol.I, pp.60-62). Only with the Venus Shrine becoming the "*New Jerusalem*" after A.D.325 did Christians call the southwest hill "Sion." The Bordeaux Pilgrim even made the association.

Before the time of Constantine, however, Eusebius was consistent in referring to the Mount of Olives as the Christian "Mount Sion." This is because the original "Church of God" had been established after the destruction of Jerusalem in A.D.70 near the site of the *cave* on Olivet.

"*The Mount of Olives* is therefore literally opposite to Jerusalem and to the east of it, *but also THE HOLY CHURCH OF GOD, and the mount UPON WHICH IT WAS FOUNDED*, of which the Saviour teaches: A city set on a hill cannot be hid, *RAISED UP IN PLACE OF JERUSALEM* that is fallen never to rise again, and thought worthy of the feet of the Lord, is figuratively not only opposite Jerusalem, *but east of it as well*, receiving the rays of the divine light, and become much *before* Jerusalem [in prominence], and near the Sun of Righteousness himself" (*ibid.*, VI,18 emphases mine).

This account of Eusebius shows that the Holy Church of God "*was founded on the Mount of Olives.*" This is a statement of great importance to the modern historian of the New Testament Church because this is the opinion of no less than Eusebius himself, the first ecclesiastical historian of the Christian faith and one who was a native of Palestine and the curator of the large library at Caesarea. He said that "the Holy Church of God" of Christendom came into being *on the Mount of Olives!* What could he mean by this other than the fact that this is where Christ was crucified, buried and resurrected from the dead, and also that the Jerusalem Church built the "Mother Church" of all Christendom on the Mount of Olives right after the destruction of Jerusalem in A.D.70? Most significantly, Eusebius made this remarkable historical observation several years *before* Constantine and his mother Helena came on the scene to insist (by visions, dreams and supposed miracles) that Christendom was really founded in the direct opposite direction from Olivet.

But Eusebius doesn't stop with this revealing bit of information. He went on to say that the "Holy Church of God" on the Mount of Olives was "raised up instead of Jerusalem" to be the city on the hill that Christ spoke about. This was to Eusebius a *new* city -- a *new* mount, and one that was to be exalted *before* the Jerusalem of old. Indeed, Eusebius in the plainest of words (in this pre-Constantine work) said that the Mount of Olives was the place where a *new* "House of God" [a synonym for a *new* Temple or Sanctuary of God] was built *after* the destruction of Jerusalem in A.D.70. Eusebius said that the Scriptures "tell of a *new Mount, and the righteousness of ANOTHER HOUSE OF GOD*, besides the one in Jerusalem" (*ibid.* II,3).

What was established on the Mount of Olives was a type of *new* city (a city set on a hill that Christ spoke about) which was raised up instead of the old Jerusalem. Eusebius is consistent with this theme.

"And *this Mount of Olives* is said to be over against Jerusalem, because it was established by God *after the fall of Jerusalem*, INSTEAD OF THE OLD EARTHLY JERUSALEM" (*ibid.*, VI,18).

After A.D.70, the Mount of Olives became the new site of the "House of God" that was taking the place of the old city of Jerusalem. That Mother Church, being on Olivet, became geographically indistinguishable from the Mount of Olives itself. Eusebius himself was fully aware of this and makes the parallel identification.

"His Church which is metaphorically called *the Mount of Olives*" (*ibid.*).

"And *this* mount of the Lord *was the Mount of Olives*, which is called Asael in the Septuagint. And this word in Hebrew is 'Work of God'...[it represents] *the Christian Church and the work of God*" (*ibid.*).

"*The Mount of Olives* is therefore literally opposite to Jerusalem and to the *east* of it, but [it is] *also the Church of God*, and the mount on which it [the Church of God] is founded" (*ibid.*).

Since Eusebius before the time of Constantine believed that the Church of God was located atop the Mount of Olives, it can be seen why Christians of the time began to call the Mount of Olives the *new* "Mount Sion."

The Scriptures "tell of *a new mount, and the manifesting of another House of God*, besides the one in Jerusalem" (*ibid.*, II,3).

"The Word announces this to the daughter of Sion, calling the Church of God by that name" (*ibid.*, VI,17).

"The Church of God might be called the daughter of Sion" (*ibid.*).

This is certainly the reason why the Mount of Olives prior to Constantine was the only site in all Jerusalem where pilgrims from around the world came to worship. The principal area of interest, so Eusebius tells us, was the *cave/tomb* which was located near the southern summit of the Mount of Olives.

"And *this Mount of Olives* is said to be over against Jerusalem, instead of the old earthly Jerusalem and its worship...*believers in Christ congregate from all parts of the world*...that they may worship *at the Mount of Olives* opposite the city...*TO THE CAVE that is shown there*" (*ibid.*, VI,18).

Note again (and this point bears emphasizing), Eusebius said *nothing* at this pre-Constantine date about Christian pilgrims from around the world coming to Jerusalem to worship at or near the Temple of Venus (which after A.D.325 became the *new* "Golgotha") or even that they paid any attention whatever to locations on the southwest hill. Their only interest, as far as this early evidence of Eusebius is concerned, was the *cave* on the Mount of Olives. And in this period the Mount of Olives was also being called the Christian "Mount Sion." This fact is made even clearer by Eusebius when he referred to the law going forth from Mount Sion in Isaiah 2:2-4. He gave the Christian interpretation of that prophecy in Book I, Chapter 4.

"This law going forth from Sion, different from the law enacted in the desert by Moses on Mount Sinai, what can it be but the word of the Gospel, *going forth from Sion* through our Saviour Jesus Christ, and going through all nations? For it is plain, that it was in Jerusalem *AND MOUNT SION ADJACENT THERETO* (*where our Lord and Saviour for the most part lived and taught*) that the law of the new covenant began *and from THENCE* went forth and shone upon all, according to the commands which he gave his disciples when he said: 'Go ye, and make disciples of all nations, teaching them to observe all things, whatsoever I have commanded you'."

Though the command of Jesus that Eusebius quotes was given in Galilee (Matt.28:16-20), no one ever thought that the Mount Sion of the New Covenant was located that far north. This *new* Mount Sion of Eusebius was somewhere near Jerusalem and it is not difficult to understand where Eusebius placed it. It was clearly on the Mount of Olives. On Olivet was a place called "Viri Galilee" around which many fourth century Christians thought some of the post-resurrection teachings of Christ took place, and this particularly applied to Matthew 28:16-20 (Hoade, *Guide to the Holy Land*, p.253). But more to the point than this, is the fact that Eusebius said this *Mount Sion* of the New Covenant was the "*MOUNT SION* (*in which our Lord and Saviour spent so much time*)" (*ibid.*, VI,13).

There is no doubt that Eusebius is referring to the Mount of Olives in his description because the New Testament plainly tells us that the predominant region in which Christ lived and taught while in the area of Jerusalem was on Olivet. It was his "habitual" place for meeting with his apostles (Luke 22:39), and "where he many times met there with his disciples" (John 18:2), and "by day he was teaching in the Temple, but by night he would go out and lodge *on the Mount of Olives*" (Luke 21:37). Even the village of Bethany where he sometimes resided was on the eastern slopes of the Mount of Olives (Mark 11:1).

The *Mount Sion* of Eusebius was the *Mount of Olives*. He said: "Mount Sion *adjacent thereto* [to Jerusalem] (*where our Lord and Saviour for the most part lived and taught*)" (*ibid.*, I.4). And, of course, the Mount of Olives was directly *adjacent* to Jerusalem, or as Eusebius said twice in another section of the *Proof of the Gospel*: "this Mount of Olives is *over against* Jerusalem" and also "the Mount of Olives *opposite* the city" (*ibid.*, VI,18). It was on this Mount of Olives that the "Mother Church" of all Christendom was built after the fall of Jerusalem in A.D.70 and Eusebius said the Scriptures called it "a *new* mount, and the manifesting *of another House of God*, besides the one in Jerusalem" (*ibid.*, II,3).

What was this *new* "House of God" that Eusebius referred to? Other writings of Eusebius show that he meant a church building as well as an administrative center. In his *Oration* he said "churches are called *the Houses of the Lord*" (XVII,4). This was the common designation of such church buildings (see *Eccl.Hist.*, IX,10). And after the fall of Jerusalem in A.D.70 he stated that the "House of God" was located on the Mount of Olives. Indeed, he made a direct statement to this effect. "The Mount of Olives is therefore literally opposite to Jerusalem and to the *east* of it, but also *the Holy Church of God*" (*ibid.*, VI,18).

This region must have been the most important area in pre-Constantine Jerusalem. Even the bishops of Jerusalem were buried near the *cave/tomb* on the Mount of Olives and it was significant enough in the early history of Christianity that Constantine had a church built over this site (the Eleona Church) shortly after A.D.325. And sometime in the second century, a tomb chamber was carved out of the rock adjacent to the *cave* itself (with spaces for five bodies). It appears from this that some people felt inspired to be buried near the *cave/tomb*. Dr. Wilkinson states: "It is hardly likely that this particular chamber was used for burying the bishops of Jerusalem, since it is a crude affair, which obviously existed before Constantine's church. We are told, however, that their tombs [those of the bishops] were at the church, and therefore they cannot have been far away" (*The Jerusalem Jesus Knew*, p.122).

Since bishops were ordinarily buried in the most important church grounds (or cemetery), it is remarkable that the early bishops of Jerusalem chose their burial spots very near the *cave/tomb* on Olivet. The reason for this should be clear. If one believes Eusebius' statements that the "Mother Church" of all Christendom was built in this very region shortly after A.D.70, then it can be easily seen why ecclesiastical authorities of the Christian church in Jerusalem would want to be buried somewhere near that important "Mother Church."

There is also another reason why Christians in the first century were very interested in the Mount of Olives. This is because it was believed that the Shekinah Glory of God (the Spirit or Presence of God) which supposedly dwelt inside the Holy of Holies at the Temple *left the sanctuary* and went to the Mount of Olives and hovered over that spot at the time of the Roman/Jewish War which ended in A.D.70. The fact that the Shekinah Glory left the old Temple and migrated to the top of the Mount of Olives was an important event to Eusebius. Notice some aggregate quotes from Eusebius which come from Book VI, Chapter 18 (288) of his *Proof of the Gospel* which show its significance.

> "Believers in Christ congregate from all parts of the world, not as of old time because of the glory of Jerusalem, nor that they may worship in the ancient Temple at Jerusalem, but...that they may worship at the Mount of Olives opposite to the city, *whither the glory* [the Shekinah Glory] *of the Lord migrated when it left the former city.*"

Eusebius gave a prophecy that the Shekinah Glory was to leave the Temple and old Jerusalem not long before they were to be destroyed. He said the Shekinah Glory would --

"depart from it [from Jerusalem] to the mount opposite the city called the Mount of Olives. And this, too, the prophet Ezekiel anticipates by the Holy Spirit and foretells. For he says: 'And the Cherubim lifted their wings, and wheels beside them, and *the glory of the God of Israel* was on them [and] above them, and *he stood on the mount which was opposite to the city*'."

This prophecy of Ezekiel was believed by Eusebius to have been fulfilled just prior to the destruction of Jerusalem. This is why the Jewish Christians just after A.D.70 built their "Mother Church" at this site on the Mount of Olives. Even Jerome, almost a hundred years after Eusebius, acknowledged that the Cherubim carried the Shekinah Glory near the summit of Olivet and founded the church of Christ.

"Here also [the Mount of Olives] according to Ezekiel the Cherubim after leaving the Temple *FOUNDED the Church of the Lord*" (*Letter* CVIII.12).

This shows that Jerome also followed Eusebius in showing that the Cherubim "*founded* the Church of the Lord" near the summit of Olivet. And when did the Shekinah Glory leave the Temple and hover over the Mount of Olives? Eusebius states that it was during "the siege of Jerusalem" (A.D.66 to 70) that "*the passing of the Lord to the Mount of Olives*" took place (*Proof of the Gospel*, XVIII sect.294).

But Eusebius and Jerome were not the only observers who said the Shekinah Glory left the Temple before the destruction of the Temple and hovered over the Mount of Olives. A Jewish rabbi named Jonathan (an eyewitness to the destruction of Jerusalem) said the Shekinah Glory left the Temple and (for three and a half years) --

"abode on the Mount of Olives hoping that Israel would repent, but they did not; while a *Bet Kol* [a supernatural voice from heaven] issued forth announcing, *Return, O backsliding children* [Jer.3:14]. *Return unto me, and I will return unto you* [Mal.3:7]. When they did not repent, it said, *I will return to my place* [in heaven] [Hos.5:15]" (Midrash, *Rabbah Lamentations* 2:11).

There was another writer (besides Eusebius and Jonathan)

who mentioned the Shekinah Glory of God leaving the Temple at Jerusalem just prior to the war with the Romans. Josephus himself also mentioned the same thing. He said that in the Spring of A.D.66 some remarkable events took place that involved the Temple at Jerusalem. In fact, Josephus gave three miracles associated with the Shekinah Glory and the Temple and each one showed that the "Glory" was *departing* the Holy Sanctuary. In *War* VI,290 he stated that a great light shone over the altar for thirty minutes at 3 o'clock in the morning (a week before Passover in A.D.66) and then it *departed*. He said the sacred scribes interpreted this sign as a bad omen for the Temple. It was like the Shekinah Glory moving away from the Tabernacle in the wilderness as a sign to disassemble the Tabernacle and transport it to another location. This may have been fine for the Tabernacle (which was portable), but it was impossible to move the Temple which had been constructed with unmovable stones and timber.

Then, a few days later (during Passover itself) the enormous brass gates of Nicanor, requiring twenty men to open and close them, opened at midnight of their own accord (*War* VI,293-295). This was also interpreted as showing a desolation coming upon the Temple. And then, about fifty days later, on Pentecost, the final sign was given which definitely showed that the Shekinah Glory was *departing* the Temple as the other signs indicated.

"Moreover, at the festival which is called Pentecost, the priests on entering the inner court of the Temple at nightfall, as their custom was in accomplishment of their ministrations, stated that they first became aware of a commotion and a roar, and after that the voice of a great multitude saying *'We are departing hence'*" (*War* VI,299).

This is the testimony of Josephus (who was an eyewitness to these times) that the Shekinah Glory left the old Temple on that Pentecost day in A.D.66. When we couple this information with that of Rabbi Jonathan (also an eyewitness), we find that the "Glory" went directly to the Mount of Olives and in some manner remained over the top of Olivet for 3 and 1/2 years (this would mean from late Spring in A.D.66 to about December of A.D.69, nearly eight months before the Temple was destroyed) and then it went back to heaven, according to Rabbi Jonathan, and it had not returned to earth up to the time he wrote.

This was highly significant to Christians. It certainly was to Eusebius in his early work *The Proof of the Gospel.* This meant that the Shekinah Glory which made the Temple holy in the first place retreated from the Temple and positioned itself directly over the very region where Christ died for mankind and where he was resurrected from the dead. From that region it apparently manifested itself as a divine apparition from time to time (as it once did when it was associated with the Temple) and, according to Rabbi Jonathan, it gave its warnings to repent to the people of Jerusalem over a period of 3 and 1/2 years. Now if people wish to believe that all of this was a figment of imagination for Rabbi Jonathan, then they can dismiss the matter (or criticize away his statement) but this is what the Jewish Rabbi stated and I have no reason to doubt that the Shekinah Glory could have done the very thing Jonathan said. At least, Eusebius himself believed the "Glory" retreated to the Mount of Olives just prior to the destruction of the Temple (as Rabbi Jonathan stated) and he made this an important point in calling the Mount of Olives the *new* Mount Sion.

This means that the Shekinah Glory went, after leaving the Temple, to the very region where Christ died and was resurrected from the dead. This was also the area from which Christ prophesied the ruin of Jerusalem (Matt.24). And this was the spot where Eusebius said the Christian "House of God" was *founded* (along with Jerome) just after the destruction of Jerusalem in A.D.70. Indeed, Eusebius connected the final sign given to the twenty-four priests at Pentecost in A.D.66 with an oracle given to Christians at this same period which warned them to abandon Jerusalem.

"The whole body of the church at Jerusalem having been commanded by a divine revelation, given to men of approved piety before the war [the 24 priests who entered the Temple on Pentecost], removed from the city and dwelt in a certain town beyond Jordan called Pella" (*Eccl.Hist.*, III,5; *cf.* Epiphanius, *Haeres. Nazaraeorum,* 7).

But then, not long after the war was over in A.D.70, Eusebius reports that Christians returned to the region of Jerusalem and that fifteen Jewish bishops ruled in the city for the next 62 years (*Eccl.Hist.*, IV,5). Once the Jewish Christians returned to the Jerusalem area from Pella, they installed their first bishop to head the Jerusalem church. They selected Simeon, the brother of James and one of the children of Joseph and Mary (Simeon was a "half-brother" of Jesus by physical descent). These Jewish Christians, according to Eusebius, established their church headquarters on the Mount of Olives. Notice his *Proof of the Gospel.*

"And *this Mount of Olives* is said to be over against Jerusalem, because it was established by God *after the fall of Jerusalem, instead of the old earthly Jerusalem*" (VI,18).

"*The Mount of Olives* is therefore literally opposite to Jerusalem and to the east of it, *but also* [is located] *the Holy Church of God, and the mount on which it is founded*, of which the Saviour teaches: 'A city set on a hill cannot be hid, *raised up in place of Jerusalem* that is fallen never to rise again'" (VI,18).

These references of Eusebius show that the Jewish Christians after their return from Pella *did not* select a site as their headquarters on the southwest hill. They also avoided the area where the Temple of Venus was built after the time the emperor Hadrian constructed the city of Aelia on the site of Jerusalem after A.D.135. And within that 62 year period (from A.D.70 to A.D.132) it would have been perfectly allowable, one would think, to erect a church or to recognize as a "holy place" the spot where the Temple of Venus was later built after A.D.135. But, according to Eusebius, those Jewish Christians were not persuaded to do anything of the kind. Those Christians, right after A.D.70, homed in on only one area in the environs of Jerusalem as being geographically important to them. That was the southern summit of the Mount of Olives. The reason for this is because it was on the Mount of Olives where Christ was crucified and resurrected from the dead and the area the Shekinah Glory selected as the place of "holiness" just before Jerusalem was destroyed.

There were also other reasons why these Jewish Christians picked the Mount of Olives for their headquarters. When the Jewish Christians returned to the area of Jerusalem after A.D.70, they were able to observe that most of the city on the western hills which comprised the Temple region, the old aristocratic area on the southwest hill and all the western areas that once represented the old city of Jerusalem were now in utter devastation. So thorough was the ruin of Jerusalem that a visitor to the area would never have believed that a city once graced the former metropolitan precincts. Josephus gave an eyewitness account of the devastation. He said: "Now as soon as the army had no more people to slay or plunder, Caesar gave orders that they should now demolish *the entire city and temple* [except a few towers and parts of some walls] but for the rest of the wall encircling the city, it was so thoroughly laid even with the ground by those who dug it up to the foundation that there was nothing left to make people who came later to the area to believe that the region had ever been inhabited" (*War*, VII,1-3).

The city of Jerusalem was completely demolished. On the western and southwestern hill the camp of the Tenth Legion of the Roman army was established. As Prof. Mazar describes it, Jerusalem was "hardly more than a military base for the Roman garrison" (*The Mountain of the Lord*, p.233). And this was true. Indeed, no walls were left around the city (and the city remained without walls until the end of the second or the beginning of the third century) (Mazar, *ibid.*, p.237). Without walls to protect the city, no region in the environs of Jerusalem offered any protection to people who wished a normal security. The whole region was an open one. And after A.D.70, the Tenth Legion began to construct brick barracks on most of the southwestern hill. With the Roman military camp in that area, who would want to build a church in that region? Or, even more to the point, what Roman military commander would allow a Christian church to be constructed within (or very near) his encampment? This would have been highly irregular if not impossible. In no way were the western parts of Jerusalem or the southwest hill proper places to construct a new Christian church. The Mount of Olives, however, was an entirely different proposition. That region would have been possible, and in fact, that is exactly where Eusebius said the Jewish Christians when they returned from Pella in A.D.70 built their church. It became the "Mother Church" for all Christendom.

Even ordinary Jews (that is, non-Christian Jews) had the same problem in trying to relocate their administrative offices in the desolate areas which once were Jerusalem. Not only were all the regions in abject ruins, but the area of Jerusalem itself had become nothing more than a Roman military camp. With this being the situation, the Jewish authorities decided that they had no alternative but to leave Jerusalem altogether. They finally got permission from the Roman authorities to move their administrative headquarters for Jewish affairs to the town of Jamnia near the Mediterranean coast. And that is what they did. Jerusalem proved to be an improper place for the Jews to conduct any further their religious obligations, and so they abandoned it.

This identical predicament also faced the Jewish Christians who had just returned from Pella in the latter part of A.D.70. What were they to do? It was impossible to build on the southwest hill because the Tenth Legion was encamped in that area. All the rest of Jerusalem was in desolation. So, what region could serve as a proper place to build their headquarters church? The answer was not difficult to come by.

In the Book of Hebrews (which Christians now reckoned as inspired literature), the answer was made plain. It even recommended that Christians should abandon the old city of Jerusalem and journey outside its gates and outside its camp (Heb.13:10-14). To be outside the camp of Jerusalem meant that they had to be at least 2000 cubits (about 3000 feet) away from the former Holy Place in the Temple. And indeed, the author of Hebrews made it clear, from his continual reference to the Tabernacle in the wilderness (at the time of Moses), that *the* gate [that is, the *single* gate] through which Christians should retreat from Jerusalem was the *eastern* gate, because in the Tabernacle there were only gateways opening on its *east* side. To go through *the* gate [that is, the outer gate of the sanctuary] that the author of the Book of Hebrews commanded Christians to do, meant that Christians had to go *eastward* -- through the *east* gate. This would have led them away from old Jerusalem and directly up to the summit of the Mount of Olives. And that is exactly where Eusebius said the Jewish Christians built their new "House of God" (and headquarters) right after the destruction of Jerusalem in A.D.70. There would have been no more logical region.

Thus, Eusebius gave us some very revealing information in his early work *Proof of the Gospel* that the Christian "House of God" (the "Holy Church of God") was erected at the top of the Mount of Olives (VI,18). This church continued to exist as the center of Palestinian Christendom until the beginning of the fourth century. In fact, that church was still in operation when Eusebius wrote his historical work called *Proof of the Gospel.*

It must be recalled that there were no walls surrounding Jerusalem after A.D.70, and the historical evidence shows that no walls were built to enclose the city until the start of the third century. Speaking of an event in the early third century, Eusebius mentioned that there were then "gates" to the city (*Eccl.Hist.*, IX,11). It was no doubt felt unnecessary to construct walls around Aelia (the name for Jerusalem) as long as the Tenth Legion occupied the southwest hill and dominated the former areas of the city. The Tenth Legion remained headquartered in the southwest region of Jerusalem until about A.D.285 when it removed to Eilat on the Red Sea (Mazar, *ibid.*,p.237).

Once the Roman army ceased to occupy the southwestern area, it is possible that a small Christian church was built on the southwest hill and this could have been referred to by Epiphanius in the next century (*Weights and Measures* 14). Though a small church could have been constructed in the region, it is difficult to believe that it could have survived the destruction of churches and other Christian buildings in the Diocletian persecution that began in A.D.303 and lasted for ten years. This is because Eusebius (who was an eyewitness to affairs in Palestine at the time) said that there was a total devastation of all Christian churches in the region (*Eccl.Hist.*, VII,30,32). In no way could Epiphanius' "small church" have survived this utter desolation of the churches in Palestine. "In the nineteenth year of Diocletian's reign an imperial decree was published everywhere, ordering the churches to be razed to the ground" (*ibid.*, VIII,2). Or, as Eusebius said: "No longer satisfied with the old buildings, they raised from the foundation in all the cities churches spacious in plan" (*ibid.*, VIII,1). And, "I saw with my own eyes the places of worship thrown down from top to bottom, to the very foundations" (*ibid.*, VIII,2). Such destruction would have included, of course, any church on the southwest hill, but it also included the grandest church of all in Jerusalem, the "Mother Church" which had existed on the Mount of Olives from shortly after A.D.70.

What must be understood, however, is the fact that before the Diocletian persecution which began in A.D.303 (and the destruction of all the churches in Jerusalem), the only place that Christians worshipped was near the *cave/tomb* on the Mount of Olives. It was there that the building called the "House of God" was built. And this is the area to which the Shekinah Glory hovered for 3 and 1/2 years before Jerusalem was destroyed in A.D.70 to point out where the real region of "holiness" was located around the city of Jerusalem. This is where Christ was crucified and resurrected from the dead. It is no wonder that the Mount of Olives became known to early Christians as the *new* Mount Sion.

It is also significant that in the period before A.D.303, there is not the slightest mention that the region of the Temple of Venus in the western part of Jerusalem, or the area of the southwest hill, were in any way important. It was only after Constantine came on the scene as the first Christian emperor of the Roman Empire that these western locales began to be looked on as holy places.

It is also important to realize that Eusebius wrote the main part of his *Proof of the Gospel* just before (or during) the year of A.D.303. This was the very year that the Diocletian persecution began. But what does Eusebius describe was the historical environment in his *Proof of the Gospel*? At this early time, pilgrims were able to travel from around the Roman world to visit Jerusalem and Bethlehem [Book VI, 18 (288)]. But Eusebius made it clear that during the ten years of what is called the Diocletian persecution it was not possible to navigate the Mediterranean (*Eccl. Hist.*VIII.15.1). This continued until Constantine secured domination over the eastern half of the Roman Empire. But before A.D.303 (when Eusebius wrote the *Proof of the Gospel*) he was saying that "men still hasten from the ends of the earth" to visit Palestine [*Proof of the Gospel*, I.1 (4)] and that people were then flocking from abroad to come to the Holy Land [*ibid.*III.2 (97)]. And when Eusebius wrote this work there were then enormous churches found everywhere in the world [*ibid.*III.7 (138)]. But this prosperous condition that Eusebius was describing in his *Proof of the Gospel* changed in the very year he was writing this book. In spite of the prosperity that was then evident, he began to say that persecution was setting in [*ibid.*III.5 (119)]. From these historical indications it is pretty easy to date the writing of Eusebius' *Proof of the Gospel* to the year A.D.303. The reasons this is important is to show that the Christianity of A.D.303 that Eusebius was writing about in his *Proof of the Gospel* was very different from that which emerged with Constantine a short 25 years later.

In the next chapter we will show just why the attention of Christians was finally directed away from the Mount of Olives on the *east* of Jerusalem, and why they turned *westward* to the area of the Temple of Venus and the southwest hill. It was not because of any historical evidence described in the teaching of the New Testament that prompted these later Christians to make the change, nor was it because of early records maintained by the Jerusalem Church. No, it was none of these things. The reason for their selection of the Temple of Venus in the time of Constantine was because Christians began to pay heed to (and to trust in) many *new* spiritual revelations which began to come to Christian authorities through the medium of dreams, visions and wonders. The following chapter will explain.

B.C., before Constantine, the only Jeru area of Chr. significance was Olivet. That changed in 325 AD. Only now did the SW hill come to be called "Mt Zion" (where last supper is said to have taken place & acts 2 upper room). This was a change from the E. Jerusalem to W. Jeru. Until 325 Mt Zion was Olivet (Eusebius) after 70 AD, he says, the spiritual height of the Xd was Olivet. a church called "the Mother Church" near the cave was built there, the new Jeru. (Heb 12:13) The old Mt Zion was the temple mount, 77 never the SW hill.

9

Visions, Dreams and Signs

It has become customary since A.D.326 for the majority of the Christian world to accept the site now occupied by the Church of the Holy Sepulchre as the area for the resurrection of Christ. The reason this location was selected rests solely with the opinions of one man. That person was Constantine the Great who became the first emperor of the Romans to publicly accept Jesus Christ as his Savior and Lord. Of course, once Constantine became convinced that the Venus Shrine in the western part of Jerusalem was the true place of Christ's passion, he was able to persuade a number of people that his proofs were legitimate. And one must remember that the emperor's authority was supreme and people found it prudent not to arbitrarily question his convictions.

Did Constantine, however, select the correct spot? What prompted him to pick the region of the Venus Shrine? There is really no difficulty in answering these questions if we pay attention to the documentary evidence written during and immediately after the time of Constantine. The prime information comes from the top theologian and historian living in that period. This was Eusebius Pamphilus, bishop of Caesarea on the Palestinian coast.

The decision to select the Venus Shrine in Jerusalem as the site of Christ's resurrection was Constantine's alone. There was no theologian, or any council of theologians prior to A.D.326 (as recorded in the accounts we have available), who recommended to Constantine that the Venus Shrine was historically proper nor did anyone suggest that a memorial church should be built there. So surprising was Constantine's discovery to Eusebius that when the knowledge of it reached him, he said that the tomb of Christ located in that region was "*contrary to all expectation*" (*Life of Constantine*, III.28). Simply put, Eusebius was astonished at the revelation of Constantine. And he wasn't the only one who expressed surprise. When Eusebius said the location was "*contrary to all expectation*," his expression signified (by his use of the word "*all*") that no other theologian or historian of the fourth century had considered the Venus Shrine either. This interpretation of Eusebius' text is not my reading something into his statement that is not there. This is plainly what Eusebius was conveying to his readers.

But what prompted Constantine to insist that this western area was correct? Eusebius was well aware of why the emperor did what he did, but it still baffled him why he would insist that the Venus Shrine was the proper place when the Holy Scriptures and history did not support his interpretation. Constantine had a profound reason why he selected the western site. The emperor believed himself to possess special and superior intelligence that gave him an almost infallible assurance that he was correct in his decisions concerning matters such as these. His conviction that the Venus Shrine was proper was based on visions and dreams given to him (according to Constantine) by no less than Christ himself. It was visions and dreams that were more important to Constantine than what the Holy Scriptures had to say or what the historical records related as shown to him by men of lesser rank than he, including the testimonies of the theologians and bishops of the Church. Constantine thought he was in possession of *secret* knowledge that even the ordained bishops did not have.

Eusebius called attention to this belief of Constantine at the time the Church of the Holy Sepulchre was dedicated at Jerusalem in A.D.336 (some ten years after the spot was selected by Constantine). In Eusebius' speech of dedication, he petitioned the emperor to inform him and the other Christian bishops why he insisted on *this* spot as the place for Christ's resurrection. Though Constantine was not present at the ceremonies (an official was in Jerusalem who represented him), Eusebius nonetheless directed his dedicatory remarks to the emperor himself. In Eusebius' closing statement of his oration, he asked the emperor (as the spokesman for the combined assembly of ecclesiastical dignitaries who had come from most of the Roman world) to reveal to his bishops the *secret* intelligence that only he seemed to possess which caused him to select the Venus Shrine. And though Eusebius was aware that Constantine was utterly convinced that he was correct in his selection of the Venus Shrine, he wanted to know *why* he was convinced.

Eusebius commenced this summing up of his dedicatory remarks in chapter XVIII of his *Oration* by mentioning the profound convictions of Constantine regarding the site of the Holy Sepulchre: "*convinced as you are by FREQUENT and PERSONAL experience of our Saviour's Diety*." Because of supernatural experiences which so frequently accompanied the emperor, Eusebius made a plea to Constantine that at some future time when he had the leisure to explain more about his extraordinary intelligence concerning divine things that he might "relate *to us* [the bishops of the Christian Church] the abundant manifestations which your Saviour has accorded you of His presence, and the *oft-repeated VISIONS of Himself* that have attended you in the hours of sleep. I speak not of those *secret* suggestions *which to us are unrevealed:* but of those principles which He has instilled into *your own mind*, which are fraught with general interest and benefit to the human race. . . . You [Constantine] will, it may be, also detail *to us* [the bishops] those particulars of His favor *which are SECRET to us, but known to YOU ALONE,* and treasured in your royal memory as *in SECRET storehouses.* Such, doubtless, are the reasons, and such the *convincing proofs* of your Saviour's power, *which caused YOU to RAISE UP that sacred edifice* [the Church of the Holy Sepulchre which was then being dedicated] which presents to all, believers and unbelievers alike, a trophy of victory over death, *a holy temple of the Holy God*" (*The Oration of Eusebius,* XVIII emphases mine).

In simple language, Eusebius was asking Constantine to explain to his bishops why his supernatural visions had directed his attention to *this* place then being dedicated?

Eusebius knew that Constantine was convinced in the reliability of his visionary experiences, but to Eusebius and the bishops then assembled in Jerusalem it was not clear to them why the area of the Venus Shrine was selected. None of them had been graced with such "secret" knowledge. Indeed, such particulars, said Eusebius, "*are secret TO US, but known to YOU ALONE.*" Eusebius petitioned Constantine to show them "*the convincing proofs . . . which caused YOU to RAISE UP that sacred edifice* [the Church of the Holy Sepulchre]."

Note that Eusebius couched his queries to Constantine amongst a great deal of laudatory language designed not to infuriate the emperor's sensitivities regarding his spiritual opinions and certainly not to question the visions or their genuineness. After all, Eusebius and the other bishops were quite interested in maintaining the top part of their anatomies attached to their nether parts. And this appraisal is no exaggeration because at this time of Constantine's life he was very stern in his demeanor with his subjects.

The truth is, there was not the slightest biblical or historical evidence to sustain the selection of this western site as the proper place of Christ's passion. Indeed, just the opposite was the case and Eusebius provides the evidence (as will be shown) which demonstrates this fact. Yet, Constantine's opinion prevailed while he remained alive. And fourteen years after his death a celestial event took place (explained in chapter eleven) that convinced many people that Constantine's selection of the Venus Shrine was correct.

But what must be understood by us of modern times is the fact that the present Church of the Holy Sepulchre in Jerusalem was selected as the site of Christ's passion exclusively through the agency of *visionary signs* and *dreams* that Constantine had experienced. This is attested by the historian Sozomen about a hundred years after Constantine. Notice what he said in Book Two, chapter one.

> "It was no easy matter to discover the Lord's sepulchre...however the place was discovered...*by means of signs and dreams*; for I do not think that human information [that is, any historical record] is required when God thinks it best to make manifest the same" (*Eccl.Hist.*,II.1).

The supernatural signs and dreams to which Sozomen was referring came from Constantine and his mother Helena. His mother had been sent to Jerusalem for the express purpose of discovering the true site of Christ's resurrection. And she found the exact spot all right (at least to her satisfaction), and she did it through visions and dreams, not through biblical or historical records.

Constantine had earlier been interested in the "holy places" in Jerusalem. He issued an edict to his eastern subjects after the defeat of Licinius (about A.D.324) which included a remarkable prayer to God in which he asked that there might be a "restoration of Thy most holy dwelling-place" (*Life of Constantine*, II.55). This prayer showed Constantine's desire to rebuild the Temple in Jerusalem at this early date. The edict was taken with joy by the Jews and they even began to rebuild the Temple. This rebuilding activity is mentioned by John Chrysostom in his oration *Against the Jews*, VI. But after the Nicean Council in the summer of A.D.325, Constantine began to have an hostile attitude to the Jews and he caused them to cease their rebuilding of the Temple. It was then that the emperor's attention turned to another project that had been occupying his mind for some time. Instead of rebuilding the Temple of the Jews as an honor to God, he decided to erect a memorial in Jerusalem to the resurrection of Christ. Eusebius explains.

"After these things [after the events resulting from the Nicean Council], the pious emperor addressed himself to another work truly worthy of record, in the province of Palestine. What was this work? He judged it incumbent on him to render *the blessed locality* of our Saviour's resurrection an object of attraction and veneration to all. He issued immediate injunctions, therefore, for the erection in that spot of a house of prayer: and this he did, *not on mere natural impulse* of his own mind, but *being moved IN SPIRIT by the Saviour himself*" (*Life of Constantine*, III.25).

But even before the Nicean Council took place, Eusebius said Constantine had a visionary experience "that a house of prayer worthy of the worship of God should be erected near the Saviour's tomb" (*ibid.*, III.29). "This object he had indeed *FOR SOME TIME* kept in view *AND HAD FORSEEN* as if by the aid of a superior intelligence, that which should afterwards come to pass" (*ibid.*). Professor T.D.Barnes gives the correct translation of Eusebius' *Oration* (11:1) to show that Constantine was used to "frequent divine visions" (*Constantine and Eusebius*, p.368).

Indeed, Constantine was long used to visionary experiences. From the year A.D.312 they had become a regular part of the emperor's life. From that year he had frequent supernatural occurrences happening in his career. And what is extraordinary, according to Constantine, he never had a reversal in his affairs if he heeded his visions.

The start of his trust in the supernatural happened at a momentous time in Constantine's life. Just before the battle at Milvian Bridge outside Rome which gained for him the mastery of the western part of the Roman Empire, he witnessed (along with his troops) a parhelion of the sun which appeared to him as a cross in the heavens. He noticed with the cross the Greek letters (Chi Rho) accompanied with the words "by this sign conquer." That evening he said that in his sleep "the Christ of God" came and told him to adopt the sign of the "Chi Rho" as a symbol to protect him and his armies and that he would ever be victorious (*Life of Constantine*, I.29). Constantine immediately had his army portray on their shields this sign of the "Chi Rho" which became the Labarum (a Roman shield symbol) for his conquering armies. And, amazingly, Constantine from that time forward never lost a decisive battle but he blazed forth with victory after victory until he became emperor of the whole Roman Empire. He came to believe that this "Chi Rho" symbol represented the first two letters in Greek of "Christ." And he felt it symbolized the Christ of the Christians. It was this extraordinary "supernatural sign" (as Constantine believed it was) that prompted the emperor to think he had been divinely selected to bring in a universal kingdom that would recognize the deity of Christ Jesus and that it was through Christ (and his servant Constantine) that divine salvation and peace would finally be brought to the world.

This visionary experience had a profound effect upon Constantine. In the following years he featured himself as the divinely chosen instrument of God to bring in the universal (catholic) kingdom to the totality of the world. It gave Constantine great confidence that he was a special and elect vessel of God himself. And all the battles that Constantine fought from A.D.312 onward, with what he called the salutary sign of the "Chi Rho" in the advance of his armies, convinced him that he was indeed that special person selected by God to bring to pass the universal kingdom of Christ on earth.

Not long after the visionary experience at Milvian Bridge, Constantine began to conceive of himself as a *new* Moses to lead the true people of God into a *new* world kingdom with Constantine as its head (*ibid.*, I.12). He reckoned that he was the instrument to inaugurate the "new Jerusalem" of the prophets (*ibid.*, III.33). And to accommodate Constantine's identification with Moses, he had a special tent constructed in the form of a cross which he, like Moses, placed "outside the camp" (alluding to Exodus 33:7). Into this tent only he and his trusted advisors would enter before any engagement with the enemy. It was there that he sought divine counsel to direct him in what he should do. "And making earnest supplications to God, he was *always* honored after a little while with a manifestation of His [God's] presence. And then, as if moved *by a divine impulse*, he would rush from the tent, and suddenly give orders to his army to move at once without delay, and on the instant to draw their swords. On this they would immediately commence the attack, fight vigorously, so as with incredible celerity to secure the victory, and raise trophies of victory over their enemies" (*ibid.*, II.12).

Constantine was always in the habit of consulting his heavenly advisors and he was not disappointed in his petitions. Things were "miraculously revealed by God *through VISIONS to His servant* [Constantine]. For He [God] *freqently* vouchsafed to him manifestations of Himself, the Divine presence appearing to him in a most marvelous manner, and according to him *manifold intimations* of future events. Indeed, it is impossible to express in words the indescribable *wonders of Divine grace* which God was pleased to vouchsafe to His servant [Constantine]" (*ibid.*, I.47).

And very *frequent* indeed were the manifestations that Constantine received from his celestial advisors. Eusebius said that Constantine's visions and other supernatural encounters became such a regular part of his career that "a *thousand* such acts as these were *familiarly* and *habitually* done by the emperor" (*ibid.*, II.14 compare with 12). Constantine's life was replete with visions, dreams and supernatural wonders and they were a dominant factor in all his major decisions. There was no exception to this procedure in his selection of the Venus Shrine in Jerusalem as being the "true" spot of Christ's passion. There was not any biblical or historical teaching that prompted Constantine to select this western area for the location of Christ's tomb nor was there any biblical encouragement for him to build a memorial church in that place. Eusebius informs us that it was "not on the mere natural impulse of his own mind [that he picked the Venus Shrine in Jerusalem], but *being moved in spirit by the Saviour himself*" (*ibid.*, III.25). Eusebius simply reported that Constantine selected the location because of supernatural signs given to him.

The decision to build a church at the place of Christ's resurrection was made by Constantine in A.D.326 probably while he was in Rome (and after he executed his son Crispus and his wife Fausta and felt sorry for his deeds). As a means of atoning for his actions against his own family (and to get over his melancholy attitude that was afflicting him at the time) he came to the conclusion that it was necessary to raise up a monument to Christ's passion in Jerusalem. Indeed, his initial desire to build such a memorial church at the site appears to have occurred to him even before A.D.326. Eusebius mentions that some kind of supernatural impulse had long before inspired Constantine to build a memorial church at the place of Christ's tomb. Note what Eusebius said on the matter: "This object he had indeed *for some time* [in the past] kept in view, *and had FORESEEN*, as if by the aid of a superior intelligence, that which should afterwards come to pass" (*ibid.*, III.29).

But in A.D.326, and in a sense of urgency, he sent his

mother Helena to Jerusalem to discover the spot that he "*had foreseen*" as the place of Christ's resurrection. To Constantine "foreseeing things" was nothing new. As an example of this, Eusebius records that at one time while Constantine was in his imperial palace some 700 miles away from Lebanon, and like an eagle that could look down and see distant objects which no ordinary human could perceive, the emperor was able to observe quite vividly a foul Venus Shrine in the mountains of Lebanon. What Constantine saw in vision (or in a dream) was a school for training initiates in the religious debauchery of the mysteries of Venus. The emperor was so incensed at what his visionary experience revealed to him that he gave an immediate command to utterly destroy that secret Venus Shrine. This was done as soon as Constantine's orders reached his army in Lebanon (*ibid.*, III.55; *The Oration of Eusebius*, VIII.5,6). Eusebius himself was amazed at the supernatural power of Constantine to observe things at a great distance that no other ordinary humans could perceive. Interestingly, no one in the metropolitan area of Lebanon knew that such a Venus Shrine existed in their mountains. But Constantine far away in Constantinople was able to describe the details of the debauchery that were going on at the site, and his description was with such precision that even Eusebius was amazed at the emperor's perceptions. But this was no uncommon thing to Constantine. Eusebius said that such supernatural "forethought" of Constantine was a frequent characteristic of the unusual psychic powers that the emperor seemed to possess with his determinations (*The Oration of Eusebius*, VIII.7).

The Shrines to Venus which were located throughout the Roman Empire were particulary offensive to Constantine (as they would be to any decent person who respected commonsense morality). Though Constantine gave an order to destroy all heathen shrines in the empire, he was foremostly hostile to the pagan temples that advocated orgiastic rites and at the top of his list for destruction were Venus Shrines. Those sacred areas of debauchery were in the "first" category for annihilation in the opinion of Constantine (*The Oration of Eusebius*, VII.3). Most other pagan temples which simply honored the national gods and goddesses of the various peoples of the empire were normally allowed to continue their rites, yet the ones which advocated orgiastic activities with effeminate men as priests and temple prostitutes as their chief protagonists (especially the Venus Shrines where such things were commonly done) were especially abhorrent to Constantine and he levelled them to the ground.

The common practice of Constantine was to destroy the most offensive of pagan temples and build in their locations Christian churches. He suppressed the immoral practices at a pagan temple in Heliopolis of Lebanon and built a church in its place (*ibid.*, III.58). It was recognized that Constantine overturned many celebrated temples to raise churches upon their ruins. Thus, when Eusebius saw the army of Constantine tearing down the Temple of Venus in Jerusalem, this would have caused him little surprise (and even if Constantine gave the orders that a Christian church was to be built there), but when it came to Eusebius' attention that Helena, who in late A.D.326 was in Jerusalem, began to call the site of the Venus Shrine the place of Christ's sepulchre, Eusebius began to express concern. This must be the case because somewhere in this very period Eusebius urgently sent a message to Constantine *begging* him for permission to present to him a scriptural discourse "on the subject of our Saviour's sepulchre" (*ibid.*, IV.33). Eusebius was so anxious to present his teaching about this matter that he informed those who were reading his work *The Life of Constantine* that this was one event "I must by no means omit to record." He made a special journey from his home in Palestine to the imperial palace in Constantinople to present this material on Christ's tomb to the emperor himself.

Upon his arrival at the palace and in the midst of the emperor and a large number of Constantine's advisors, Eusebius commenced his discourse on the subject of Christ's sepulchre. All seemed quite in order except for one thing. While Eusebius lectured, the emperor refused to sit down! Constantine remained standing with fixed attention on Eusebius. This attitude of the emperor was disturbing to Eusebius (as it would be to anyone trying to present a subject of importance to those in his audience). The body-language of Constantine was rather easy for Eusebius to read. "I entreated him, but in vain, to seat himself on the imperial throne which stood near, but he continued with fixed attention to weigh the topics of my discourse" (*ibid.*, IV.33). And up to this point in Eusebius' lecture the emperor gave his assent "to the truth of the theological doctrines it contained," but he still refused to sit down and he exhorted Eusebius to continue his presentation. So, Eusebius proceeded with his essential teaching about Christ's sepulchre. And what did Constantine do? He continued to stand with fixed attention and he weighed every word Eusebius was saying. Now notice what happened.

"After some time had passed, the oration being of considerable length, I was myself desirous of concluding; *but this he would not permit*, and exhorted me to proceed to the very end. On my again *ENTREATING HIM TO SIT*, he in his turn was displeased and said that it was not right to listen in a careless manner to the discussion of doctrines relating to God; and again, that this posture [of standing with fixed attention] was good and profitable to himself, since it was reverent *TO STAND* while listening to sacred truths. Having therefore, concluded my discourse, *I returned home and resumed my usual occupations*" (*Life of Constantine*, IV.33)

This was a most unnerving experience for Eusebius. There was nothing courteous to Eusebius by this action of Constantine. Indeed, it was an overbearing display. Revealingly, Eusebius stated three chapters before (*Life of Constantine*, IV.29) that when the emperor was in the habit of standing erect at the time sacred topics were discussed he would then assume "a grave aspect and subdued tone of voice." The truth is, when Constantine remained standing throughout the long discourse of Eusebius about Christ's sepulchre in Jerusalem, he was showing forth an obstinate and fixed attitude toward the topic being discussed. In a word, Eusebius was being intimidated! And what was the outcome of this crucial conference about Christ's sepulchre that brought Eusebius all the way to Constantinople to present to the emperor? The emperor won the day! Eusebius summed it up very well. In a curt and matter-of-fact way, Eusebius (in so many words) said: "With Constantine in the attitude he was in, I packed up my belongings and went on home to Palestine where I continued my usual occupations." Eusebius apparently got nowhere with the emperor!

At this point in history there was no turning back for Constantine. He had now identified, to his satisfaction, the exact area where Christ had been resurrected from the dead. Visions, dreams and miracles had succeeded! In his letter to Macarius, the bishop in Jerusalem, Constantine admitted it was a "wonderous circumstance" that had revealed the site of Christ's passion (*Life of Constantine*, III.30). The emperor acknowledged to Macarius that the place had "remained *unknown* for so long a series of years" but now the site had once again been discovered by Constantine. The emperor called it "*this miracle* as far transcends the capacity of human reason as heavenly things are superior to human affairs" (*ibid.*). In other words, human reasoning [what he meant was "historical documents" and ordinary proofs that most humans accept as evidence] was not the proof that Constantine had for substantiating that his site for Christ's sepulchre was correct. Indeed, the emperor said that the location was being confirmed "by fresh wonders" revealed in Constantinople (not in Palestine) that made the location certain in the opinion of Constantine. The emperor simply told Macarius that it was by divine knowledge that the place where the Venus Shrine stood had been legitimatized as Christ's sepulchre. In his official orders to Macarius to build a church at the site which was to be "the most marvelous place in the world" (*ibid.*, III.31), Constantine said "I have disencumbered that sacred spot *under divine direction*" and he informed Macarius that he had "a clear assurance" that his determination of the spot was correct (*ibid.*). Eusebius wrote that Constantine was the "discoverer" (and no one else) of the sacred places in Palestine (*ibid.*, III.41). and that he was "under the guidance of the divine Spirit" in accomplishing this (*ibid.*, III.26).

But by what authority did Constantine sustain his beliefs even when Eusebius and the other bishops had no evidence of a biblical or historical nature to vouch for such teachings? That is not difficult to determine. Constantine felt himself to be of higher authority in making judgments on religious matters than even the theologians and bishops of the church. After all, it was Constantine who approved the final decisions of the bishops at the Nicean Council and he put the edicts into effect. Eusebius records that "once on the occasion of his entertaining a company of bishops, he let fall the expression, 'that he himself too was a bishop,' addressing them in my hearing in the following words: 'You are bishops whose jurisdiction is within the Church: *I am also a bishop, ordained by God* to overlook what is external to the Church'" (*Life of Constantine*, IV.24).

Truly, Constantine came to feel that his prestige was far more eminent than the authority possessed by the bishops. He even reckoned himself as equal to the apostles of Christ. When he designed a church in Constantinople in honor of the twelve apostles, he placed twelve coffins in the midst of the church. But in the middle of them (with six on one side and six on the other) he placed his own monumental coffin in which he was placed after death. This is because, as Eusebius tells us, the emperor felt that he "shared his title with the apostles themselves" (*ibid.*, IV.60). And interestingly, the Greek Church to this day recognizes Constantine as "Equal to the Apostles" (Hastings, *Dict. Religion and Ethics*, vol.IV,p.78). The fact is, how could anyone in the fourth century disagree with the emperor who thought himself to be an "apostle" of Christ? Constantine had such an exalted opinion of his authority (and this was recognized by others at the time) that he saw his rule within the Roman Empire as being like that of Moses at the time of the Exodus (*ibid.*, I.12) and better than that of Cyrus or Alexander the Great. No one in the world (including Eusebius or even the bishop of Rome) could approach Constantine's "divine stature" in the authority he thought he had.

Eusebius, however, speaking at the dedication of the Church of the Holy Sepulchre in A.D.336 asked Constantine to reveal to his bishops the reason *why* he selected the Venus Shrine for the site of Christ's resurrection? Eusebius was not insubordinate in his request. He said that he and the other bishops in Jerusalem were not "presuming to instruct *you*

[Constantine] who is yourself taught of God; nor to disclose to *you* those secret wonders which He himself, not through the agency of man, but through our common Saviour, and the *frequent light* of His divine presence *has long since revealed and unfolded TO YOUR VIEW*" (*The Oration of Eusebius*, XI.1). At this dedication, Eusebius acknowledged that the Church of the Holy Sepulchre and its adjacent buildings were "lofty and noble structures, imperial monuments of an imperial spirit, which you [Constantine] have erected in honor of the everlasting memory of the Saviour's tomb, *the cause*, I say, of these things *IS NOT EQUALLY OBVIOUS TO ALL*" (*ibid.*). It was not discernible to Eusebius and the other bishops *why* Constantine picked *this* spot. In fact it did not seem obvious to anybody except Constantine. Of course it was realized that the emperor was guided by supernatural signs to pick the place then being dedicated. "These works are the result, to appreciate the *more than human impulse* by which our emperor *was guided* to admire his piety toward God, and to believe his care for the memorial of our Saviour's resurrection to be a desire *imparted from above*" (*ibid.*, XI.6).

To Eusebius there was no obvious reason which most humans relied on (such as historical documents) for erecting the monuments to Christ's resurrection at the location where the Venus Shrine formerly stood. That's why he asked Constantine at this dedication of the Church of the Holy Sepulchre, "convinced as you are by *frequent* and *personal experience*. . . .that you will at a time of leisure to relate to us [the bishops of the Church] the abundant manifestations which your Saviour has accorded you of His presence, and the *oft-repeated VISIONS of Himself* which have attended you in the hours of sleep. . . . You will, it may be, *also* detail to us [the bishops] those particulars of His favor *which are SECRET to us,* but *KNOWN TO YOU ALONE*, and treasured in your royal memory as in *secret storehouses*. Such, doubtless, are the reasons, and such the convincing proofs of your Saviour's power, *which caused you* [Constantine] *TO RAISE THAT SACRED EDIFICE* [the Church of the Holy Sepulchre] which presents to all, believers and unbelievers alike, a trophy of his victory over death, a holy temple of the holy God" (*The Oration of Eusebius*, XVIII emphases mine).

In other words, Eusebius and the assembled bishops in Jerusalem saw no obvious reason why Constantine would have picked the site of the Venus Shrine as the place for a church to the memory of Christ's resurrection. The selection of the spot came through *secret* visions and supernatural revelations known only to Constantine. The emperor's opinions, however, prevailed. He claimed to possess divine knowledge, just like the apostles, and those visionary experiences gave him the essential teachings which he thought to have as their source his Saviour and which he considered necessary for all the Christian Church (including the bishops) to follow.

But where did Constantine get his authority to make decisions on such matters? True, Constantine was assured he had the power. Note that he even proclaimed himself a bishop along with the other bishops of the Church, and indeed, he thought himself of more exalted rank than the bishops because he reckoned himself as being an apostle of Christ (and in his burial he outranked all the original apostles of Christ). And to demonstrate this authority that Constantine thought he possessed, he presided (and made the ultimate decisions on doctrines) over the first ecumenical meeting of the Church since the time of the apostles which was held at Nicaea. There was no individual (including the bishop of Rome or the bishop of Constantinople) who held more power in the Christian Church than that which Constantine thought himself to have. But note this. While all this authority of Constantine was being exercised within the Christian Church, Constantine himself *was not even a baptized member!*

The fact is, Constantine did not become a member of the Church through the normal ceremony of baptism until he was on his death bed. But in spite of this lack, it was he who made all the important decisions in matters concerning the Christian Church from A.D.326 until his death in A.D.337.

These extraordinary procedures show how a secular ruler of the Roman Empire (though he was giving lip-service to a belief in Christ) could completely dominate the ordained "ministers of Christ," even in deciding on crucial theological matters about which only the bishops of the Christian Church supposedly had authority to decide upon. And ever since Constantine took over essential control of the Christian Church, all Christians have had to be wedded to those decisions instigated by the emperor Constantine on prime theological matters affecting the Christian Church.

What actually happened is that Constantine was able to persuade some bishops that his visions, dreams and signs were proper. If only the principal bishops would have had in their hands the teachings of St. John of the Cross who lived in the 16th century about the real dangers of trusting in visions, dreams and signs, they could have been spared the great falsehood concerning the whereabouts of Christ's sepulchre that was being perpetrated upon some of the bishops of the Church (*Ascent of Mount Carmel*, Bk.II, XVI through XXIX). No one in early times has given a better appraisal of how dangerous and foolish it is to trust in visions, dreams and signs than the appraisal of St. John of the Cross. His classic evaluation should be read by all people today who rely upon such manifestations as visions, dreams and miracles as a means for establishing doctrines or religious principles. Such procedures are some of the most dangerous imaginable in their ability to produce falsehood and deception amongst the unwary. Had there been a "St. John of the Cross" at the time of Constantine (with the warnings he so ably presented to the theological world of the 16th century), and had he been believed, then the Christian Church would not have been saddled with the supposedly "divine" teachings of Constantine and his advisors about the need to accept the place of the Temple of Venus as the place of Christ's passion. It would have been understood that visions, dreams and miracles are the most unreliable "proofs" for demonstrating historical, geographical and theological truths.

But in actual fact, there was indeed, at the time of

Constantine, a "St. John of the Cross" who warned Constantine (and the Christian Church) of the dangers of the teachings that were being accepted because of the visionary experiences of Constantine. But his appeal for biblical and historical commonsense on these matters was not received by Constantine and his chief advisors. Who was this person? It was none other than Eusebius himself! That's right. Eusebius actually stood up for the truth and he has left us with an abundance of information to show how wrong Constantine was in his decisions that have dominated Christian belief ever since. X

In the next chapter it will be shown how Eusebius recognized the problems that the actions of Constantine had brought upon the Christian Church in the fourth century and we will see the methods Eusebius adopted to combat the anti-biblical teachings that were being dispensed by Constantine.

This ch. explains the basis of Constantine's decision to bld a Xch to X's death on the Venus site. The info comes fr. Eusebius of Caesarea. Constantine, like charismatics, (p93) who was [illegible] by X. He did not consult the Xch, [illegible] visions & dreams; [illegible] his [illegible] 98 96, 104, 94. The Xch was dedicated [illegible] trad. [illegible], but his secret [illegible] 95. Eusebius speech. 95. At 1st Constantine edicted the Jews to [illegible] 336 A.D. rebuild the temple, but after Nicea rescinded it & decided to bld the Xch instead — also guilt fr. murder of wife. 100 One of Constantine's vision was "by this sign conquer" 98 He was convinced it was he who was called to Christianize the world, a "Moses" who speaks [illegible] "outside" & thus being X's return. He saw himself as a [illegible]. Vision of the evil of his military camps" 99-100 (cf Reagan's astrology). Vision of the evil of the Venus shrine made him order its destruction. 101, because of orgies w/ homosex priests & temple prostitutes. On their sites he bld Xchs. Eusebius made a special trip to Constantinople to dismiss the error, but Constantine was bored. 102. intimidating Eusebius. 103 saw himself as one of the apostles. 105, buried w/ them, superior to the bishops. yet he was not yet a baptized member of the Xch, until his death in 337.

Beware of visionaries & dreams. 108.

10

The Counterfeit Golgotha

When it was realized by Eusebius that Constantine had abandoned the teaching of the Holy Scriptures in favor of the information he received from visions, dreams and signs, he decided on a different format of instruction for those who believed in the teaching of the Bible. What he did was to provide a way in which those trained in the Holy Scriptures could recognize his *real* teachings from the counterfeit. He began by combining an oration given at Constantine's death with the discourse that he gave at the dedication of the Church of the Holy Sepulchre in Jerusalem. He made one document out of the two separate works and it has become known as *The Oration of Eusebius.* He provided an introduction to the whole work (the first chapter) then from chapter two to chapter ten (inclusively) he recorded his *Oration to Constantine* as a eulogy at the time of his death, then from chapter eleven to the end of chapter eighteen he recorded the discourse that he gave in Jerusalem at the dedication of the Church of the Holy Sepulchre. It was in his last chapter (XVIII) that he asked Constantine to tell him and the bishops *why* his visions had him select the region of the Venus Shrine as the place of Christ's passion.

The most important part of the two "*Orations*," however, is the "Introduction" itself. It is a powerful testimony of Eusebius that gives his own opinions on what the *truth* really was concerning the activities of Constantine. Though these two "*Orations*" are filled with much laudatory praise about Constantine (indeed, Eusebius gave excessive flattery to the point of *ad nauseam*), it appears to me that this maneuver of Eusebius was a literary device to get his readers' attention.

The fact is, this style of writing was so out-of-character with Eusebius. Never had he resorted to such honeycombed fawning of a person. This was so *unlike* Eusebius! And that is no doubt the exact appraisal that Eusebius wanted his readers to make. Anyone who would have known Eusebius before the time of Constantine (and those familiar with his early writings) would have said: "*This* is *NOT* the Eusebius that we have known in the past." With this in mind, Eusebius was actually saying to his readers: "Anyone reading these *Orations* should know me better than this, so don't take me seriously in these teachings about Constantine." He gave two major "keys" in the text of the *Orations* to show this.

In his Introduction Eusebius gave some instructions on how to interpret what he was actually meaning. Once this first "key" to his type of discourse was understood, Eusebius then informed his readers not to deviate from that "key." This "key" would show that the Church of the Holy Sepulchre as the place of Christ's passion is a counterfeit manufactured by Constantine. To recognize this first (as well as his second) "key," one must strip away all of his sycophant comments about Constantine that he gave in his Introduction and in the two "*Orations*," and one will be left with some revealing information that shows the real character of Constantine and the actual type of government Eusebius thought Constantine was introducing. Eusebius shows that Constantine and his government were contrary to the simple teachings of the Holy Scriptures.

Eusebius starts out his Introduction by saying: "I come not forward prepared with a fictitious narrative, nor with elegance of language to captivate the ear, desiring to charm my hearers." The fact is, Eusebius wanted to tell the truth, but it would not be understood by "the common crowd." He said that he was "leaving the common track of men to pursue the untrodden path which it is unlawful to enter with unwashed feet," but those who are truly tuned in with the holy teachings of God would perceive what the truth really is. He said his teaching was only for those "who are *initiated* into the universal science [the queen of sciences, *real* theology], and have attained to Divine as well as human knowledge." And though in the Introduction Eusebius shows (with excessive laudation) that Constantine was great and noble and had celestial wisdom with things in reference to God, Eusebius was really telling the *initiated* something quite different. These are the people to whom Eusebius was appealing. He said: "Let those, however, who are within the sanctuary, and have access to its inmost and untrodden recesses, close the doors against every profane ear, and unfold, as it were, *the secret mysteries* of our emperor's character *TO THE INITIATED ALONE*." To Eusebius, only those who were *initiated* would be able to perceive the *secrets* of Constantine's character. And who were the "*initiated*"? The true "*initiated*" were those who obtained their instruction from "*the sacred oracles* [the Holy Scriptures], *given not by the spirit of divination, or rather let me say of madness and folly, but by the inspiration of Divine truth,* [let them] *BE OUR INSTRUCTORS in these mysteries*."

As plain as Eusebius could make it, he directed his readers to the one standard by which all mysteries can be understood. He told his readers to let the Holy Scriptures "*be our instructors*" *and never to deviate from them!* This is the "key" that Eusebius was giving to his readers. He insisted that only the Holy Scriptures should be consulted and relied on for the understanding of secret mysteries and not "the spirit of divination, or rather let me say, of madness and folly" that was prompting Constantine and his advisors. Eusebius taught that one should stay with the Holy Scriptures to discover all matters of divine truth. Doing this would allow his readers to discern "*THE COUNTERFEIT COIN*." Or, as Eusebius closed his Introduction, "With these oracles [the Holy Scriptures], then, *to initiate* us in the knowledge of the sacred mysteries, let us essay, as follows the commencement of our divine mysteries."

It was quite common in this period (and several centuries before) for many authors to record information in their works that only their *initiates* would understand. As for Eusebius he called attention to this literary device that he thought was used even in the Scriptures and was also utilized by Plato to record his true feelings concerning any subject if he found it prudent to do so. This is how Eusebius thought the Holy Scriptures were written (as well as Plato). It was one thing to read the outward teaching and gain excellent information, but the wise were advised to dig beneath the surface and find secret communications which only the *initiated* could understand. Note what Eusebius said.

"But the deep and hidden reason of these things [in the Scriptures] they [the prophets] left to be sought out and learned *in secret communications* by those who were capable of being *initiated* in matters of this kind. It will be well, however, to describe in a general way a few points in the contemplation of these matters, and to show that herein also Plato entertained the sentiments which were dear to the said people" (*Preparation of the Gospel*, Bk.XI.7).

And to show this principle adopted by Plato to instruct those *initiated* into his *real* doctrines, Eusebius said that the philosopher actually believed that there was in reality a singular God but that he commonly referred to the Deity in the plural when he was talking to the uninitiated.

"But that he [Plato] had a knowledge of one God, even though in accordance with the custom of the Greeks he commonly speaks of them as many, is evident from the *Epistle to Dionysius*, in which, giving marks to distinguish his letters written in earnest from those thrown off at random, he said that he would put the name of 'The gods' as a sign at the head of those which contained nothing serious, but the name of 'God' at the head of those which were thoughtfully composed by him. Accordingly he thus speaks word for word: 'With regard then to the distinctive mark concerning the letters which I may write seriously, and those which not, though I suppose you remember it, nevertheless bear it in mind and give great attention to it. For there are many who bid me to write, whom it is not easy for me openly to refuse. So then the serious letter begins with *God*, and the less serious with *gods*'" (*ibid.*, XI.13).

Eusebius had the same problem Plato encountered. He was also called on to give orations and to write discourses by those "whom it is not easy openly to refuse." The bishop found himself having to resort to this common stratagem in order (not simply to preserve his life, which was no doubt a factor) but that his early writings might be preserved for posterity. Had Eusebius been *utterly plain* in his dealings with Constantine, there was a chance that not only he, but his writings as well would have been destroyed. His historical works were most important for those of the future who would need to know the truth of what was happening to Christianity at this period of time. Eusebius was used to resorting to the literary devices that most authors and teachers were forced to apply if they found themselves within an hostile environment to the teaching of their truths. So, Eusebius tells his readers of the Introduction to his "*Orations*" that those who are truly *initiated* into the divine and secret mysteries of the Holy Scriptures will be able to identify the true character of Constantine and the actual source of his government which he was then forcing on the Christian world and the Roman Empire itself. But to do so the *initiated* would have to pay attention to the "key" that Eusebius provides to understand his *true* teaching. And what is that "key"? He said:

> "Let those, however, who are within the sanctuary, and have access to its inmost and untrodden recesses, close the doors against every profane ear, and unfold, as it were, the secret mysteries of our emperor's character *to the initiated alone*. And let those who have purified their ears in the streams of piety, and raised their thoughts on the soaring wing of the mind itself, join the company which surrounds the Sovereign Lord of all [God], and learn in silence the divine mysteries. Meanwhile *let the sacred oracles* [the Holy Scriptures], given not by the spirit of divination, or rather let me say of madness and folly, but by *the inspiration of divine truth*, be our instructors in these mysteries; speaking to us of the sovereignty, generally: of him who is the Supreme Sovereign of all, and the heavenly array which surrounds the Lord of all; of that [true] example of imperial power which is before us, *AND THAT COUNTERFEIT COIN*" (*The Oration of Eusebius*, I.4,5).

Eusebius told the *initiated* to stay away from the madness, the folly, the spirit of divination and the counterfeit coin and remain solidly with the teachings of the Holy Scriptures (which he called "the sacred oracles"). Eusebius provided much *secret* teaching if the *initiated* retained the interpretation which came solely from the Holy Scriptures. Note this. When he gave his *Oration* concerning the thirtieth anniversary of Constantine's coming to power in the Roman Empire, Eusebius said this number of years represented "the revolution of three cycles of ten years" (*The Oration of Eusebius*, VI.1). And then he went into a long discourse on the numbers 1, 2, 3 and 4 and that in a special way the number 4 produces 10. But how can 4 lead directly to the number 10? Eusebius gave the answer: "The number four produces the number ten. For the aggregate of one, and two, and three, and four, is ten" (*ibid.*, VI.5).

The whole of his sixth chapter is devoted to the discussion on the significance of these numbers and the importance of a triad of tens which equals thirty (the number of years of Constantine's rule). The commentator of the *Nicene and Post-Nicene Fathers* (vol.I, p.587) did not know why Eusebius saw significance in the numbers 1, 2, 3 and 4 giving an aggregate of 10, but he thought the concept was probably Pythagorean in origin. He called attention to the fact that Philo in the first century (*de Mund.Opif.* ch.15) also mentioned that the sum of the first four numbers produced 10 (and that it was significant in matters dealing with creation). Did Eusebius have the same thing in mind? Without doubt he did! It is pretty clear what Eusebius was trying to show his readers what was being *created* right in front of their eyes in the middle part of the fourth century *if* they would simply let the Holy Scriptures (not Pythagoras) be their inspired guide.

All of those *initiated* into the divine mysteries of the Sacred Scriptures should have been able to know what Eusebius was talking about. It is not difficult for us to see as well. In the Book of Daniel we have an example of the numbers 1, 2, 3 and 4 leading directly to 10. Using the interpretation of Daniel's *four* kingdoms and *ten* toes (horns) as understood by Eusebius (*Proof of the Gospel* 15 Fragment 1), the number 1 represented Babylon, number 2 was Medo-Persia, 3 was Macedon, and 4 was the Roman Empire, and this led directly to number 10 which was the empire of "iron mixed with miry clay" (the last heathen empire of 10 kings prophesied to exist just before Christ's Second Advent).

In his *secret* teaching to those *initiated* into the teachings of the Holy Scriptures, Eusebius was saying they were seeing the culmination of the heathen empires proph-

14 Dan.

esied by Daniel in the emergence of Constantine's empire. Indeed, Eusebius made it clear in his use of the number 10 that he wanted his readers to realize that it represented the *final* number, and no matter how many series of 10's that they would witness in the future, the present "10" (which came from the the 1, 2, 3 and 4; that is, from Babylon, Medo-Persia, Macedon and the Roman Empire of Augustus) would remain as a unit and a steadfast empire until that "10" would be destroyed by the Second Advent of Christ. Look at how Eusebius said that *this* "10" of Constantine was the *final* "10" no matter how many cycles of 10's would exist in the future.

"For the unit is the tenth of ten, and ten units make up a decade, which is itself *the limit* [the *final* number], the settled goal and boundary [the terminus] of units; it is that which *terminates* the infinity of number [that is, the number 10 reaches out to infinity], *the term AND END* of units" (*The Oration of Eusebius*, VI.16).

It was this 1, 2, 3 and 4 leading to 10 that Eusebius associated with Constantine's empire. But it did not end there. The particular *Oration* that Eusebius was presenting (of which we have been speaking) was that given at the thirtieth anniversary of Constantine's rise to power. And Eusebius had a great deal to say about this thirtieth year of Constantine. It was, to him, a direct outgrowth of the "mysterious" 1, 2, 3, 4 and 10 that he was referring to in his chapter six. Continuing from the quote above, Eusebius said:

"Again, the triad combined with the decade, and performing a threefold circuit of tens, produces that most natural number, thirty. For as the triad is in respect to units, so is the number thirty in respect to tens" (*ibid.*, 17).

In simple language that the *initiated* would understand Eusebius was informing his readers that even Constantine's thirtieth year was a part of the 10 kingdoms mentioned in the Book of Daniel. It did not make any difference how many series of decades there would be in the future, the philosophy that governed the Empire of Constantine would continue until the 10 kingdoms of Daniel would be destroyed at Christ's Second Advent. And more than that, the present thirtieth anniversary of Constantine was important because it was a triad of decades that equalled the course of the *moon*. Constantine's thirty years, according to Eusebius, was under the influence of the *moon*. Continuing with his discourse in chapter six he said:

"Again, the three combined with ten, and performing a threefold circuit of tens, produces that most natural number, thirty. For as the triad is in respect to units, so is the number thirty in respect to tens. It is also the constant limit to the course of that luminary which is second to the sun in brightness. For the course of the moon from one conjunction with the sun to the next, completes the period of a month; after which, receiving as it were a second birth, it recommences a new light, and other days, being adorned and honored with thirty units, three decades, and ten triads" (*ibid.*, VI.16,17).

This may appear as an exercise in philosophical nonsense (and many have accepted it as primitive reasoning on numerology which characterized the age of Eusebius), but Eusebius was telling his readers something in what appears as "mumbo-jumbo" on the surface. He identified Constantine's empire with the 10 antichristian kingdoms that the Bible says will exist just prior to Christ's advent. And he said that the past thirty years of Constantine's reign was under the influence of the *moon*. Anyone knowing the symbolic usage of the *moon* in the Book of Revelation understands that this is the luminary equated with Satan the Devil and his government (Rev.11:2, 13:5). The Book of Revelation also shows that the heavenly virgin who gives birth to the man child destined to rule all nations with a rod of iron (Christ Jesus), dominates the *moon* by having it "under her feet" (Rev.12:1). To Eusebius, Constantine's "*lunar*" empire will be eclipsed by that of the true Christ.

There is yet another "sign" that Eusebius gave to his readers to show when he was giving *secret* teaching in his outward discourses designed for public consumption. Note this: In Eusebius' early works (composed primarily *before* the ascendancy of Constantine over all the Roman Empire) it was common for him to use the name "Jesus" (or its various combinations, such as "the Lord Jesus Christ") with complete freedom and with an attitude of adoration and worship. His *Preparation of the Gospel*, *The Proof of the Gospel* and his famous *Ecclesiastical History* contain the name "Jesus" (or its combinations) in all circumstances where it would have been natural to use it. But in the works intended for the general public (which we have been discussing) written *after* Constantine came to full power within the Roman Empire and after he began his campaign of governing the Christian Church (including its building activities and theological discussions), Eusebius *NEVER* used the name "Jesus." Thus, in his *Life of Constantine* and his two "*Orations*" in praise of Constantine the name "Jesus" *is conspicuous for its ABSENCE!* As Professor T.D.Barnes astutely observes in regard to Eusebius' work *Praise of Constantine*, he "deliberately aschews exclusively Christian terminology, never uttering the name Jesus or the word 'Christ'" (*Constantine and Eusebius*, p. 253).

And though Eusebius was willing to use the title "Christ" in his *Life of Constantine* (and only in chapter XVI of the "*Orations*"), the normal titles he used in place of "Jesus" were "Saviour, Lord, Logos, Sovereign, Son of God and the Son." But it is easily recognized that *all* these titles were equally used by priests of the pagan world to refer to their own deities. Though Eusebius honored the title "Christ" (he had a long discourse on its significance in *Proof of the Gospel*, IV.15,16), he showed that "Christ" could refer to many humans (priests, prophets, kings), but the name "Jesus" was in a higher classification. The "mere mention of the Name of Jesus" could drive away all the work of the demons, and "every demon and unclean spirit shudders at the Name of Jesus" [*ibid.*, III.6 (132,133)]. Eusebius called specific attention to the fact that "in the name of Jesus every knee should bow" [*ibid.*, III.7 (136)].

The title "Christ" was not as important to Eusebius as the name "Jesus" (or combinations of titles with it). When it became obvious to Eusebius that Constantine was more interested in his visions and dreams than in what the Holy Scriptures themselves taught (note his long journey to Constantinople to give a scriptural discourse on the tomb of

Christ but he got nowhere with Constantine), Eusebius *then* had second thoughts about Constantine. Eusebius began to see very early that the Christian Empire of Constantine was going to be controlled not by the teachings of the Holy Scriptures but by the visionary experiences of Constantine and those near him. Thus, the whole demeanor of Eusebius in his writing (his style and contents) changed drastically *after* Constantine assumed full authority over the Roman Empire. So altered was his style and content that one would almost wonder if the same man wrote the later works which were so different from his former. But he was the same person all right. After A.D.326, he simply had to couch his writings and discourses in a literary style that only those who were *initiated* into the secrets of the Holy Scriptures would understand.

So, what was Constantine's Empire in the interpretation of Eusebius? He saw it as the 1, 2, 3 and 4 (its head was Babylon, followed by Persia, Macedon and then the Roman Empire) which had developed under Constantine into the 10 (the antichristian kingdom of the prophet Daniel). If one stays squarely with the Holy Scriptures for the interpretation of these mysterious numbers of *creation* put forth by Eusebius, then one is led directly to Daniel's account of the various world kingdoms of the heathen that would continue on earth until the coming of the Kingdom of God. Constantine's thirtieth year was, to Eusebius, a triad of decades which answered to the course of the *moon* and this signalized the power which motivated his government. Thus, Eusebius saw Constantine's Empire as *lunar* in origin (associated with darkness), and not that of the *sun* which represented God's (Mal.4:2). Because of this, Eusebius simply refused to use the holy name of "Jesus" (the one that all people must use to be saved -- Philippians 2:10,11) in his later works meant for the general public. He instead resorted to the use of the normal heathen titles that most people in the Roman Empire were accustomed to using for their pagan deities. In a word, Eusebius was saying that Constantine's Empire *was not* the Kingdom of our Saviour and Lord *Jesus* Christ.

The above indications were some of the factors that

represented Eusebius' "keys" (his use of the word "*Jesus*," or its lack of use, being the main one). This is what he used to teach the *initiated* after A.D.326. Thankfully, by this stratagem Eusebius was able to preserve his former (and *true*) writings for us today. If he would have been too plain with his personal feelings and would have objected most strenuously to the interpretation of the visions and dreams of Constantine, he would at the best have been sent into exile or at worst to a premature death, but (more importantly to Eusebius, I am sure) he knew that such openness of his beliefs to Constantine would have meant the destruction of all his writings and the world would no longer have had these valuable documents to retain the truths that he thought were essential for preservation.

It was even essential to Eusebius that his early writings be edited so they would not be in danger of destruction after his death. It is well known that Eusebius was in the habit of bringing his works up-to-date when occasion merited it. And if there was ever a time to edit his earlier works, it was after A.D.326 when Constantine began to establish his type of Christianity based on his visions and dreams. Eusebius' early historical works in many cases gave information which was counter to what Constantine was obtaining from his visionary experiences. For example, in no way was the real sepulchre of Christ on the western side of Jerusalem. This important event actually happened near the southern summit of the Mount of Olives and not where the Venus Shrine was later built. And in his early work called *Proof of the Gospel*, Eusebius made it clear that the real "Mother Church" for all Christendom was at the *cave* (which was really a *cave/tomb*) on the Mount of Olives. Even Jerome, a hundred years later, acknowledged that the Lord's Church was *founded* on Olivet (*Letter* CVIII.8). The Mount of Olives actually represented the spiritual "Mount Sion" for Christians, and before the time of Constantine it was to the *cave/tomb* on Olivet (and *only* to that spot) that Christians came from around the world to worship God. But after A.D.326, everything changed! All attention shifted to the western area of Jerusalem where the Venus Shrine had been built by the emperor Hadrian.

Now note an important point. Whereas Eusebius' early work called the *Preparation of the Gospel* was in fifteen complete books (all of which have come down to us), his sequel to that work called the *Proof of the Gospel* (which was at one time found in twenty books) is deficient in its latter TEN BOOKS. Eusebius' books eleven to twenty of his *Proof of the Gospel* have not come down to us. Why do we have only the first ten books of *Proof of the Gospel?* What happened to the last ten?

It ought to be obvious what happened to the latter portion of this early work of Eusebius if one looks closely at the subject matter that Eusebius was beginning to discuss at the end of book ten and the start of book eleven. Look at this point carefully. Eusebius in the first ten books of his *Proof of the Gospel* had just reached the history of Christ Jesus *up to the time of his crucifixion!* And right at the end of book ten, which was the very time we need the plain teaching of the historical records which Eusebius was referring to regarding the place of Christ's crucifixion, burial and resurrection, *all the teaching of Eusebius is* ABRUPTLY BROKEN OFF! The events which Eusebius had written about concerning Christ's crucifixion and resurrection (and the subsequent events leading to the establishment of the Christian Church at Jerusalem) *are not brought down to us!* In a word, those last ten books of Eusebius' *Proof of the Gospel* are missing. And the missing section began at the very time Eusebius began to write about the place of Christ's crucifixion and the events that succeeded that momentous occasion. But why were the latter ten books of *Proof of the Gospel* taken out of this important work of Eusebius? The answer is not difficult to understand.

The problem was, Constantine had selected a place for Christ's passion that was utterly contrary to the historical accounts that Eusebius had recorded in his early writings. This historical material which Eusebius had preserved that showed the essential truths of where Christ was crucified and resurrected was either taken out of his *Proof of the Gospel* by Eusebius, or by later people shortly after Eusebius' death who destroyed the last ten books so that Constantine's *new* Golgotha (the one selected by his visions and dreams) would be retained as authoritative for the Christian Church.

Interestingly, however, if it was actually Eusebius himself who "hid" his latter ten books to his *Proof of the Gospel* (in order that the fifteen books of his *Preparation of the Gospel* and the first ten books of his *Proof of the Gospel* could be saved from destruction), then it would pay us to look carefully at what Eusebius finally presented to the world by his editing of those early *twenty-five* books. And no one will be disappointed if one looks carefully. It was in those early works that Eusebius was still able to show that the "Mother Church" of all Christendom was on the Mount of Olives and that Olivet itself was indeed the spiritual "Mount Sion" of the early Christians before the time of Constantine. And not only that, notice what he said in *Proof of the Gospel* Book VI, chapter 18. Amongst a host of words that the superficial reader would pass over, Eusebius couched four central points that, when put together in a sequential pattern, identifies the actual spot of Christ's crucifixion and resurrection from the dead. At the commencement of section 294 of chapter 18 he said (point one) that Christ's "spiritual blood has fallen" in Jerusalem, and that (point two) this saving knowledge would "go forth from Mount Sion," and that (point three) as the Shekinah Glory (the Holy Spirit) left the old Temple in Jerusalem and went "to the Mount of Olives," and that from the Mount of Olives there came forth (point four) "*the events of the day of His passion*, and the living water, flowing into all the world, and to crown all, the Kingdom of the Lord ruling over all the nations, and His One Name, filling all the earth."

What this conclusion to chapter 18 shows (of Eusebius' Book VI of his *Proof of the Gospel*) is that (when the four points he raised are put in a sequential sentence format) we have a remarkable testimony of Eusebius himself where the actual crucifixion and resurrection of Christ took place. Condensing his four points into a simple sentence that all can understand, Eusebius said: "Christ's spiritual blood fell on the spiritual Mount Sion which is the Mount of Olives to which the Holy Spirit retreated after its departure from the Temple at Jerusalem and that the events of Christ's holy

atonement

passion took place at that Mount Sion." It takes a careful analysis of the concluding part of chapter 18 to comprehend the teaching of Eusebius on this matter, but those *initiated* into the secrets of the Holy Scriptures, according to Eusebius, would be able to discover the truth without difficulty.

In short, Eusebius was showing that Christ was crucified and resurrected from the dead near the southern summit of the Mount of Olives. And, of course, this is exactly what the Holy Scriptures show as the truth as we have demonstrated in the early chapters of this book. Eusebius in his later works is stating that anyone who is *initiated* into the principal factors of scriptural interpretation can know what the *truth* is in regard to the *true* place of Christ's resurrection from the dead. But more importantly, Eusebius was showing that the *initiated* will also be able to discover the truth of the type of government that Constantine was then establishing and it was *not* in accordance with the teaching of the Holy Scriptures. As he said in his introduction to his *Oration in Praise of Constantine* that the *initiated* would be able to discover what is true from the counterfeit. And to Eusebius the "truth" was exactly opposite of what Constantine was then advocating.

What Eusebius was able to see was that Constantine had not only conquered all secular opposition to his rule within the Roman Empire, he had effectively taken over control of the Christian Church as well. With his visions, dreams and signs Constantine positioned himself within the Christian community as the overall "bishop" with an apostolic rank which he concluded was higher than the original apostles (including Peter) because at his burial he positioned himself higher in rank than the apostles themselves.

Constantine established in the fourth century what became known as *Caesaro-papism* (Caesar is Pope). So different had the Church become from that of the apostles that St. Bernard (died 1153) called it the Church of Constantine, not that of Peter (McBrien, *Catholicism*, pp.612,825). Interestingly, while Constantine dominated the Church from A.D.325 until his death, his control was accomplished *while he was unbaptized and not even a member of the Church!*

In effect, what Constantine established in the fourth century was a politico-religious empire based on philosophical and theological principles that were completely contrary to the doctrines of the Holy Scriptures and the early teachings dispensed by the original apostles. This is what Eusebius was able to observe without the slightest difficulty and why he explained this fact in his *Oration of Eusebius*. In those eighteen chapters, Eusebius told those who were truly *initiated* into the teachings of the Holy Scriptures what the real character of Constantine was like and that he was actually being motivated by *the spirit of divination* (which, to Eusebius, was an expression of madness and folly) (*The Oration of Eusebius*, I.4,5). In the next chapter it will be explained why the majority of the world finally went over to the interpretation of Constantine and his mother Helena that the site of the Temple of Venus was the place for Christ's crucifixion and resurrection from the dead. It is an interesting matter indeed.

Explanation of Eusebius flattery of the emperor — hoping the initiated would recognize the spoof. He thot even " " " interp Scrip that way. i.e. deeper meanings. Also Plato — This strategem Eusebius wrote to save his life. 114f on here 1+2+3+4=10 — 4 of Daniel: end of heathen empires, with Constantine. He also so used Rev. to = Const. w/ Satan — 117 Because "went w/ visions & dreams, not Scripture. Just all the while Constantine was unbaptized

11

Accepting the Site of the Temple of Venus

The evidence in this book demonstrates that the site of Christ's crucifixion was on the Mount of Olives. Even Christian traditions down to the time of Constantine show that the only area reverenced by Christians as having any sign of holiness was the *cave/tomb* on the Mount of Olives. But the queen mother Helena and Constantine selected a spot at the Temple of Venus built by the emperor Hadrian right after A.D.135. This region was in *the exact opposite* direction from Jerusalem and the Temple in which the Holy Scriptures placed Christ's crucifixion and entombment. In doing this they had to resort to dreams and visions to determine the site (and the church historian Sozomen about 100 years later said this was the safest method in deciding such issues, *Eccl.Hist.*II.1). Another historian who wrote slightly earlier admitted that Helena, in trying to locate Christ's sepulchre, finally "*after much difficulty*, by God's help, she discovered it" (Socrates, *Eccl.Hist.*I.17). Sozomen recorded the same belief: "It was no easy matter to discover the Lord's sepulchre" (*ibid.*). One wonders why locating the tomb was so "difficult" and "no easy matter" if there had been a consistent and prevailing tradition among the Christians in Jerusalem that the site of the Temple of Venus was where Christ's passion took place? The truth is, there were no traditions whatever that the pagan shrine was the proper place. This is one of the main reasons why Constantine and Helena relied on visions and dreams to discover the "true" sepulchre. As a matter of fact, Sozomen related that Helena not only relied on the intervention of God with supernatural signs but she also sought professional human help as well.

> "Some say that the facts [about Christ's tomb] were first disclosed by a Hebrew who dwelt in the East, and who derived his information from some documents which had come down to him by paternal inheritance" (Sozomen, *Eccl.Hist.*II.1).

It was actually more than a single Jewish man that she consulted. Paulinus of Nola in A.D.403 gave the following explanation of how Helena uncovered the lost tomb of Christ.

> "She became eager to obtain information solely on the site of the crucifixion. So she sought out not only Christians full of learning and holiness, *but also the most learned of the Jews* to inform her of their native wickedness in which, the poor Jews, they even boast. Having summoned *them* she assembled *them* in Jerusalem. Her resolve was strengthened by the unanimous witness of all about the site. There was then, undoubtedly under the impulse of a revelation she had experienced, that she ordered digging operations to be prepared on that very site" (*Letter* 31.5).

Again, one might wonder why Jewish leaders, who had been summoned from around Palestine, would be eager to point out the Temple of Venus as the place of Christ's crucifixion? Whatever the case, Paulinus of Nola said the Jewish authorities told Helena that the pagan shrine was the proper place. But if Helena had to rely on the knowledge of Jewish scholars, why would this have been necessary if a realization of the true sepulchre had been handed down by Christian people in Jerusalem from generation to generation? What Helena apparently wanted from the Jewish authorities was a confirmation of the visions and dreams which she and her son Constantine had experienced. So she called in the Jews to substantiate the reliability of her persuasions. She no doubt thought the "wicked Jews" had kept a record of the site and had been hiding it from Christian knowledge. And what happened? The Jewish authorities obliged the queen mother with their expert understanding on the matter! They pointed out the Temple of Venus as the true site -- or rather, it was one of their spokesmen who apparently had the actual documentation handed down to him from his parents which could prove the Temple of Venus to be the real place of Christ's passion. Only this *one man* had the documentation.

Interestingly, the individual who supposedly had the

historical evidence was a Jewish man whose name was *Judas*. This Judas told Helena that the Temple of Venus was the proper site of Christ's crucifixion. Helena then, "by an impulse of a revelation" (as Paulinus of Nola supposed it to have been), had her attendants dig into the ground at the place which Judas told her. And amazingly, they came upon three crosses superimposed upon one another. But that wasn't the end of it. Nearby was found a tablet which had upon it the exact words which the New Testament said Pilate placed above Christ's head. Also found in the same spot was a sponge and a reed like those associated with Christ's passion. How such delicate items could survive some 300 years buried in the earth was apparently not questioned!

Finding these wonderful artifacts in the place which Judas told Helena was the site of Christ's crucifixion was an outstanding discovery as far as the queen mother was concerned. But this didn't finish the story. Which of the three crosses was the one on which Christ was crucified? The answer soon came. They found a woman who was sick nigh unto death. They took the three crosses to her bedside and placed one on her. Nothing happened! They placed the second. Nothing happened! They placed the third on the woman and she was supposedly healed at once. This, to the Christian people of the fourth century, was proof positive that they had indeed found the true cross on which Christ was crucified. (One other tradition says they put the final cross on a dead man and he was restored to life.)

From this time forward, there was no turning back for many of the Christians in Jerusalem and the world (when they heard what happened). But it is most remarkable, and something that has surprised scholars for years, that the great historian Eusebius as well as the Bordeaux Pilgrim (who were in Palestine during this period) said not one word about this so-called "discovery" of the crosses which were "so conveniently" located several feet underground at the Temple of Venus. These significant omissions by these observant eyewitnesses have caused many modern scholars to call into question the so-called discovery of the crosses themselves (*e.g.* E.D.Hunt, *Holy Land Pilgrimage in the Later Roman*

Empire, pp.38-42). And no wonder, because we will show in chapter 14 that Christ was not even crucified on a Latin or a Greek cross. He met his death on an entirely different form of executionary instrument that was nothing like some boards of timber nailed together in the form of a cross.

But, getting back to the story at hand, once these crosses were found in the very region that Judas had pointed out, there was no turning back for many Christian believers (and this was especially so when an event occurred at Jerusalem in the year A.D.350, some 24 years later, which proved to be the catalyst that secured the belief that Judas was right in what he told Helena). Finding this "true" cross pointed out by Judas was the proof that "Golgotha" had been discovered. No matter what people may have thought about the importance of the Mount of Olives before this time, the queen mother and the emperor Constantine (with Judas) now bestowed their authority on the Temple of Venus.

It is interesting that the historical records written not long after these events credit this Jewish man, named Judas, with the actual discovery of the "true" cross.

"The venerable wood of the cross was discovered through the zeal of Helena, *the Hebrew Judas revealing the spot*, who was afterwards baptized and named Quiriacus" (Gregory of Tours, *History of the Franks*, I.36).

It was Judas (a man who was not even a Christian at the time) who was responsible for all of Christendom since that time revering the site of the Venus Shrine as the most holy place on earth. Of course, there were also the visions and dreams of Helena and Constantine who provided the first incentive that the Venus Shrine was correct, but the discovery of the three crosses (which Judas said would be found under the pagan shrine) was the clincher! So famous did Judas become in the Christian world for the discovery, that he was even made a bishop of Jerusalem.

"The altar in the middle is dedicated to St. Helena, and that on the left to St. Quiriacus, *whose name was also Judas*, who showed the cross . . . and was made Bishop of Jerusalem" (The Palestine Pilgrim's Text Society, *Anony. Pilgrim*, II (12th cent.], vol. VI, p.6).

Isn't it interesting that the Jews were the only ones in the the time of Constantine, and this *Judas* in particular, who supposedly knew where Christ was crucified and buried? This was in spite of the fact that all Christian records show that no Jews were allowed in Jerusalem or its environs for almost 200 years (from A.D.135 to the time of Constantine). This does not mean that Jewish people were unaware of important geographical sites in Jerusalem (after all, it was *their* holy city), but would they not have been more interested in remembering Jewish holy places than Christian ones? And what is remarkable is the fact that only *Judas* seemed to know the exact place of Christ's crucifixion while Christian authorities (who lived in Jerusalem and Palestine at the time) were unaware of the importance of the Temple of Venus. Indeed, Eusebius, the chief spokesman for the Palestinian Christians, found *Judas*' suggestion to be "contrary to all expectation" (Eusebius, *Life of Constantine*, III.28). Of course, it must be remembered that Judas' so-called documentation agreed with the visionary experiences of Constantine and his mother Helena. This amazing coincidence gave the documentation of Judas (handed down supposedly from his parents) a notable ring of truth (as understood through the spiritual principles accepted by many Christians living at the time).

This brings up a significant point to consider. We should ask a question about this Judas (the only man in Palestine who supposedly had any documentation on the matter of Christ's crucifixion). Could it be that Judas pointed out the Temple of Venus as the place of Christ's crucifixion for a particular reason? Christian authorities (including Eusebius) did not possess any historical knowledge that would support the site. In fact, Eusebius showed that the Christian "Mount Sion" before the time of Constantine was actually the Mount of Olives and in his clandestine way Eusebius showed that the summit of Olivet was, in reality, the place of Christ's crucifixion. Since this is the case, it may mean that Helena, the mother of Constantine (and even Constantine himself), was deceived by this man called Judas concerning this *new* site for Christ's crucifixion. The fact is, Judas may have had definite reasons for misleading them. (This point will be discussed in more detail in the next chapter.)

Whatever the case, practically the whole Christian world went over to the belief that the place selected by Judas (along with the visions and dreams of Constantine and Helena) was indeed the correct place for Christ's crucifixion and resurrection. This belief was further strengthened because of an event that occurred in Jerusalem in the late Spring of A.D.350. Let us now look at that event which clinched Christian belief that the true site of Christ's passion had now been found in the western part of Jerusalem at the Temple of Venus.

In the year A.D.350 Cyril became bishop of Jerusalem. And at the very beginning of his bishopric (on May 7th) a most significant celestial phenomenon occurred in the skies over Jerusalem. So elated was Cyril at the event that he immediately dispatched a letter to the emperor Constantius (the son of Constantine) to tell him of the wonderous sign given to the people of Jerusalem. What all the people saw was a parhelion of the sun which astonished the whole population of the city. Here is what Cyril said: "During these holy days of the holy Paschal [Passover] season, on the Nones of May [May 7th] at about nine in the morning, a gigantic luminous cross was seen in the sky above holy Golgotha, extending as far as the holy Mount of Olives; not seen by one or two only, but clearly visible to the whole population of the city; nor, as might be expected, quickly vanishing like an optical illusion, but suspended for several hours above the earth in the general sight of all and by its dazzling display conquering even the rays of the sun" (Cyril, *Letter to Constantius* 4).

This was a normal parhelion of the sun which is a well-known type of halo phenomenon seen at various times when cirrus (ice crystal) clouds are in evidence in the upper atmosphere. Almost always one observes a large circle of 22 degrees width, but in the interior of the halo there is often a refraction of light that gives the appearance of a cross in the heavens. As Van Nostrand's Scientific Encyclopedia states: "Much supernatural lore was built by such displays by the ancients" (p.228). But these phenomena are easy to explain. From the years 1950 to 1954 my job was in the Air Weather Service of the United States Air Force (I was sent by the United States government to the University of New Mexico to become a meteorologist, which profession I would still be in today had I not taken an interest in biblical history). These displays of solar activity in the form of various types of halos are quite common and there need be nothing supernatural about any of them.

Of course, these natural phenomena were not understood properly by the ancients and they almost always thought them to be a sign from God (or some supernatural being) that something special and significant was being given to mankind. Constantine just before his battle at Milvian Bridge saw such a parhelion (with an optical effect of a "cross" seen in the sky). It seemed completely providential to Cyril and the people of Jerusalem that this same type of solar halo as formerly seen by the emperor Constantine had now happened in the skies over Jerusalem in the late Spring of A.D.350. So spectacular was this parhelion to Cyril that he immediately came to the conclusion that God was now vindicating the *new* site of "Golgotha" that had been pointed out by Judas (and the visions of Constantine and his mother Helena). And though Cyril did not mention it, there must have been in his mind the similarity of this *type* of heavenly display that "God" had apparently given to Constantine. The comparision must have seemed too close to be a mere coincidence. Whatever the case, in the mind of Cyril and the Christian people of Jerusalem, the true site of Christ's crucifixion and resurrection had now been properly identified from heaven itself!

To Cyril, and the people of Jerusalem, this heavenly display was proof positive that the *new* site for "Golgotha" was correct. And even though there was not the slightest historical or geographical evidence to support the supposition, this celestial halo (in the form of a cross that stretched from the former Temple of Venus up to the Mount of Olives) was the final evidence that they needed that Constantine's "Golgotha" was proper! This was the "heavenly sign" that the people of Jerusalem were waiting for and they got it on May 7th, A.D.350. With this "heavenly approval" there remained no doubt in the minds of Christians in Jerusalem that they had found the true site of the passion of Christ. Constantine, Helena and Judas (who pointed out where the "true" cross was located) had won the day. And from then on there was no turning back for the majority of Christian opinion. Visions, signs and dreams were then the criterion for the establishment of important biblical sites and artifacts. Look at the following evidence that proves this point.

If there was ever a time in history when dreams, visions and signs were used to locate holy places and the long lost tombs of prophets, etc., it was the fourth century. Such "miraculous" events were held in much higher esteem than documentary evidence found in the historical records. The principal authors of the fourth century (and at the beginning of the fifth century) were Cyril, Socrates, Theodoret, Evagrius and Sozomen. The latter historian could serve as their spokesman when speaking of Christ's crucifixion.

"The place was *discovered*, and the fraud about it so zealously maintained was detected [the "fraud" was done by Hadrian who covered up the site with the Venus Shrine]; some say that the facts were first disclosed by a Hebrew who dwelt in the East, and who derived his information *from some documents* which had come to him by parental inheritance; but it seems more accordant with truth to suppose that God revealed the fact *by means of signs and dreams*; *FOR I DO NOT THINK that human information is required* when God thinks it best to make manifest the same" (*Hist.* II.1).

To people of the fourth century historical evidence went by the wayside as important in determining geographical sites associated with Christ, the apostles and the earlier prophets. Dreams, visions and miraculous signs had come into vogue in finding such important sites (as well as artifacts accompanying the holy men of the Old and New Testaments). As an example of this, notice how the tombs of Micah and Habakkuk of the Old Testament were discovered.

"The relics of the propto-prophets, Habakkuk, and a little while afterward,

Micah, were brought to light about this time. As I understand, God made known the place where both these bodies were deposited *by a divine vision in a dream to Zebennus*, who was then acting as bishop of Eleutheropolis" (Sozomen, *Hist.*, VII.29).

But this did not stop the wonderful discoveries! The people of the time were able to locate the tomb of Zechariah the prophet and the New Testament martyr Stephen.

"Among other relics, those of Zechariah, the very ancient prophet, and of Stephen, who was ordained deacon by the apostles, were discovered; and it seems incumbent on me to describe the mode, *since the discovery of each was marvelous and divine*. . .the prophet stood beside him *in a dream* and manifested himself" (*ibid.*, ch.2).

There is even more. In chapter two of this section just quoted, Sozomen shows how the empress Pulcheria beheld a vision of forty early martyrs who disclosed the whereabouts of their graves and they were discovered where her vision informed her. "Then the princess returned thanks to God for having accounted her worthy of so great a manifestation and for attaining the discovery of the holy relics" (bk.IX, ch.2).

But this did not end the matter. By dreams, visions and signs to various people at the end of the fourth century, almost every artifact associated with Christ, the apostles and the prophets of old was "miraculously" discovered for people to adore and to treasure for their wonderous powers and effects. Notice this. The people of the fourth century found the very column to which Christ was bound when he was whipped by the Roman soldiers, the anointing horn for consecrating the kings of ancient Israel, the lance that pierced Christ's side, the stones that stoned Stephen, the stone on which the cock stood when it crowed before Peter at Christ's trial, the chalice used by the apostles at the last supper, the tomb and the skull of Adam which were located at the *new* Golgotha selected by Constantine, Helena and Judas (e.g. Hoade, *Guide to the Holy Land,* p.306).

The "discoveries" even went beyond these just mentioned. Great miracles began to happen in regard to the "true" cross that was pointed out by Judas. It wasn't long until pieces of it were sent to all parts of the Christian world (Cyril, *Cat.*xiii.3). And what is most remarkable, the "true" cross had the unusual powers, so the story goes, of replenishing itself when pieces of it were sent to individuals or to churches throughout the world. So many pieces of this "true" cross were "supernaturally" multiplied that John Calvin in his time estimated that 300 men could not carry all the fragments. Indeed, virtually *every* item minutely associated with Christ, the apostles or other biblical personalities was "discovered" and placed in churches over the world -- including even milk from Mary's breasts and several foreskins of our Lord (*Ency.Rel.Ethics*, vol.X,pp.653-658).

All rational people today realize that all such "discoveries" are nothing more than pious frauds. But what needs to be recognized is that the so-called "true" cross was equally spurious. This is especially true since it can be demonstrated (as we will show in a later chapter) that Christ was not even crucified on a Latin or Greek cross.

People should realize that Judas Quiriacus was simply an opportunist and they should have dismissed his so-called "discovery" of the cross of Christ. But that was an age of credulity -- when dreams, visions and signs ruled the day. The common people, and even theologians, began to accept the evidence afforded by this great outpouring of "miracles" in the fourth century, and to the people living at the time such supernatural occurrences proved to be of more authority in locating Christian holy places and artifacts than historical documents.

If people would have, as Eusebius suggested to his readers, depended upon the teachings of the Holy Scriptures to be their guide in determining these matters than the visions, dreams and signs which were replete at the time, then the world would not have been subjected to the hoax provided by Judas Quiriacus to satisfy the "visions and dreams" of Constantine and his mother Helena. In actual fact, if people in the fourth century would have paid proper attention to the teaching of the Holy Scriptures, it would have been understood that "visions and dreams" are not always the vehicles by which divine truths are revealed to mankind. The prophet Ezekiel chastised the prophets of Israel who came in the name of Yahweh (the true God of Israel). The prophet Ezekiel called the majority of prophets in Israel as "foolish prophets" because they were depending on lying divination (Ezek.13:3-6). Such lying prophets were seeing numerous *visions* to substantiate their claims of representing God (Yahweh himself). Ezekiel was angry with the teachings of these prophets. He said that Yahweh was against "the prophets of Israel which prophesy concerning Jerusalem and which *SEE VISIONS* of peace for her, and there is not peace, saith the Lord God" (Ezek.13:16).

To the prophet Ezekiel the prophets of Israel were seeing many visions (and they were all showing *peace* for Israel) and he was condemning them for their *visions* which were not true. What we find in the scriptural revelation is that it is not always wise to trust in the visionary experiences of individuals, especially if those supernatural manifestations lead people away from the simple historical and geographical teachings afforded by the biblical revelation. Moses even commanded Israel to have nothing to do with "dreamers of dreams" and "miracle workers" who directed people away from the true worship of God (Deut.13:1-5). And Jesus was equally adamant that even people who came in his name (and doing wonderous signs and uttering prophecies) were not necessarily his representatives (Matt.7:21-23). It was considered essential by Christ and the apostles that people tell the truth in matters concerning the teaching of Christianity (John 17:17).

If only the Christian Church at that time would have had (and believed) the later teachings that St. John of the Cross, given in the 16th century about the dangers of trusting in visions, dreams and miracles, the Church of the fourth century would have been spared the nonsense that Constantine and his advisors were forcing on the Christian Church. And let me state once again, the teaching of St. John of the Cross on the perils of trusting in visions, dreams and miracles to establish essential truths of the Gospel is one of the most important discourses on the subject. Anyone desiring to believe such "divine evidences" should read (and with utmost attention) what St. John of the Cross said (*Ascent of Mount Carmel*, Book II, XVI to XXIX). The only reason I mention his teachings on these matters is that they have *never* been improved on to this day. True, the visions given in the Old and New Testaments are valid, but St. John of the Cross shows *how* they are true and also *how* so many visions, dreams and miraculous signs since the time of the apostles have led people into the most profound errors that can be imagined. Constantine's visions are an example.

What St. John of the Cross said (as well as Eusebius in the fourth century) is that the teachings found in the biblical revelation can always be relied upon. Eusebius tried to tell his readers that those who trust implicitly and explicitly in the Holy Scriptures will have the real "key" to comprehend all essential truths that have been given to mankind by the Father and Christ Jesus.

What the New Testament actually shows is that Christ was crucified on the Mount of Olives. And Eusebius (before Constantine began to assert his visionary authority in determining religious sites) showed that the Mount of Olives was not only the place of Christ's crucifixion and resurrection, but it was also where the "House of God" (the headquarters church of Jerusalem) was built right after A.D.70. Eusebius indicated as well that the Mount of Olives was the new (and spiritual) Mount Sion for Christians. No wonder Eusebius said nothing about the discovery of the "true" cross which was found under the Shrine of Venus (as disclosed by Judas Quiriacus) because he knew it was a hoax concocted by Judas from the very beginning.

Indeed, even if one accepted the parhelion as observed by the people of Jerusalem on May 7th, A.D.350 as a divine sign (in which a cross was seen stretching from the newly discovered "Golgotha" to the Mount of Olives), it could just as well have been interpreted that God was telling the people to abandon the *new* "Golgotha" located in the western part of Jerusalem and return to the true site of the crucifixion on the Mount of Olives!

Be this as it may, Cyril (the bishop of Jerusalem) decided that the parhelion was a wonder from heaven that the *newly* selected "Golgotha" was correct. This prompted him to deliver a sermon in the *new* Church of the Holy Sepulchre that would demonstrate that the *new* site was proper. The biblical evidence he gave was a mystical interpretation of the Song of Songs (the scriptural song written by King Solomon). He felt that the evidence for the *new* location for Christ's crucifixion had long been hidden in that book written almost 1000 years before the birth of Christ (see Parrot's *Golgotha and the Church of the Holy Sepulchre*, pp.56,57 for more information on this interesting point). The truth is, however, Cyril did not have any substantial proof from history or the Bible that the former Temple of Venus was the real site for Christ's crucifixion. 14

What this means is that visions, dreams and signs were the determining factors in convincing Christians in the middle and later fourth century that the *new* "Golgotha" of Constantine, Helena and Judas Quiriacus was correct. Sound historical and geographical proofs given in the New Testament and later documents were substituted for "supernatural proofs" and people in the world have been subjected to the teachings of Constantine ever since.

In the next chapter we will show why Judas Quiriacus (and especially the Jewish authorities in Jerusalem) pointed out the Temple of Venus as the place of Christ's passion. There was an important reason why this was done. It was one of the most clever subterfuges ever accomplished and the deception has held fast unto our modern times.

Quiriacus 134

The Temple of Venus was built by Hadrian in 135 A.D. Helena sought advice also fr. a number Jews, incl. Judas. They advised [illegible] so as to protect fr. pagan hands their Holy ground on Olivet. She went w/ them rather than the tradition because they played along w/ her visions, and the [illegible] [illegible] [illegible] [illegible] it healed (?) a woman. But [illegible] was not crucified on such a cross. (ch 14) The Jew, tho a non Xian ∴ was made a bishop of Jerusalem. Her vision was further strengthened by an celestial event in 350 AD, Parhelion of sun. cross in sky. p130. cf Milvian [illegible] 4th cent was given to visions etc. 132 f. Relics [illegible] carry cross so many would make a cross [illegible] 300 men could not carry [illegible] [illegible] Mary's breast. 2 of X's foreskins. Eusebius knew it was (Calvin) a hoax done by Judas. It was however a deception & a subterfuge.

12

Why the Temple of Venus?

The main attraction to objective historians today that there may be a kernel of truth in believing that the Temple of Venus in Jerusalem stood over the former site of Christ's crucifixion is because they think it reasonable that people living in Jerusalem from A.D.70 to A.D.326 would have retained numerous traditions that *this* was the true site. This belief, on the surface, makes perfectly good sense. But what many scholars have not considered are the teachings of Eusebius that in the pre-Constantine period it was common for Christians to call the Mount of Olives the *spiritual* Mount Sion; also that Christians from around the world came to visit the *cave/tomb* on the Mount of Olives (and no other site in Jerusalem was indicated as having any significance); that the "House of God" (the headquarters church for Jerusalem) was located on the Mount of Olives until it was destroyed in the Diocletian persecution beginning in A.D.303; and that Eusebius said the Shekinah Glory of God left the old Temple at Jerusalem and went to the top of the Mount of Olives just before the destruction of the city in A.D.70. Eusebius said *nothing* (nor did anyone else) about the Temple of Venus site. In actual fact, *before* the time of Constantine, the *only* place in the Jerusalem area that was sanctified as being important in Christian tradition was the *cave/tomb* near the southern summit of Olivet.

And while Eusebius said that by the early third century there was a trend for people to journey to Palestine "to examine the historic sites" (*Eccl.Hist.*6:11), we have no evidence that people saw any efficaciousness in the sites themselves, or that they would afford some spiritual benefit to the people who attended them. In the New Testament and the writings of the Apostolic Fathers in the second century there is no evidence that Christians saw any special significance to the sites associated with Christ or the apostles. But with the time of Constantine, all that changed drastically. We find that the places (or artifacts) supposedly associated with people of the biblical period began to take on unique spiritual and physical powers in themselves. People then began to journey to the Holyland to worship at what became known as the "holy places." It even went further than that. The places themselves began to take on a sanctification and "miracles" became associated with the sites and with certain artifacts connected with the holy men of old. Christians then started to visit the "holy places" for the spiritual amenities that the sites themselves could afford.

This all commenced in the time of Constantine and the ardor has not diminished to this day. Indeed, wars and arguments have taken place over the past 1500 years to secure in proper hands the custodianship of those "holy places." One of the main reasons for the Crusades (which dominated the activities of most European nations from A.D.1096 to 1291) was to recapture and put in Christian hands these sacred areas in Palestine -- and this especially applied to the Church of the Holy Sepulchre that Constantine selected as the spot of Christ's crucifixion.

Such interest did not abate even with the failure of the Crusades to secure proper guardianship over the areas sanctified since the time of Constantine. As late as the middle of the last century there were many disputes concerning the "holy places" between European nations and the Turks (who were then controlling Jerusalem). The main contention concerned who had the authority to protect and supervise these revered areas in Jerusalem -- and, again, this particularly applied to the Church of the Holy Sepulchre. So heated did the arguments become (especially when the Czar of Russia began to express his divine right to be protector of the Church of the Holy Sepulchre) that major hostilities broke out between the claimants and the conflict became known as the Crimean War. England, France and Turkey went to war with the Russians over this very matter.

Though the war was concluded in a little over a year, the outcome was a defeat for the Russians. It finally ended with what has become known as the *status quo* regarding who has protection and supervision over the various "holy places" in Palestine. This especially applied to the parties who claimed to have the right to control certain parts of the Church of the Holy Sepulchre. Indeed, the matter of the "holy places" is still a major bone of contention between many Christians, Moslems and Jews. It is interesting that the Church of the Holy Sepulchre (over which most contention has centered) is not even the proper area of the crucifixion and resurrection of Christ.

The problem all began with the visions of Constantine and his mother Helena and with the so-called "documentation" provided by Judas. The truth is, these fourth century Christians selected the wrong spot. But they became confident that the crucifixion happened at the site of the Temple of Venus located in the western section of Jerusalem. What was it that prompted them (other than dreams and visions) to decide on *this* spot? There was a major reason for it. Many Christian people in the latter part of the fourth century came to believe that the emperor Hadrian (beginning in A.D.135) built the Temple of Venus over the site of Christ's crucifixion because he hated the Christians so much and wished to intimidate them by the sacrilege. While it is true that Hadrian had an utter disdain for the Jews (and he raised up a Shrine of Jupiter on the site of Herod's Temple, and probably other Jewish holy places), new research by historians over the past 50 years has raised serious doubts that Hadrian had any animosity against his Christian subjects.

Even earlier emperors were not systematically hostile to Christians (except the persecution that developed in Nero's time after the fire of Rome in A.D.64). There is not a tissue of evidence that the emperors Vespasian and Titus presecuted Christians in a general and consistent way. Even the problems under Domitian (A.D.96) have been greatly overplayed. And though there were some government reprisals about A.D.112 under Trajan, these were all local and certainly temporary. Indeed, under Trajan (98-117), Hadrian (117-138) and Antonius (138-161) there is no clear evidence of any general persecution of Christians by the imperial authorities of Rome. True enough, there was the martyrdom of Ignatius in Trajan's reign, but it must be recognized that the judgment was against Ignatius personally and that he had begged for a martyr's death. Ignatius' seven epistles make it plain that the Christian Church as a whole was under a period of general peace and safety as far as matters concerning the Roman government were concerned. Even with Ignatius (if one reads him carefully), his death could have been averted by the appeal of Christians in Rome. But Ignatius for some reason did not want them to step in to gain him clemency.

In the period of the Apostolic Fathers (95-161), their records show in the main that the Christian Church was developing steadily within an environment of peace and security in relation to the imperial government. There were the martyrdoms of prominent men such as Ignatius, Polycarp and Justin, but these were isolated occurrences and were in no way indicative of what was happening to most Christians throughout the Roman Empire. It was not until A.D.177 with the persecution in Lyons that the imperial government began actively to take an interest in persecuting Christians in general.

As a matter of fact, in A.D.112 the emperor Trajan gave a decree which for all practical purposes gave a toleration for Christian activities that were within the law. This was also reiterated by the next emperor, Hadrian, and the policy appears to have continued under Antonius to the year A.D.161. There is no evidence to show any universal Roman government hostility to Christians (no matter where they were in the Roman world) from A.D.98 to 161. The situation is summed up well by Professor Frend in his excellent work *Martyrdom and Persecution in the Early Church:*

"Even in Asia Minor, where the Church was strongest, Christianity was one of the lesser problems which confronted Pliny in his investigations into provincial mismanagement in 112-113. In Antioch and in Palestine there were isolated conflicts between authorities and the Christians, but none in Alexandria nor the remainder of the Hellenistic world. The total recorded 'incidents' in the whole empire for two generations *may be counted on the fingers of one hand*" (p.181, italics mine).

It can truly be said that under the emperors Trajan, Hadrian and Antonius the Christian Church, as far as general government policy was concerned, was not being systematically persecuted or in serious jeopardy.

But wait a moment! Does that mean that Christians had very little persecution? *No, not in the least!* What we have been discussing are relations between Christians and the Roman imperial government, *not* between Jews and Christians or Christians and other Christians. The fact is, between Jews and Christians there are abundant indications to show continuing and often violent contentions among the two groups between A.D.70 and 161. There was such a prevailing hatred between the two religious societies that it was almost an impossible task to convoke any harmony between them. Only on rare occasions (like the dialogue of Justin the Christian with Trypho the Jew about A.D.140) did any civilized spirit of discussion take place. There was such a deep cleavage in religious belief with Jews and Christians that only an open belligerence and persecution prevailed among them. (It should be mentioned that there were also squabbles and fights within the Christian communities among those expressing diverse and contrary doctrines from others, but the Roman government itself was in the main tolerant of Christian affairs.)

What has all this to do with our present discussion about the site of the Holy Sepulchre and the place where Christ was crucified? Very much. This is because there is a belief among scholars today (and among many theologians of the late fourth and early fifth centuries) that Hadrian built the Temple of Venus over the site of Christ's passion because he supposedly hated Christians so much that he wanted to desecrate their object of chief devotion. But in no way is this theory correct. The truth is, Hadrian had his quarrels *with Jews*, and *not* with Christians. This point is very important to the issue we are discussing and it will help us to pay close attention to it.

Truthfully, Hadrian had no animosities towards Christians. If anything, he found them allies with him (or at least sympathetic to him) in his wars with the Jews. The reason for this is clear. Since the A.D.66-70 Roman/Jewish War there had been a deep rupture in Jewish and Christian relationships, and this especially applied to Jewish Christians. Professor Frend has a long section surveying the ordinary Jewish attitude towards Jewish Christians from A.D.70 up to 135 (pp.178-181). And, as stated before, it was one of utter hostility. After all, the Jewish authorities had reckoned that the Jewish Christians in particular had deliberately abandoned and forsaken the principles of proper religion when they accepted Jesus as their Messiah. One thing that irritated them among other things was the Christian refusal to join them in their conflicts for independence from Rome in the wars of A.D.66-70, 115-117 and 132-135. These three wars were in one way or another inspired with a Jewish belief that the political Messiah of the Old Testament (as the Jews understood him) would come to destroy the Romans and raise up a Jewish world kingdom.

But real believers in Jesus Christ could not participate in those wars of the Jews against the Romans without Jesus himself returning from heaven to bring in the Messianic kingdom. This particularly applied to the Roman/Jewish War of A.D.132 to 135. During that war the Jewish people had come to the conclusion that a man by the name of Simon (who was the general in charge of the Jewish armies) was indeed the Messiah, and he was called "Simon Bar-Kokhba" (the Son of the Star). No Christian in any way, shape or form could have accepted such a man as the Messiah, and they didn't! Even in the time of Domitian (about A.D.96) it is recorded that the grandsons of Jude (the brother of Jesus) were brought before the emperor for interrogation. They were dismissed when it was discovered that they were farmers having no revolutionary tendencies and that they proclaimed the Messianic kingdom would be manifested in the future when Christ would return from heaven (Eusebius,

Eccl.Hist. III.20, quoting the second century author Hegisippus).

This, and other historical factors, prove that the Christians (even Jewish Christians) would have had nothing to do in siding with the Jews against the Romans in the Bar-Kokhba Revolt (A.D.132-135). The evidence would support the Christians as being decidedly on the side of Hadrian against Jewish aspirations. This must be the case because Hadrian allowed Gentile Christians to carry on with their worship in Jerusalem (without interruption) even after the war was over. This alone shows that Hadrian had no quarrel with Christ or Christians. There is even evidence that the emperor reckoned Christ to have been a holy man and thought him to be a god. Aelius Lampridius mentioned a report that Hadrian even purposed to erect temples to Christ as one of the gods, but was deterred by the priests of Rome who declared that all the world would become Christians if he did (*Alexander Severus*, 43). This clearly indicates that Hadrian would not have been prone to desecrate a Christian "holy place" with his Temple of Venus as the Capitol of his new city called Aelia. But there was every reason for Hadrian to humiliate Jewish "holy places" or monuments.

Since the builders of the Church of the Holy Sepulchre found a tomb (and adjacent tombs) associated with the Venus Shrine, what if it were an important "Jewish tomb" that Hadrian was endeavoring to humiliate in A.D.135? This is surely the answer to the whole matter. Remarkably, the authorities (both ancient and modern) who have examined the tombs in and around the immediate site of the Church of the Holy Sepulchre agree that the tombs date to the period of the Second Temple. This means they were constructed before A.D.70. and it gives us archaeological evidence that the tombs under the Venus Shrine were indeed Jewish. The way the tombs were situated seems to show one central tomb with others as subsidiary. This arrangement could very well be indicating that the main tomb was of a prominent Jewish person. *But whose tomb was it?*

The Bordeaux Pilgrim in A.D.333 said that this "Calvary" located at the former Temple of Venus was then a small hill that apparently stood out around an area of flat ground. This made the hill or any structure built on it a prominent one. The site must have had a natural geographical eminence or Hadrian himself would not have placed the Capitol of his new city which he called Aelia. The early descriptions of the site show that it represented a prime landmark which was easily recognized by the people of Jerusalem. Could it have been a conspicuous tomb/monument that was there in the time of Christ? There is every reason to believe that this was the case.

Since Josephus saw this area and described it before the Romans destroyed Jerusalem in A.D.70 (and Josephus' description would have given a reasonable approximation to that which existed in the time of Christ), we should ask if Josephus mentioned such a significant tomb/monument in this area? He most certainly does.

This region in Christ's time was sparsely populated (*War* V.260) and consequently there were only a few houses and other buildings within the general vicinity. This factor would tend to make this Jewish tomb to stand out as a central landmark. And this is exactly what Josephus states. There was a tomb/monument in this very region which had geographical prominence. He referred to it four times in his description of the war with the Romans, and on all four occasions he used the location of the tomb/monument as a landmark to identify the places where major events took place. It was the *Tomb of John Hyrcanus* -- the famous and respected High Priest ruler of the Jews who reigned from 135 to 104 B.C. He was the son of Simon (the first ruler of the Hasmonean dynasty) and the one who was most responsible for creating a prosperous Jewish Commonwealth that was the envy of other Middle Eastern powers. His father could be considered the "George Washington" of the new Jewish nation, while he himself might be called the "Thomas Jefferson." So important was he to the Jewish people that at his death a splendid monumental tomb was made for him.

It is important to note that John Hyrcanus had the deep respect of most Jews and he was one who was a proper example of righteousness. John Hyrcanus was also a recent

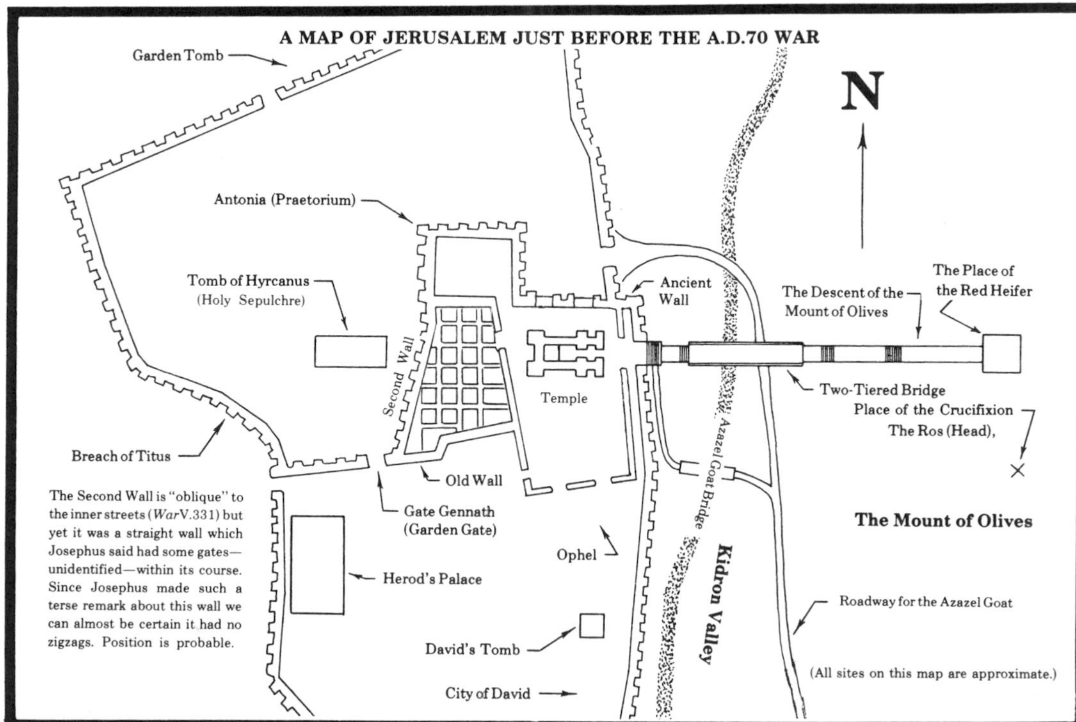
A MAP OF JERUSALEM JUST BEFORE THE A.D.70 WAR
N
Garden Tomb
Antonia (Praetorium)
Tomb of Hyrcanus
(Holy Sepulchre)
Second Wall
Temple
Ancient Wall
The Descent of the Mount of Olives
The Place of the Red Heifer
Two-Tiered Bridge
Place of the Crucifixion
The Ros (Head),
Breach of Titus
Old Wall
Gate Gennath
(Garden Gate)
Azazel Goat Bridge
Kidron Valley
The Mount of Olives
Ophel
Herod's Palace
David's Tomb
City of David
Roadway for the Azazel Goat
(All sites on this map are approximate.)
The Second Wall is "oblique" to the inner streets (War V.331) but yet it was a straight wall which Josephus said had some gates—unidentified—within its course. Since Josephus made such a terse remark about this wall we can almost be certain it had no zigzags. Position is probable.

hero who epitomized the valiant quest for Jewish liberation from their Gentile oppressors. His example could very well have been a rallying point around which the liberators of A.D.132 gained confidence to overthrow the Roman yoke. The former monument area of John Hyrcanus (being a revolutionary Maccabee) could have provided a patriotic sense of encouragement to the fighters of Bar-Kokhba. Since the former buildings which made up Jerusalem before A.D.70 had all been destroyed, the freedom fighters could have symbolically used the site of John Hyrcanus' Tomb as their own "Jefferson" or "Lincoln" Memorial.

Where was this prominent tomb/monument located in Jerusalem? Josephus used it as a benchmark to identify the place where the Roman general Titus (later emperor) penetrated the western wall of Jerusalem which had been built by Agrippa (*War* V.258-260). Since the place of the breach is reasonably known, we can use this breach of Titus as a means of discovering the site of Hyrcanus' Tomb. Titus broke through the western wall (which was built in a northwest/southeast direction) about 300 yards north and west of where the Old Wall began near the present Jaffa Gate. Since Josephus stated that Titus' breach was *exactly opposite* the Tomb of John Hyrcanus, we can rationally say that the Tomb was located about 300 yards north of the Old Wall. This would place it on an east/west line which connects precisely with today's Church of the Holy Sepulchre.

We are later told (*War* V.304) that the Jewish forces of Simon held the Second Wall *near the Tomb of John Hyrcanus*. From this northern point of the Second Wall, Simon controlled the Second Wall itself southward until it intersected with the Old Wall east of the Water Gate of the Hippicus Tower (which is near the present Jaffa Gate). With Josephus saying that Simon's northern limit of occupation was on the Second Wall *opposite Hyrcanus' Tomb*, this indication in itself puts his position on a line directly opposite the Church of the Holy Sepulchre.

But there is even more. Directly south and alongside Hyrcanus' Tomb, Josephus said that Titus raised an embankment to provide a ramp in order to bring up his engines of

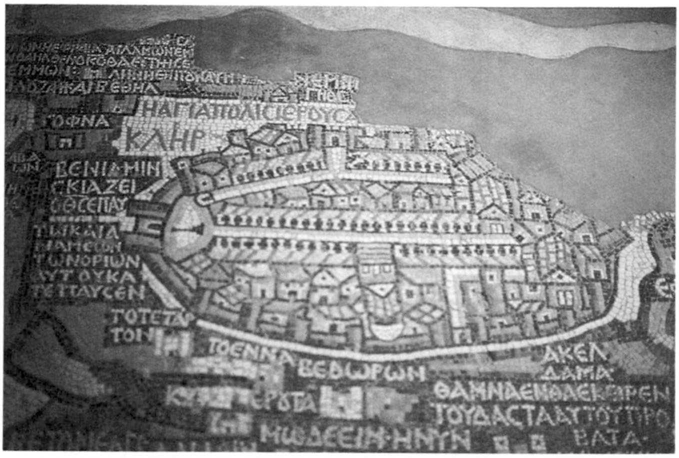

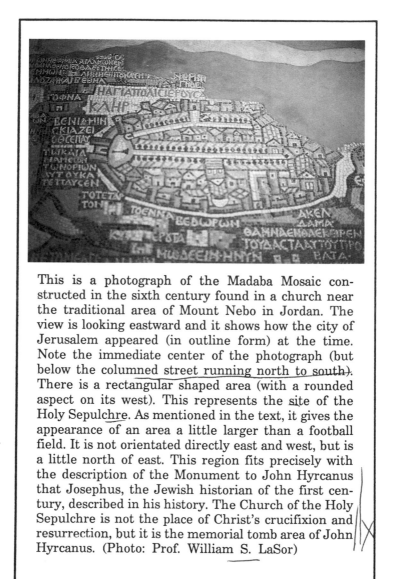

This is a photograph of the Madaba Mosaic constructed in the sixth century found in a church near the traditional area of Mount Nebo in Jordan. The view is looking eastward and it shows how the city of Jerusalem appeared (in outline form) at the time. Note the immediate center of the photograph (but below the columned street running north to south). There is a rectangular shaped area (with a rounded aspect on its west). This represents the site of the Holy Sepulchre. As mentioned in the text, it gives the appearance of an area a little larger than a football field. It is not orientated directly east and west, but is a little north of east. This region fits precisely with the description of the Monument to John Hyrcanus that Josephus, the Jewish historian of the first century, described in his history. The Church of the Holy Sepulchre is not the place of Christ's crucifixion and resurrection, but it is the memorial tomb area of John Hyrcanus. (Photo: Prof. William S. LaSor)

destruction to breach the Old Wall to the south (*War* V.356). To be "alongside" (as Josephus stated) suggests that the tomb area of Hyrcanus was in a rectangular shape much like a football field today (with its broadside oriented east/west). But also, the Tomb of Hyrcanus was positioned *opposite* a gate in the Old Wall (probably the Gennath, which means the Garden Gate) because a Jewish soldier came out to do single combat with a Roman soldier "opposite Hyrcanus' Tomb" (*War* VI.169). The Garden Gate no doubt led to the gardens surrounding the monumental Tomb of Hyrcanus.

We should note that the Madaba mosaic near Mount Nebo in Jordan also shows the original area of the Church of the Holy Sepulchre to have been rectangular in shape and this would agree with what Josephus indicated about the Tomb of John Hyrcanus. And since it is well known that the Church of the Holy Sepulchre was built over some kind of tomb area with its origin before Jerusalem was destroyed in A.D.70, this also gives reasonable evidence that the site was actually that of John Hyrcanus' Tomb.

What should be understood is that Jewish people at the time of Constantine must have been well aware that this area (at which the Temple of Venus was constructed by Hadrian after A.D.135) was the tomb area of John Hyrcanus. The man Judas Quiriacus must surely have known this! What seems evident is the fact that the Jewish people in the time of Constantine (through Judas their intermediary) pointed out the Tomb of John Hyrcanus to Helena as the place for all Christians to adore as the tomb of Christ. But would not Christians in Jerusalem have known this site was wrong and that the evidence pointed to the Mount of Olives as the true place? Yes, that is true. Indeed, we even have Eusebius making a journey all the way to Constantinople begging the emperor to hear him out on this matter of the Holy Sepulchre. But the people of the time were more interested in what visions, dreams and signs afforded as proof. And when Judas Quiriacus was able to show three crosses, along with the tablet of Pilate, the sponge and the reed supposedly associated with Christ's crucifixion, and especially when on May 7th, A.D.350 a parhelion of the sun pointed out "Golgotha" with a "cross" that stretched all the way to the Mount of Olives, all further inquiry on the matter was closed. The former importance of Olivet became totally eclipsed by these "wonderful signs" that God had supposedly given to the fourth century Christians.

What we find is that Christians after A.D.326 were more "led by the spirit" in finding the holy places than relying on historical and geographical facts. It is well known that this technique resulted in enormous blunders in trying to locate the early sites associated with Christ, the apostles and Old Testament prophets. As an example, they moved (with utter confidence so it seems) the hill of Sion from its actual location on Jerusalem's southeast ridge up to the large southwest hill just south of the *newly discovered* "Golgotha" in the western part of Jerusalem. And note this. Since all early manuscripts of Josephus fell into Christian hands, it appears that the Christians of the fourth century even changed the text of Josephus (*War* V.137) to make him supposedly say the citadel of David was on the southwest hill, but they forgot to alter what Josephus said in his *Antiquities* VII.65-67 where he indicated that the actual "Mount Sion" was the lower southeast hill. And, as explained in chapter 9 of this book, Eusebius and even Jerome explained in their writings that the real "Mount Sion" of the Bible was on the southeast hill of Jerusalem (and by extension to the Temple mount itself). In no way would Josephus have said that the southwest hill was the "Mount Sion" of King David! There is not the slightest indication in the Bible that this is true.

Such tampering with the text of Josephus is not only unfair with history and geography, it represents a deliberate fraud against the original writings of Josephus. Whatever one thinks of the motives of such people, they cannot be accepted as honorable by anyone who respects the teaching of the truth. The fact is, the Christian editors of the fourth century had no justification (either morally, ethically or historically) for altering Josephus to make him support the later visions, dreams and miracles associated with Constantine, Helena and Judas Quiriacus.

But this did not end the matter in identifying other

holy sites or artifacts. The people of the fourth century came to the conclusion that they did not need historical evidences to show them where such things could be discovered. The "Holy Spirit" (as they conceived it to be) was able to reveal the location of such things. Eusebius himself became very concerned about Constantine's selection of the Temple of Venus as the site of Christ's crucifixion, but he ran up against a brick wall in convincing Constantine that his visionary experiences were in error. Even he and the assembled bishops at Jerusalem asked Constantine to provide them with the evidence that his visionary experiences were proper, but the appeal of Eusebius had little effect on Constantine. The important things to the emperor and his mother were visions, dreams and signs (and we must not forget the discovery of the "true" cross and other artifacts by Judas Quiriacus under the Shrine of Venus).

What we find is that visions, dreams and signs won the day! From the time of Constantine, it was open season on the acceptance of many miraculous discoveries. But were these so-called signs telling the truth? Let us look at the facts. People who could not find ten acres of Sion and misplaced David's Tomb by half a mile, were still able to identify the precise pillar Christ was tied to at his scourging, the place where Mary stood when Christ was anointed after his death, the Tomb of Adam, that of Melchizedek, and even the stone on which the cock crowed at Peter's denial. I hope my friends who rely on these traditional "discoveries" will forgive me for expressing doubt in their authenticity. No wonder fourth century Christians needed visions, dreams and miracles to locate such "holy places." They claimed to have the Holy Spirit to tell *where* these important events took place, and it was not felt needful to rely on biblical or historical documents to identify the spots.

It is a sad commentary, but the credulity shown by Christian authorities at the time of Constantine (and the hundred years that followed) was at an all time high. It was an age in which religious "proofs" took precedence over the type of objective evidence that most historians utilize today. The church historian Sozomen was very candid in stating that dreams and visions were more able to show truths than historical documents.

"The place [of Christ's crucifixion] was *discovered*, and the fraud about it so zealously maintained [that the emperor Hadrian had hidden the site] was detected; some say that the facts were first disclosed by a Hebrew who dwelt in the East, and who derived his information *from some documents* which had come to him by paternal inheritance; but it seems *more accordant with truth to suppose* that God revealed the fact by means of signs and dreams; *FOR I DO NOT THINK that human information is required* when God thinks it best to make manifest the same" (*Hist.*II.1).

Though Sozomen did not think that documents were on a par with signs and dreams, it was believed that Judas the Hebrew had such documents to justify the site of the Venus Shrine as the site of Christ's crucifixion. Interestingly, we find that Christians themselves in the fourth century possessed no such documents. However, the Christians and Jewish authorities that Helena assembled in Jerusalem agreed that Judas had picked out the right place (Paulinus of Nola, *Letter* 31.5). And what a significant spot they selected! It was really the tomb area of the Maccabean priest/king, John Hyrcanus. He was one of the greatest Jewish heros from the past. What "luck" that the cross of Christ (and the other artifacts associated with the crucifixion) were conveniently found under the soil at the Venus Shrine. And now, every Christian in the world, including the Roman emperor himself, would be bowing in reverence before the monumental Tomb of John Hyrcanus.

There can really be no doubt that the Jewish scholars would have known that the Venus Shrine was actually the Tomb of John Hyrcanus (or very near the spot) and that it was not actually the place of Christ's crucifixion. The Jewish authorities would have remembered the location of *every* significant site in pre-70 A.D. Jerusalem. After all, it was *their* Holy City (not some common city such as Rome, Alexandria or Antioch). Even Hadrian's restriction which forbad any circumcised person from entering Jerusalem was of no relevance because the decree did not apply to *women* or young Jewish men posing as Gentiles (who could always be circumcised at a later time in their lives.)

One might ask why the Jewish authorities were willing to oblige Helena and Constantine with the wrong spot, and the Tomb of John Hyrcanus at that? It may have been in retaliation for Constantine's unfair persecution. We find that the emperor, upon becoming sole ruler at the defeat of Licinius in A.D.324, issued a decree which included his prayer to God for "the restoration of thy most holy dwelling-place" [that is, that the Temple of God in Jerusalem could be restored] (*Life of Constantine* II.55). But he had a change of heart at the Nicean Council in A.D.325. With advice from his Christian bishops, Constantine developed a hostile attitude towards anything Jewish, and this even included his decree of a year earlier that the Temple of God could be rebuilt in Jerusalem. At the Council of Nicaea he reversed his opinion of giving full religious toleration to the Jews. From A.D.325 onwards, it was: "Let us have nothing to do with the detestable Jewish crowd" (*ibid.* III.18).

And what happened? When the Jews in Jerusalem got the first decree of Constantine in A.D.324 that the Temple of God could be rebuilt, they immediately commenced its reconstruction. But by late A.D.325, Constantine's mind had changed drastically on this matter. What he did was to order a stop to such building activities and he had the ears of the Jews cut off who were doing the construction. Since the Scriptures demanded that no maimed person of the Jews (including the priests) could take part in Temple rituals, this effectively put a stop to this rebuilding of the Temple in A.D.325 (John Chrysostom, *Against Judaizing*, Disc.V.10; VI.2).

With such imperial afflictions lashed out against the Jewish people, it can be understood why they soon retaliated by pointing out the "true" site of Christ's tomb to the queen mother in A.D.326. They, along with their spokesman named Judas, simply pointed out the Tomb of John Hyrcanus (which was then covered by the Temple of Venus) as the proper spot. And queen Helena bought their story hook, line and sinker! She was more than prone to do this because she and Constantine had received visions, dreams and signs that *this* must have been the true site of Christ's passion. And when the "true" cross (and the other artifacts associated with the crucifixion) were conveniently discovered after digging into the soil at the site, there was then no turning back. This was enough to "prove" that the holiest spot in all Christendom had been found! And ever since, Christians from around the world have been reverently worshipping at the Tomb of John Hyrcanus!

But, as explained in chapter 9 of this book, Eusebius (on discovering what was happening in Jerusalem) hastily went to the emperor in Constantinople "and begged permission to pronounce a discourse on the subject of our Savior's sepulchre in his hearing" (*Life of Constantine* IV.33). Eusebius, however, was thoroughly rebuffed by the emperor who would not even give him the courtesy of sitting down while he spoke! Constantine had made up his mind and there was no changing it. The only thing that Eusebius could do to justify the site was to call *this* "Golgotha" a "*new* Jerusalem" which had nothing to do with the history or geography of the Jerusalem that existed in Christ's time. He said: "And *it may be* that this was that *second* and *new* Jerusalem spoken of in the predictions of the prophets, concerning which such abundant testimony is given in the divinely inspired records" (*Life of Constantine* III.33).

In other words, Eusebius could not find the slightest historical proof to show that the Venus Shrine was the place of Christ's crucifixion, so he simply said *it may be* reckoned the prophesied *second* or *new* Jerusalem, because it certainly had nothing to do with the history and geography of the Jerusalem here on this earth! Even as late as the dedication of the *new* Church of the Holy Sepulchre in A.D.336, Eusebius was still asking Constantine for some real and substantial evidence *why* he insisted on *this* spot (*The Oration of Eusebius* XVIII)? The fact is, Eusebius, and several other bishops at the time, knew that the Jewish authorities (particularly Judas who showed where the "true" cross of Christ was located) were not telling the truth to Constantine and Helena. But the opinions of Eusebius went counter to the visions, dreams and signs that Constantine had experienced, and for the next 1600 years (unto our time today) Christians have been subjected to calling the Tomb of John Hyrcanus the holiest place on earth.

In closing this chapter, one might ask why the Jewish authorities (and Judas in particular) were so willing to point out the site of the Temple of Venus as the place of Christ's passion? It wasn't simply to get back at Constantine for his cruel behavior to them (which some people might think was justification alone), but their motives were prompted for more serious reasons. By directing Christians to the Venus Shrine, it kept the area of the important Miphkad Altar at the summit of the Mount of Olives free from Christian shrines. The Jews knew that if the Temple of God were ever to be rebuilt (as the prophecies in the Bible said that it would be), then not only the Temple mount but the top of Olivet had to be free of foreign and, to them, unauthorized shrines and holy places.

Indeed, at the same time these Jewish authorities began pointing the Christians to the wrong locations, they also started to say that the place where the ashes of the sin offerings were placed was to the *north* of Jerusalem. In no way was this true (as I have explained in chapter 3 of this book). The Jews even went along with Christian belief and perpetuated the *new* teaching that the southwest hill (which has not the slightest significance with Old Testament rituals) was actually the "Mount Sion" of David. Anyone with any historical and geographical sense would have known this to be wrong. But this was a time when visions, dreams and signs ruled the day, and the Jews simply capitalized on the credulity of Constantine and the other Christians. One would find it difficult to blame them because of the way they had been recently treated by Constantine.

And what was the outcome of this subterfuge? From that time forward, Christian attention was directed *away from* the *REAL* Mount Sion (located on the southeast hill of Jerusalem and by extension it embraced the Temple mount). And, by pointing out the site of the Temple of Venus as the place of Christ's crucifixion, it had the effect of turning Christian attention *away from* the Miphkad Altar area on the top of the Mount of Olives (which had to be free of non-authorized shrines in order for a new Temple to function properly).

So, for the Jewish authorities to direct Christians of the fourth century to the southwest hill as being "Sion" and that the Tomb of John Hyrcanus underneath the Temple of Venus was the "true" site of the crucifixion of Christ made good practical sense to them. This subterfuge must be reckoned the most ingenious plan for the safe keeping of Jewish holy places ever found in the records of history! And for the last 1600 years their plan has worked! Most Christians around the world are still calling their most holy place on earth the Church of the Holy Sepulchre while it is actually the Tomb of John Hyrcanus!

Mother Church, situated on Olivet, until destroyed by (303) Diocletian. Sites: relics were not imp. to Xians till after Constantine. This led to the Crusades, & the later Crimean war w/ Russia.

A further reason for the selection of the Venus site: 4th cent Xians that Hadrian had blt the Venus shrine over the place of X's crucifixion in his effort to desacralize Jeru. But, tho Hadrian later [illegible] Jews, he did not so the Xians, (p. 140 ff) must correct about Roman persecution of Xians overall. It was the Jews who persecuted Christian at 1st. Hadrian saw Xians as allies to his hate of the Jews. The Jews hated Xians not only on theological grounds, but because they refused to join the Jewish wars of liberation from Rome 143 Hadrian even wanted to bld a shrine to X. 144 It was a Jewish tomb Hadrian wanted to desecrate by the Venus shrine. A conspicuous ornament in tomb of John Hyrcanus. X 145 147 (Josephus) Gardens surrounded it.

So the churches are really warring over the grave, not of X, but Hyrcanus. Why would the Jews, Judaism, so advise the emperor re: Venus site. To keep Xians away fr Olivet, sacred to the Jewish Temple. 155 To keep it free for rebuilding of Temple 152

So also Constantine. p153

13

Burial Grounds in Jerusalem

The Tomb of John Hyrcanus located just outside the Second Wall of Jerusalem in the time of Christ was the site chosen by the emperor Hadrian to build his Temple of Venus. This area was later selected by Constantine for his Church of the Holy Sepulchre. The situation of this tomb, however, was *within* the 2000 cubits' radius from the Holy of Holies which designated the *camp of Israel*. In other words, John Hyrcanus' Tomb was *within the camp* in the time of Christ and this prohibits the area from being considered as the site of Christ's crucifixion since the author of the Book of Hebrews said Christ was executed "*outside the camp*" (Heb. 13:11-13). Indeed, Hyrcanus' Tomb was not the only one positioned *within the camp*. So was that of his son Alexander who died in 78 B.C. (*War* V.304). And there are the monumental tombs in the Kidron Valley (traditionally called those of Absalom, Jehoshaphat, James and Zechariah) constructed in the late second or middle first century before Christ. These tombs were also *within the camp* which encircled Jerusalem in the time of Christ (the latter four are within a stone's throw of the Temple itself).

But legislation concerning tombs around Jerusalem began to change by the time Christ commenced his ministry. It then became unlawful to construct any new tombs within any district of the camp of Israel that encircled Jerusalem. Within a 2000 cubits' radius from the Holy of Holies in the Temple, it was not allowed for new tombs to be constructed. Indeed, even the older ones within the limits of the camp had to be cleansed and the remains of the dead transported to other areas *outside* the camp. These older tombs were especially a problem during Jewish festival periods. With tens of thousands of Jews assembling in Jerusalem at the beginning of the first century, it was so easy within the central area for people to accidently touch a tomb. This automatically disqualified them from entering the Temple for a seven day period (Num.19:11-21). So the authorities simply decided it would be best to cleanse all tombs in the "camp area" by removing the bones of the prophets and righteous people out of Jerusalem and to prohibit new tombs being built in the area.

Remember one point. It was even necessary to execute Christ *outside the camp* (Num.15:35,36), and it was also considered essential in Christ's time for his burial (which took place a short distance away) to be *outside the camp*. It was this outer limit of the camp that represented the city limits of Jerusalem. Burial was only permitted beyond 50 cubits from what was considered the outer boundaries of the city (Tosefta, *Baba Bathra* 1:11). But many old tombs and graves were located within the camp area just before the time of Christ and they presented problems to the Jerusalem authorities. It wasn't that the tombs themselves were the difficulty, but it was the bones within the tombs or graves that made them ritualistically unclean. It was possible *to cleanse* them if the bones and other body remains could be removed. There is archaeological and historical information which reasonably shows that shortly after A.D.16 there began to be a lot of activity to remove the bones and other remains from these tombs and to place them in new tomb areas outside the region of the camp. Notice it.

In 1953 an extensive cemetery containing more than 500 burial places was discovered at the Franciscan sanctuary of the Dominus Flevit which is located half way down the slope of the Mount of Olives and it was well *within the camp* in Christ's time. For the Second Temple period we find the coins unearthed in these tombs are dated before A.D.15/16 (Finegan, *The Archaeology of the New Testament*, p.243). This suggests that no more burials were allowed in this area after A.D.16 (or somewhere soon after that date). This gives us good information that the ban against burying people within the 2000 cubits' radius surrounding the central Temple at Jerusalem only started about A.D.20 and lasted until the destruction of the Temple in A.D.70.

The reason I say "ban" is because a rule was legislated (somewhere near the time Christ began his ministry) that no more tombs could be built so close to Jerusalem and that even the existing ones that were above ground had to have the bodily remains of the dead removed to places *outside the camp*. "In Jerusalem it was not permitted *to leave tombs* [within Jerusalem] with the exception of those of the house of David and that of the prophetess Hulda" (Tosefta, *Baba Bathra*, 1:2). By tombs, the rule meant that the bones in the tombs had to be transported to other non-sacred areas, not that the physical tombs themselves were removed (many of which were carved in solid rock). The Jewish authorities at Jerusalem simply enacted a law which made it illegal for Jews "*to leave tombs*" within the city limits of the holy city. It became custom to place the bones of those buried within the city limits in specially designed chests of wood or stone called ossuaries. These were then transported out of the sacred regions of Jerusalem and *outside the camp* into *newly built* tomb areas on the outskirts of Jerusalem.

These ossuaries were small chests of wood or stone (about 20 to 32 inches in length, 11 to 20 inches in width, and 10 to 16 inches in depth). Ossuaries were used as *secondary* burials. Many of them have been found. One is most interesting because it illustrates the custom near the time of Christ of not leaving tombs (or the bodily remains in the tombs) within the city limits of Jerusalem. Inscribed on one of these ossuaries is the following: "Hither were brought the bones of Uzziah, king of Judah -- do not open" (Thompson, *Archaeology and the New Testament*, p.336). This reference is very important to our present discussion because the early king Uzziah became a leper and was buried, in the first place, *outside* Jerusalem. His original tomb was located in the field and not among the royal sepulchres in the City of David (II Chron.26:23). But near the time of Christ, having a tomb "in the field" (though outside the walls of Jerusalem) was then being reckoned as still *within the camp*. This is why it was thought necessary to transfer his bones *outside the camp* of the larger Jerusalem that existed in Christ's time. The bones of King Uzziah were placed in a *newly made* tomb area beyond the sacred limits of Jerusalem. There must have been several of these outer tomb areas that were designed not only for the burials of important people living in the first century but also to house the bones of the early prophets and righteous people who had been buried *within the camp* of Israel inside and surrounding the city of Jerusalem.

The building of these *new* tomb areas is mentioned by Christ as occurring at the very time he was preaching the Gospel in Jerusalem. Notice what he said: "Woe unto you, scribes and Pharisees, because *you are building* [present tense] the graves of the prophets and *you are decorating* [present tense] the tombs of the righteous" (Matt.23:29). Since the prophets had died centuries before, it is ridiculous to think the Jewish authorities were building their tombs for the first time. What Christ was referring to was the making of *new tombs* for them. The tombs of all the prophets and righteous people *within the camp* of Israel that surrounded Jerusalem were (in Christ's time) being transferred to other areas outside the city limits. Until the bones and other remains of those dead were removed, it was customary to whitewash their tombs within the sacred area of Jerusalem in order that people would be able to distinguish them so that they would not become ritualistically unclean by touching them (Matt. 23:27). But the Jewish authorities were at the very time of Christ in the process of *building* [present tense, and the text means *presently building*] the tombs of the early prophets (this is also mentioned in Luke 11:47,48 as well as Matthew 23:29). The transferral of the bones of the righteous dead (including the early prophets) outside the camp of Jerusalem was going on right at the time of Christ's preaching in early A.D.30.

It appears that there were two principal regions (which archaeologists are able to locate) that represent these areas for the re-burial of the early prophets and righteous. One of the main sites has become known as the Sanhedriyya Tombs located a little over a mile northwest of the Temple Mount

This is a photograph from the Israel Museum which shows the tomb slab of Uzziah the early leper king of Jerusalem. It is written in the Aramaic (the common language spoken by many of the Jews in the Jerusalem area in the first century of our era) and it says: "Hither were brought the bones of Uzziah, king of Judah -- do not open." Scholars date this tomb slab to about the first century A.D. and what we have shown in this book, the greatest activity for the removal of bones from earlier tombs located "within the camp" at Jerusalem was precisely at the time that Christ was preaching. He said: "*You are building* [present tense] the graves of the prophets and *you are decorating* [present tense] the tombs of the righteous" (Matt.23:29). The bones of the righteous were then being transported to other tomb areas located "outside the camp" encircling Jerusalem.

and well outside the limits of the "camp." The contents found in those tombs were dated from the beginning of Herod's reign (36 B.C.) to the fall of Jerusalem in A.D.70. And since Christ said that the authorities were *decorating* the memorial tombs of the righteous, it is interesting that the Sanhedriyya Tombs have at their entrance various carvings of acanthus leaves, pomegranates and citrons. These may have been the very *decorations* to which Christ had reference. But besides that, most of the ossuaries in which the bones of the prophets and righteous were deposited were also *decorated*. And this is precisely what Christ said they were doing in his time.

But the area of the Sanhedriyya Tombs was not the only region of re-burial. There was another to which the remains of the early Jewish dead were transferred. This was a rock-hewn chamber located on the Mount of Offence to the southeast of Jerusalem (Finegan, *Archaeology of the New Testament*, pp.238-240). It must be reckoned that the time for deposting the remains of the dead at this location was associated with that of the Sanhedriyya Tombs.

This information is important in relation to the execution and burial of Christ Jesus. Obviously, if old tombs were then being relocated *outside the camp*, it cannot be imagined that new ones could be placed *inside the camp*. In fact, we have information that major tombs (that is, *new* ones) which were constructed within twenty or so years after Christ were built a little distance *outside the camp* which surrounded Jerusalem. One such tomb was that of Queen Helena of Adiabene. She was a convert to Judaism and died about thirty years after Christ. It is significant that her royal tomb area was located north of Jerusalem about 300 yards from the boundary of the "camp." It is important to note that archaeologists have *not* found *one tomb* which was built from the time of Herod to the fall of Jerusalem *north* of the wall of Jerusalem up to the tomb area of Helena (*Biblical Archaeological Review*, March/April, 1986, pp.51,52).

Had tombs been permitted inside the camp at that time, one would imagine that Queen Helena would surely have been granted a site near the Temple or somewhere near the City of David. But, since we know that even the prophets, as well as other righteous people, were having *new* tombs built for them outside the city limits in the time of Christ, we can understand why Queen Helena had her own tomb area constructed well to the north and *outside the camp*.

This rule also applied to the Herodian family tomb located southwest of the Temple. These tombs were situated almost the same distance away from the Sanctuary as was the tomb area of Queen Helena. These Herodian tombs which were referred to by the Jewish historian Josephus (*War* V.507) were not those associated with Herod the Great because he was buried at the Herodian located about 10 miles south of Jerusalem. This tomb complex no doubt belongs to Herod Agrippa the First (Acts 12:1) and he lived near the same period as Queen Helena of Adiabene. If this is the case, and it seems to be so, then this also shows that the royal tombs of even Herod Agrippa had to be located outside the limits of the camp which were reckoned at the time to be 2000 cubits from the central part of the Temple. The tomb of the High Priest Ananus was located about the same distance southwest of the Sanctuary as Herod's tomb (*War* V.506).

Since these royal personages were required to build their tomb areas outside the 2000 cubits' zone which represented the "camp," it can be readily understood why Joseph of Arimathea, though a rich man and a member of the Sanhedrin, also had to have his *newly hewn* tomb located outside the 2000 cubits' zone. And, of course, the area just south of the southern summit of the Mount of Olives fits the requirements precisely! This region was situated not far south of the Miphkad Altar where the Red Heifer was burnt to ashes (which had to be offered according to the biblical revelation just *outside the camp*). Thus, the summit of Olivet was just outside what was considered the city limits of Jerusalem. But the site of the present Church of the Holy Sepulchre and the Garden Tomb were well within the camp.

What is certain is that no one could officially be executed "in the middle" of the city of Jerusalem during the time of Christ. This must be emphasized because there is a second century account by Melito of Sardis that Christ was crucified "in the middle" of Jerusalem (*On Pascha* 72,94), even "in the middle of the Broadway and in the middle of the city" (para.94). Since Melito made a journey to Jerusalem (then called Aelia) about A.D.160, some scholars have believed that this indication may show that the Church of the Holy Sepulchre could have some credentials because the Temple of Venus which Constantine and his mother selected as the site of Christ's passion was, in the time of Melito, "in the middle" of Jerusalem. See the article *Melito and Jerusalem* by A.E.Harvey in *JTS*, n.s. 17 (1966), 401-404.

While this suggestion may appear reasonable on the surface, there are major difficulties with such an appraisal. Actually, there was no city called "Jerusalem" in Melito's time. On its site was a thoroughly pagan city called "Aelia" and no Jews were permitted to step foot within its boundaries (or even to approach sight of it). Melito's "Jerusalem" to which he had reference was the one that existed in Christ's time. He called *his* Jerusalem "the city of the Hebrews" and it is certain that the Aelia of Melito's time was clearly *not* any "city of the Hebrews." Melito was criticizing the Jews in his work *On Pascha* in the same context that Christ himself gave his rebuke to them in Luke 13:33-35. Christ said that it was not possible for prophets to be killed *outside* Jerusalem. Notice what Christ said.

> "For it cannot be that a prophet perish *outside* of Jerusalem. Jerusalem, Jerusalem, that killeth the prophets, and stoneth those sent unto her. How oft would I have gathered your children together, even as a hen gathereth her own brood under her wings, and you would not."

Melito's castigations and his reference to Jerusalem were so similar to those of Christ. Certainly, it is not to be imagined that Christ in Luke 13:33 intended to be geographically specific in his statement that it was impossible for righteous persons or prophets to be killed "outside Jerusalem" (for many of them were, and even he was crucified "outside the camp"). Christ simply meant that his own death would occur in the heart of Israel's society (at the very capital itself!). Christ did *not* mean, of course, that his death would occur *inside* Jerusalem (which, of course, was prohibited in the first place).

Melito meant the same thing. He did not literally mean (nor did he intend his readers to understand) that Christ was actually killed in the middle of Aelia. This has to be the case because Melito also said that Christ's death occurred "in the *middle* of the day" (para.94) and it would be absurd to think he meant that Christ died precisely at *noontime*, and this is especially so since he stated in paragraph 71 that his death happened in the Hebrew *evening* (which was understood as our *afternoon*). What Melito meant was that Christ was crucified *in broad daylight* and in view of all the people gathered in Jerusalem for the Passover season.

The reference of Melito was not the Aelia which existed in his time (A.D.160). He meant the Jerusalem before its destruction in A.D.70 -- "the city of the Hebrews" (which Aelia *never* was). This fact is even reinforced by his reference to it as the "city of the law. . . the city accounted righteous" (para.94). In no way could Aelia of the second century (a thoroughly pagan city in every facet of its existence) have met those descriptions of Melito. What Melito had in mind was the Jerusalem in the time of Christ! And his reference that Christ was crucified "in the middle" of Jerusalem was not to be understood literally. He was simply referring to Luke 13:33 and *not* that Christ was executed at the site of the Temple of Venus which in his day was "in the middle" of Aelia.

Melito did mention a point that should be noticed. He said Christ was crucified "in the middle *of the Broadway*" (para.94). This is interesting because the two witnesses referred to by the apostle John in Revelation are also prophesied to be crucified where their Lord was killed. Many have not noticed this significant point but Revelation 11:8 says that these future witnesses would be killed "*where* their Lord was *ALSO* crucified." Note the word "*also*." It shows that the two witnesses will *also* be crucified, but Revelation 11:8 states as well that their bodies would be exposed to view for three days and a half "*where* their Lord was *also* crucified." This was *on* or *beside* "the Broadway of the Great City."

The word "Broadway" in the Greek is *plateia* and it means a wide thoroughfare associated with Jerusalem, not simply the streets and lanes of the city. Could it be that the apostle John is describing a main "Broadway" into the city or into the Temple beside which Christ himself was earlier crucified? Remember that it was Roman custom to crucify people in prominent places, especially alongside major roads. Quintilian said: "the most crowded roads are chosen [for crucifixions]" (*Declamationes*, 274). In *Alexander Severus*, 23:8 we read: "as a deterrent to others he had them crucified on the street which his slaves used most frequently." And we are told that Pilate placed the title above the head of Jesus because many Jews were passing that area. The apostle John said "the place where Jesus was crucified was near The Place [the Temple] of the City" (John 19:20, Greek). This means the site of Christ's crucifixion was in a well-travelled place where many people could witness his execution.

As we have shown in the earlier chapters of this book, Christ was crucified near the southern summit of the Mount of Olives and beside a major thoroughfare leading into Jerusalem and the Temple. The apostle John in the Book of Revelation refers to this by saying that the two witnesses will have their dead bodies displayed "*where* their Lord was *also* crucified." This location was *on* (or better, *beside*) "The Broadway" (one of the principal boulevards which was a part of the city of Jerusalem).

The only thoroughfare that fits the evidence we have been presenting in this book is the "Broadway" which came from the east over the summit of the Mount of Olives (going through the village of Bethphage and near the place of the Miphkad Altar). The roadway descended down the western slopes of the mountain, across the Kidron Valley by the two-tiered arched bridge and through the Gate Beautiful into the eastern precincts of the Temple. From the summit of Olivet into Jerusalem Luke called it "The Descent of the Mount of Olives" (Luke 19:37).

This "Broadway" must have been very beautiful to behold. In no way could it have been a dirt or a gravel track leading into the Temple and the city of Jerusalem. It was especially holy and constructed in such a manner so that no ritualistic impurities could possibly be allowed on or near it. The one responsible for building this roadway and the bridge was no doubt Herod called the Great (though it was priestly funds that paid for it, *Shek.*4:2). He was responsible for constructing the Temple and its adjacent buildings and this certainly included the roads into Jerusalem and the Sanctuary. The fact is, Jerusalem was one of the most beautiful cities on earth in the first century. Josephus took considerable pains to describe the sumptuousness of the kingdom of Herod (the many cities, aqueducts, gymnasiums, theaters, etc. that he constructed) (*War* I.401-428). And this grandeur especially applied to his capital city of Jerusalem. So rich had Jerusalem become in the time of Christ that Josephus said it was the envy of the world (*War* VI.408).

But Jerusalem and Judaea were not the only areas made glorious by Herod. His generosity spread even to foreign lands. The same type of "Broadway" leading into the city of Antioch was once in need of massive repair, so Herod had two and a half miles of it paved "with polished marble, and as a protection from the rain, adorned it with a colonnade of equal length" (*War* I.425).

If Herod was so generous with Syrian Antioch in providing them with such a beautiful "Broadway" leading up to their city, it can hardly be imagined that he did less for his own capital city which was considered one of the most majestic urban areas in the Roman Empire! With this in mind, let us recall that the dead bodies of the two witnesses were prophesied by the apostle John to be displayed beside "The Broadway of the Great City" (Jerusalem) "*WHERE ALSO their Lord was crucified*" (Rev.11:8).

If one reads the text strictly, the apostle John is telling his readers that this main street of Jerusalem was "*the* Broadway" of the city itself. The use of the definite article by John suggests that *this* "Broadway" was either the *only one* leading into Jerusalem or at least one of the principal boulevards. And since the two witnesses are prophesied to have their dead bodies displayed after their crucifixions *on* or *beside* "The Broadway of the Great City (Jerusalem)," we should ask "*Where* was this *Broadway* located?" Again, note that the apostle John said it was "*where* their Lord was *also* crucified." From the evidence we have presented in this book, it can reasonably be shown that "The Descent of the Mount of Olives" was that "Broadway."

What we find is that the summit region of the Mount of Olives fits perfectly with all the requirements of the Jews regarding the place of execution for criminals. When the evidence of the New Testament and history are brought together (as I have tried to provide in this book), we can show that Christ Jesus was crucified *east* of Jerusalem (just "*outside the camp*") and alongside the principal "Broadway" called "The Descent of the Mount of Olives" which led into the Temple and the city of Jerusalem. This was the area most crowded in Jerusalem at Passover time. And then, after his death, he was buried in the newly-hewn tomb of Joseph of Arimathea just south of the southern summit of the Mount of Olives.

The Ch. of H. Sepulchre is w/in, not "outside the gate" 157
Other famous people were also buried in Jeru. until time of XST
when it became illegal to [have] tombs w/in the camp of Israel, Jeru.
Even the others had to be removed. "unclean" 157-8 So XST had to
be buried outside the camp, not 50 cubits outside the city, Levitic.
About 16 A.D. removal of bones in ossuaries from their graves began. Pilgrims at
festivals would touch the tombs & become unclean. cf Mt 23:29 p 160
" 27 p 162
159 on the ossuaries.
So the tomb of Joseph of Arimathea would have had to have
been 2000 + cubits away. 162-3. The area just So. of the So.
summit of Olivet qualifies. p. 164 comment on Lk 13:33

166 The place of X's execution was a public place
cf Quintilian (c Severus. The "Broadway" rd over Olivet
The Palm Sunday road, a paved road by Herod. 167
~~The road~~ The Descent mt Jer. was the most populated area
during festivals.

14

The Manner of Christ's Crucifixion

One of the greatest "secrets" associated with Golgotha concerns the manner in which Christ was crucified. Almost everyone for the past 1600 years has imagined that Christ was martyred on either a Roman or Greek type of cross or perhaps a simple stake without a crosspiece. The New Testament, however, gives information on this matter that is counter to all these suggestions. The truth is, Christ was not killed on a cross which was a beam of timber on which were nailed one or more crosspieces, nor was it a single upright pole (without a crosspiece) with his hands brought together and nailed above his head. In this chapter we will discuss the actual way in which he was crucified.

What first must be understood is that Christ met his death in a garden (John 19:41). Actually, the word "garden" in the Greek has the meaning of *orchard* or *plantation* -- a place of trees. It appears that "Golgotha" (which the Bordeaux Pilgrim called a *monticulus* -- "a small hill on top of a mount") must have had trees associated with it. It was to this small hill called "Skull Place" (no doubt shaped like the bald or top part of a skull) that Christ carried his cross on which he was crucified. Many scholars today believe it is inconceivable that Christ, who had been subjected to extensive beatings and whippings, could have carried a fully assembled Latin cross that would have weighed 200 pounds or more. This certainly has to be the case. The "cross" he transported was only the upper crosspiece which was nailed to a larger and more substantial support. It was to this board plank that Christ's arms or his wrists were affixed, and this is what Simon of Cyrene carried the final distance to Golgotha. Such crosspieces associated with crucifixions were given a technical name in Latin (*patibulum*).

When Golgotha was finally reached, Christ then had his arms or wrists nailed to the *patibulum*. Both he and the *patibulum* were then hoisted upwards and the crosspiece was nailed to some substantial stock of wood large enough to support the person being crucified. It was also common to bend the victim's legs upwards and nail the feet to the stock of wood itself. Sometimes a wood block was attached to the main wooden framework near the midsection of the body on which the buttocks of the victim could rest. This probably describes the manner in which Christ was crucified.

There were also two robbers who were crucified with him. There can hardly be any doubt that the same procedure of crucifixion was adopted for them. This would mean that the two robbers were affixed to their individual *patibulums*, and then each *patibulum* was nailed to a large stock of wood. But what kind of wooden support was this that Christ had his *patibulum* and his feet nailed to? The Bible shows that it was something entirely different from what most people believe today. It was not a dead piece of timber because both the apostles Peter and Paul said that Christ was nailed to a tree. He was crucified on *a living tree!*

This fact should not appear at all unreasonable considering the circumstances connected with Christ's crucifixion. His crucifixion and those of the two robbers was a "hurry-up" affair. The main reason to get their executions over quickly was because the Passover of the Jews was soon approaching and it was biblical law that no one could hang on an instrument of death beyond sundown. Indeed, it was common in times of haste to nail criminals to trees (Hastings, *Christ and the Gospels*, vol.II,p.749).

Using a living tree as the main stock of wood for the *patibulums* of Christ and the two robbers gave the soldiers the advantage of not having to dig holes some five or six feet deep in order to secure three large standing poles to support the *patibulums* of the three men. The soldiers, at first, simply nailed their arms to the *patibulums* and then lifted each board plank up to the middle of a tree, and then each of the *patibulums* was nailed to the tree. Finally, each of the three men had his lower legs nailed to the trunk of the tree. This was an ordinary tree like any tree found in an orchard today! And this is precisely what Peter and Paul said in the New Testament. Christ was nailed to a tree (in Greek: *xylon*) -- which in this case was *a living tree!* Notice what Peter said.

"The God of our fathers raised up Jesus, whom ye slew and hanged *on a TREE*" (Acts 5:30).

"We are witnesses of all things which he did both in the land of the Jews, and in Jerusalem: whom they slew and hanged *on a TREE*" (Acts 10:39).

"Who his own body bare our sins in his own body *on the TREE*" (I Peter 2:24).

The apostle Paul spoke the same thing.

"They took him down *from the TREE*" (Acts 13:29).

In all these instances *the tree* was a living tree! Christ himself said at the very time of his crucifixion: "For if they do these things in (dative: *with*) *a green TREE*, what shall be done in (dative: *with*) the dry?" (Luke 23:31). This indication shows that Christ was crucified *with* (or *by means of*) a *living* tree (*xylon*). It was the instrument by which he was executed. Paul also emphasized this fact in Galatians 3:13.

"Christ hath redeemed us from the curse of the law, being made a curse for us: for it is written, 'Cursed is every one that hangeth *on a TREE*'."

Paul was quoting Deuteronomy 21:23 where it states that the Israelites in the time of Moses were to hang the dead bodies of criminals on the bough or limbs of a tree until sundown. In no circumstances does this mean a type of crucifixion where single poles or beams with crosspieces were used to execute people. The "tree" in Deuteronomy meant a plain and simple *tree*, and in the later examples where this type of punishment was exacted by the Israelites, the "trees" in question were all ordinary living trees (Josh.8:29; 10:26,27). And this must have been the same situation in the case of Christ. He was executed in a garden (really, in an orchard of trees). In such a location it makes perfectly good sense why a tree was used by the Romans, especially since there was an urgency to get his crucifixion over in haste.

But wait a moment. Have we not been told that Christ was crucified on a *stauros* (in Greek) which is usually translanted "cross" in most of our English versions? Yes indeed, but the New Testament usage does not demand the Latin type of cross (or any other type of cross made up of dry pieces of timber in some way nailed together). Not in the least! The Greek word *stauros* by the first century had come to have a variety of meanings.

The original significance of the word *stauros* meant simply an upright pole or a stake. Like today, even we may speak of a pole to which one tethers an animal. In such a case we almost always think of a single stake secured to the ground. But if we should say "telephone pole," we could think of a single stake or a pole with one, two or even five cross-pieces attached to it. Even our English word "pole" can have several meanings depending on the context in which the word is used. The Greek word *stauros* fits into the same category.

The fact is, words change meanings over the years and can often take on opposite significations. For example, if a person were going to England from the United States one might fly by airplane or *sail* by ship. But if one wishes to *sail* today (in 99% of the cases), one means to go on a vessel that has no *sails* at all. Indeed, in naval terminology (to use another such word that indicates a change of meaning) a captain of a ship may say he is going *full steam ahead* when he is actually burning diesel fuel or nuclear power.

These changes of the meanings of words (and hundreds more could be given) are examples of what happened to the Greek word *stauros* from its earlier usages to those of the first century. Remarkably, however, there are some religious denominations who demand that Christ was crucified on a simple upright pole or stake because that was the original meaning of the word *stauros*. Yes, that was the first meaning, but for such interpreters to say that *stauros* had that exclusive significance in the first century is to deny the abundant literary evidence which shows it did not. If they should insist on the original meaning for all usages in the New Testament, then they should also (to be consistent) demand that anyone who says he *sails* to England today must in all circumstances go on a *sailing vessel.*

Actually, the word *stauros* in the first century could refer to all kinds of executionary impalements in which individuals were nailed or tied to *any* supportive timbers or trees for judgment. Like today, we may call a very severe judge "a *hanging judge*" (if he is prone to issue the death penalty without mercy), yet the state in which the judge presides could use the gas chamber, lethal injection or the electric chair for its means of executing convicted murderers. There is an old saying in the interpretation of words within their historical contexts. It is: "An *ounce* of usage is worth a whole *pound* of etymology." How true this principle is!

In the case of the word *stauros* in first century usage this is certainly the case. It had at least three different meanings in the New Testament alone. Note that the board plank which supported the arms of Christ (called the *patibulum* in Latin) was itself called a *stauros* (Luke 23:26). But it had a further meaning. The actual pole or the tree trunk on which the *patibulum* was nailed was also called a *stauros* (John 19:19). And the whole complex together (both *patibulum* and the bough of the tree reckoned as a single executionary devise) was called a *stauros* (John 19:25).

This means that the living tree on which Christ was crucified was known itself as a *stauros*. In almost all situations where quickness was demanded for a crucifixion, it was common to nail or tie the victims to living trees. This was accepted as the easiest way to get the task done since it required less work and time for the executioners. Recall that Pilate, up to the last moment, was trying to release Christ. There was no lengthy trial that would have allowed time to dig holes into which timber beams could be placed and then crosspieces (*patibulums*) nailed to the poles. And since it was made a cardinal point in the New Testament that the Jews themselves wanted the crucifixion of Christ to be over soon because the Passover was just on the horizon and they wanted to be able to take of the Passover without defilement with dead bodies (John 19:31). This is one of the reasons why the executioners decided to crucify Christ and the two robbers to a living tree, and they did!

The early Christians who lived after the apostles were fully aware of this fact that the *stauros* on which Christ was crucified was actually a living tree. The author of Barnabas (who wrote in the late first or early second century) consistently called the *stauros* of Christ a tree (5:13; 7:5; 8:5; 12:1,5). The descriptive context which he provides shows he meant a living tree. In mentioning the ritual of the Red Heifer, Barnabas said that the priests tied a crimson thread to a tree which represented the *stauros* of Christ (8:1,5). He said that Psalm 1:3 ("He shall be like the *tree* planted by the rivers of water, that bringeth forth fruit in season, and his leaf shall not wither") signified the *stauros* on which Christ was crucified (11:1,8). Even the top crosspiece that is found in the letter "T" was acknowledged by Barnabas as a *stauros*, and even the evangelist Luke himself said the same thing by calling the *patibulum* which Christ (and Simon of Cyrene) carried to the crucifixion site a *stauros* (Luke 23:26). And Barnabas stated that the incident of Moses in making the brass serpent showed Moses nailing the serpent to a tree, not to an upright pole (12:1,2), and Christ himself said that this incident was analogous to his own crucifixion (John 3:14).

And there is even more evidence of this recognition in the early second century. Ignatius also referred to the *stauros* as a tree, and so alive was it that it even bore fruit (*Smyr.* 1:2) and that it had branches (*Trall.* 11). In the writings of Ignatius he said it was believed that the instrument of death on which Christ was crucified represented "the Tree of Life" which was mentioned in the Book of Revelation (Rev. 2:7; 22:2,14), and of course that Tree of Life was a living *xylon* (tree) just as the apostles Peter and Paul said Christ was crucified on a similar *xylon* (tree).

There are numerous other references from early Christian writings that refer to the *stauros* on which Christ was placed as a living tree. But it is not only in literature that we find this fact. It was also common in early drawings of the crucifixion to depict branches and leaves as protruding from the bough of the *stauros*. The *stauros* of Christ was shown as a *living* symbol which represented life itself.

"Early Christian art indicates a close relationship between the tree of life and the cross. The cross of Christ, the wood of suffering and death, is for Christians a tree of life. In the tomb paintings of the 2nd century it is thus depicted for the first time as the symbol of victory over death. It then recurs again and again. The idea that the *living* trunk of the cross bears *twigs* and *leaves* is a common motif in Christian antiquity" (Kittel, *Theological Dictionary*, vol.V,pp.40,41 italics mine).

There is no doubt that Christians up to the middle of the second century knew Christ was crucified on a literal tree. Melito of Sardis consistently said the "cross" of Christ was a tree. He said: "Just as from a tree came sin, so also from a tree came salvation" (New fragment, III.4). The *patibulum* of Christ was, without doubt, nailed to a living tree!

There is another important point that must be made to make the story of Christ's crucifixion properly understood by us of modern times, and it is also very different from what most people today have imagined. It may be surprising but the apostle John shows that Christ and the two robbers were crucified together on *ONE TREE*, not on three separate trees! Notice what he recorded.

"The Jews therefore, because it was the preparation, that the bodies [note the plural, *BODIES*] should not remain on the *STAUROS* [singular, the *tree* of crucifixion] on the sabbath day (for that day was an high day), besought Pilate that their legs might be broken, and that they might be taken away. Then came the soldiers, and brake the legs of the first, and of the other crucified with him. But when they came to Jesus, and saw that he was dead already, they brake not his legs" (John 19:31-33).

These verses tell us very much. They show that there were three men crucified *ON ONE STAUROS!* This is even indicated in the Greek word *sunstaurothentos* found in John 19:32. The fact is, it not only means that the two robbers were simply "with him," but both of them were crucified "*together* with him." And indeed they were "together with him" on the same *stauros* -- a single living tree!

Even breaking the legs of the two robbers shows that Christ and the two malefactors were affixed to one tree. Note that the Scripture shows that one robber was on one side of Christ and the other robber on the opposite side. "Then two robbers were crucified with him, one on his right and one on his left" (Matt.27:38). If one robber was crucified on a separate cross on Christ's left side (as is normally depicted), and the other robber on another cross on his right (so that there were *three* crosses placed side by side with one another -- with Christ Jesus situated in the middle), we then have a major problem with the deaths of the two robbers. This is because the soldiers killed first the two robbers and last of all they came to Christ in the middle to slay him. Being in the "middle" should have made Christ the second to be killed.

It was this very circumstance that caused Dr. Bullinger (in his *Companion Bible*) to reckon that the Bible indicated, at least to him, that there were actually four others besides Christ who were crucified that day. He thought that the Bible was showing that there were two others on each side of Christ who were crucified with him. Here was his reasoning. Since the New Testament called those crucified with Christ both "robbers" (Matt.27:38) and also "malefactors" (criminals) (Luke 23:32), Bullinger came to the conclusion that there were *two* "malefactors" and also *two* "robbers." This is why Bullinger believed the two malefactors on one side had their legs broken first and then the soldiers came to Christ in the midst of the *two* malefactors and *two* robbers. But there is no need for such an interpretation (though Bullinger's suggestion was ingenious). Actually, all robbers are criminals (malefactors), but it is not true that all criminals are robbers. Luke simply used the generic term "malefactors" (criminals) to refer to the *two* robbers who were crucified with Christ.

However, Bullinger had a real point. How could soldiers first break the legs of the two robbers and then come to Jesus who was in the midst of them? The answer is simple. Since we are told by the apostle John (being an eyewitness to the scene) that all three were crucified *on ONE stauros* (that is, a single *tree*), it is easy to see how the soldiers broke the legs of the robber on Christ's right side (who had his back to Christ and was located on the northeast side of him) and then they broke the legs of the robber on Christ's left side (who also had his back to Christ but located on the southeast side of him). So, preceeding from the northeast side of the tree of crucifixion, the soldiers killed the first robber, went to the southeast side and killed the second robber, but they then came to Christ who was facing (let us say) westward towards his Father's Temple. When they reached Christ they found him dead already. All of this makes perfectly good sense as to what happened.

This factor is important to show that the apostle John wants his readers to know that the three men were nailed to *one* tree (a single *stauros* -- see John 19:31). These indications show that the traditions associated with the Church of the Holy Sepulchre have nothing to do with the real crucifixion of Christ. When Judas Quiriacus revealed to Helena the three crosses (with Pilate's tablet, the sponge and reed that were supposedly those associated with Christ), he was providing the Christian world with one of the greatest hoaxes ever devised. The Bible itself and the early Christians of the second century state that Christ was crucified on a living tree, not on some dead Roman crosses. And besides that, the two robbers were crucified with Christ *on the same tree!*

This fact seems illustrated in later works. For what it's worth, the *Arabic Infancy Gospel* has Jesus prophesying to his mother at a young age: "in thirty years, mother, the Jews will crucify me in Jerusalem, and those two robbers *will be fastened to the stauros WITH ME*, Titus on my right [the supposed name of the first robber] and Dumachus on my left" (Hennecke-Schneemelcher, *The New Testament Apocrypha*, vol.I, p.408). And in a work titled "Christ's Descent into Hell," one of the robbers is reported to have said: "Truly, I was a robber, and the Jews hanged me on a *stauros WITH* my Lord Jesus Christ" (*ibid.* p.480 emphases mine in both quotes).

Whatever reliability one wishes to place on these later

(and Gnostic) works is only of academic interest, but we have the certain word of the apostle John himself that Christ and the two robbers were indeed crucified to *one stauros*, and that *stauros* was a living tree. And though some scholars may wish to see in the singular *stauros* of the apostle John a simple figure of speech (in which the singular might be stretched to signify the plural), I will let them argue the matter with John. As for me, within the grammar of John 19:31 is the clear statement that Christ and the two robbers (all three of them) were crucified on *one stauros*, and it makes perfectly good sense that this was the case.

Since all three of those men who were crucified that morning on the Mount of Olives were crucified on a single *tree*, it is an absurd proposition to imagine that all three men were nailed to *one* Latin or Greek cross (made up of dry wooden timbers nailed together). How could two robbers be nailed to ONE *stauros* (as John said they were) with Christ nailed to the same *stauros* and at the same time Christ is described as being "in the middle" of the robbers? Each of the victims would have had to display some unusual bodily contortions to accomplish such a feat.

But away with such nonsense! Actually, the Holy Scriptures state that Christ and the two robbers were crucified together on *one tree* (and anyone should realize that a normal size tree would be large enough to allow ample room for all three to be on the same *stauros*). And this is exactly what happened! Christ and the two robbers were executed on *one* living tree near the summit of the Mount of Olives. Recall again what Melito said in the middle of the second century: "Just as from a tree came sin [in the Garden of Eden], so also from a tree came salvation [at Christ's crucifixion]" (New Fragment, III.4). Indeed, there are many references in early second and third century Christian writings to show that it was a literal *tree* on which Christ met his death in Jerusalem (cf. Danielou, *The Theology of Jewish Christianity*, pp.275-288).

There are some, however, who might question the crucifixion of Christ as being on a "living tree" (*xylon*). This is because the word *xylon* sometimes means a dry piece of wood (a stock or stave) and this is even the case in the New Testament (Matt.26:47; Acts 16:24; Rev.18:12). One might think that the word *xylon* could mean, after all, that it was on some dry timber beams that Christ was crucified?

True enough, if we had no context in the New Testament regarding the events of the crucifixion to show that *xylon* means a green tree (as it does most often), then we might have to consider the possibility that the *stauros* was made up of some dry pieces of timber. But, we have a cardinal reference by Christ himself, right in the context of the crucifixion scene, that the *xylon* on which Christ was crucified was a *green and living* tree which had roots in the ground. At the very time Christ was being led up to the crucifixion site, he said to the women following him: "If they do these things in (Greek dative: *with*) a green tree (*xylon*), what will occur in (Greek dative: *with*) the dry tree?" (Luke 23:31). Christ was saying that it was *with (or by means of)* a green tree (*xylon*) that he would meet his death.

This reference in Luke's Gospel shows that the instrument of Christ's execution was a *green* tree (*xylon*) and not with some dry pieces of timber nailed together in the form of a Latin or Greek cross (or any other configuration of dry timber beams). Christ was truly crucified on a *living* tree, and in chapter 18 it will be shown why this was absolutely necessary to fulfill the symbolic teaching of the Messianic prophecies in the Old Testament which predicted the coming of the true Messiah to Israel.

But what happened to *that* tree on which Christ was impaled? The Jewish historian Josephus said that all trees around Jerusalem (and certainly on the Mount of Olives) were cut down by Titus the Roman general in the A.D.66-70 holocaust (*War* VI.1). That destruction would have put an end to *that* tree if it had continued to exist to that time. But did *that* tree remain on the Mount of Olives for the next 40 years following Christ's crucifixion? There is reason to believe that the tree itself was destroyed soon after the burial of Christ.

It should be remembered that Christ was charged by the Jewish authorities with the most heinous of crimes --

that of blasphemy (Matt.26:65). This meant that he was looked on by the people as "accursed of God" and this is exactly how the apostle Paul described him (Gal.3:13). Paul's reference was to Deuteronomy 21:22,23 where it states that such an "accursed" person defiled even the soil (the very land) where the execution of an accursed person took place. This defilement also applied to the *tree* on which a person was hanged. The apostle Paul said that the *tree* (the *stauros*) was reckoned "a shame" (Heb.12:2) and he called the crosspiece (Latin: *patibulum*) "the reproach" (Heb.13:13). All the instruments were "accursed" because they came in contact with the "accursed one."

The essential teaching on how to cleanse the land of such "accursedness" is found in Deuteronomy 21:22,23, and in the previous verse 21 it says this purging was to be done by *burning* (Hebrew: *bahgar*). In the Old Testament example of such purging, it was thought necessary to burn the possessions of such an "accursed one" because the abominable sin of the person was even transferred to the things owned by the sinner (since he had touched them and this reckoned even his possessions "accursed"). This was the case with the things belonging to Achan who sinned so grievously in the time of Joshua (Josh.7:15,24-26). What happened was that Achan himself was killed (with his children and animals) and all his "accursed" things were burnt up together with him. This practice of utter destruction was considered the only way to purify the land of Israel from such defilements.

With this as the cardinal example of what happened to an "accursed one" and the "accursed things" which he had touched, it must be that the *tree* on which Christ was crucified was consigned to be burnt to ashes. After all, it was reckoned "a shame" (itself "accursed"). To keep the land from being polluted, Christ had to be destroyed before sundown and the "accursed" *stauros* had to be burnt up so that no person could ever touch it again. The only thing of Christ that was considered worth saving was his cloak, but it must be noted that it was the Roman soldiers who cast lots for the garment since they had no scruples about Jewish matters.

What the Jewish authorities wanted to do was to take

the dead body of Christ and the "accursed" (shameful) tree and *burn them up together* just as the Israelites did with Achan in the Old Testament. This is the reason that Joseph of Arimathea gathered up courage and made a daring entrance into the presence of Pilate (in a sense of urgency) in order to gain Christ's body for burial before they could burn it to ashes (Mark 15:43). Had not Pilate given Joseph of Arimathea charge over Christ's dead body, it would indeed have been consumed in the flames along with the tree on which he was crucified.

Actually, there was a prophecy that many people at the time interpreted as referring to the Messiah and his death. It showed that the tree and the person on the tree would be destroyed *together*. Though the original teaching of this Old Testament prophecy seemed to refer to the prophet Jeremiah, later Christians came to feel that it was a direct prophecy of what happened to Christ at his crucifixion. The prophecy is found in Jeremiah 11:19.

"But I as a lamb that is brought to the slaughter; and I knew not that they had devised devices against me, saying, Let us destroy the tree *with* the fruit thereof, and let us cut him off from the land of the living, that his name may be no more remembered" (italics mine -- the subsidiary word "ox" in the King James Version is not in the original Hebrew).

The Anglican Commentary (London: 1875) gives an interesting quote from Jerome in the fourth century about this very verse.

"Jerome well says on this verse; 'All the churches agree in understanding that under the person of Jeremiah these things are said of Christ. For he is the lamb brought to the slaughter that opened not its mouth. The tree is his cross, and the bread [fruit] his body: for he says himself, *I am the bread that came down from heaven*. And of him they purposed to cut him off from the land of the living that his name should no more be remembered" (vol.V,p.395).

And though later Christians interpreted Jeremiah 11:19 in various ways, it is interesting that the Hebrew made one think that *the tree* WITH *the fruit* [the body] were prophesied to be destroyed *together!* This is a most important factor in our present discussion. While the prophecy (acknowledged by Christians as referring to Christ) has the tree of Christ's crucifixion *destroyed* WITH Christ (and this would seem to mean that both would be consummed *together* -- perhaps in a holocaust as in the case of Achan), we know that Joseph of Arimathea was able, at the last moment, to rescue Christ's body from such a fate. But this biblical reference still shows that the tree itself was *destroyed*. And typically, in the judgment rendered by the Sanhedrin against Jesus, it could be reckoned that Jesus was "destroyed" with the tree (at least he should have been destroyed *with* the tree) had not Joseph of Arimathea rescued his body from the flames. The prophecy of Jeremiah 11:19, as understood in the original Hebrew (and interpreted as referring to Christ and the tree on which he was crucified), is further proof that early Christians knew that the tree itself was not spared from destruction.

Yet after the time of Constantine many Christians began to believe that the cross escaped destruction (including the two crosses of the robbers) and that it was preserved in a miraculous way in order for it to become a relic in later times. Paulinus of Nola said:

> "It is certain that if it [the cross] would have fallen into the hands of the Jews (who were taking every precaution to crush belief in Christ), it would inevitably have been broken into pieces *and burnt*" (Letter 31).

But Paulinus thought that the cross of Christ and those of the robbers in some way were taken immediately away by Christians and hidden near the site of Christ's tomb. Paulinus did not explain why Christians thought it necessary to preserve the robbers' crosses as well. He also believed that as the decades passed, "all recollection" of where the crosses were buried passed from the knowledge of Christians until they were discovered by Helena the queen mother when the Temple of Venus was being cleared in order to build the Church of the Holy Sepulchre (Letter 31).

All of these late fourth century stories about the hiding of the crosses of Christ and the robbers, could have been put to rest as hoaxes if those later Christians would simply have paid attention to the New Testament revelation that the centurion and the others around the crucifixion site were able to *see* the curtain of the Temple tear in two. Such an indication alone is enough to jettison the *western* "Golgotha" discovered at the Shrine of Venus as even being a contender for the true site because such a scene could only have been viewed from near the summit of the Mount of Olives. And had they read (and believed) the apostles Peter and Paul that Christ was actually crucified on a *living tree* (and that Christ and the robbers were executed on a single tree), they would also have been spared the nonsense that Judas Quiriacus was foisting off on Helena, Constantine and the Christian world.

But with Constantine having seen the "cross" in the sky before the battle of Milvian Bridge and subsequently identifying the site of Christ's crucifixion with his visions and dreams (in association with the so-called supernatural revelations shown to his mother Helena), both Helena and Constantine became prime targets for Judas Quiriacus to pull off his subterfuge. The capstone for accepting all these things, however, must have come when Cyril (the third bishop of Jerusalem) said that all the city saw a great cross in the sky stretching from *new* "Golgotha" to the Mount of Olives. This parhelion of the sun (on May 7th, A.D.350) was interpreted by the Christian authorities in Jerusalem as a wonderful sign from God that vindicated the newly discovered *western* site for Christ's passion. Visions, dreams and signs had won the day! And from that time until now the world has been honoring the wrong spot for Christ's crucifixion. Most people have also accepted the wrong type of *stauros* by embracing the legitimacy of the Roman type of crosses that Judas Quiriacus unearthed for Helena. However, the actual *stauros* of Christ was a *living tree* which was growing in the ground near the southern summit of the Mount of Olives.

15

The Surprising Cause of Christ's Death

Christ was certainly crucified by the Romans but his death came about in a far different way than is normally supposed. The fact is, he did not die by crucifixion alone. Recall that Pilate wondered whether Christ had died so early because it was usually an hour or so before sundown that Jewish authorities broke the legs of those crucified in order to kill them. But it was reported to Pilate that Christ had died about two hours earlier than this (Mark 15:44). Something else caused Christ to die more quickly, and it presents us with a terrifying spectacle of what happened to him.

In one way, I almost wish we could be spared a knowledge of what took place at his crucifixion. It was most gruesome, and sad! But there is no use hiding our heads in the sand concerning the sufferings that Christ endured. After all, the description of what happened is recorded in the Holy Scriptures (though overlooked by many people over the past 1500 years) and for that reason it is essential that each of us knows what occurred at that Passover season in A.D.30. When it is fully understood, it is truly a heartbreaking and horrendous scene. But the New Testament records that a triumph and victory emerged because of the resurrection of Christ Jesus and his subsequent exaltation to supreme power at the very throne of God the Father.

To understand just what punishment Christ underwent, it is necessary to recall a prime scripture that is found in Isaiah's prophecy about the Suffering Servant recorded from Isaiah 52:13 to 53:12. The principal verse that allows us to comprehend the full meaning of the prophecy is given at its beginning in Isaiah 52:14.

"As many were astonished at thee; his visage was so marred more than any man, and his form more than the sons of men."

Also coupled with this description of the Suffering Servant is a further prophetic account in Psalm 22 (personified in the sufferings of King David). Notice Psalm 22:16,17.

"For dogs have compassed me: the assembly of the wicked have inclosed me: they pierced my hands and feet, I may tell all my bones: they look and stare at me."

While it appears that David applied Psalm 22 as belonging to himself in an allegorical sense, it was seen by the apostles as having a literal fulfillment in the person of Jesus. It is interesting, however, that these verses are usually not fully applied today in connection with Christ's crucifixion. But let us do so. Coupling these two sections of the Bible together (as certainly was done by the writers of the New Testament) gives us a further indication to the type of death that Christ encountered. Had there been no literal application of these scriptures to Christ it is difficult to see how the apostles could have defended them as describing the role of Christ at his crucifixion (which, of course, was quite *literal*).

If these prophetic descriptions in Isaiah and the Psalms are to be literally interpreted (and it appears that they were by the apostles) then we have the characterization of a man who was not only crucified but one who had some of his flesh so torn away from his bones that people looking upon him could hardly tell he was a human being. As Isaiah said: "His visage was so marred more than any man" (Isa.52:14). Even the bones of his body were able to be seen (not simply observed under his skin, but the bare bones themselves were being exposed because so much skin and flesh had been rent away from them).

This is what the prophet Isaiah was saying in his description of the Suffering Servant. His flesh was to be so mangled and his body so disfigured that it was almost impossible to recognize him as being a normal human (Isa.52:14). What did his tormentors do to him (other than simple crucifixion) that much skin and flesh were torn away from the parts of his body facing them? I realize that such a description may seem offensive to some people, but it is time for all of us to take stock of what the scriptural revelation actually says and not be squeamish about the truth of the crucifixion scene. The prophet Isaiah described the Suffering Servant with his visage and form marred more than any man. Some people may find it distasteful to imagine Christ in this fashion, but that is what Isaiah wrote and it seems reasonable to accept his description. The apostles certainly did, and several of them were also eyewitnesses to the crucifixion.

What type of judicial punishment could produce such an awful description of the Suffering Servant? The scourging that Christ was subjected to *before* his crucifixion cannot account for such mangling since Pilate intended to let him go after the soldiers had chastised him, and from this it shows that Pilate fully believed he would recover (Luke 23:22). No, it was not the beatings that Christ endured under the abuse of the soldiers. There is really only one type of execution that could fit the scriptural descriptions (which was a common one in Jerusalem at the time). Interestingly, it is the only kind of punishment that the Mosaic legislation allowed for capital crimes. What we find in these prophecies is a classic portrayal of a person who was pelted with stones.

There is no doubt that Christ experienced the torment of volleys of small, sharp stones thrown at the front parts of his naked body while he was nailed to the tree of crucifixion. The stones were hurled at his face, at his mid-section and his legs! These must have been like sharp flintstones (many of which are on the Mount of Olives) that would break the skin and dislodge the flesh but without the force to break his bones. Such volleys of stones hitting his body periodically for almost a six hour period could produce the description of Isaiah: "As many were astonished at thee: his visage [his outward appearance] was *so marred* more than any man, and his form [*so marred*] more than the sons of man."

In the Old Testament stoning was the only type of execution that was prescribed for those committing capital crimes. Notice what Hasting's *Dictionary of the Apostolic*

Church says about the Old Testament legislation concerning stoning.

> Stoning was "the pelting of stones by a mob at a person who had merited their ill-will (Exo.8:26; 17:4; II Chron.24:20ff; cf. Heb.11:37; Acts 5:26) or the infliction of the death penalty by stoning (Lev.20:2; Deut.13:10). The method which an enraged crowd took of executing vengeance with the weapons lying readiest to their hand came to be employed afterwards as a regular and legal method of inflicting the death sentence on a criminal. Stoning is *the ONLY form of capital punishment recognized in the Mosaic Law*" (vol.II, pp.528,529 emphases mine).

In the time when Christ was put to death, the Romans forbade the people of Judaea from applying the death penalty on anyone (John18:31). It was Pilate who had the only authority to execute Christ and the Roman method for crimes against the state for non-Romans was normally by crucifixion. And, without doubt, Christ was indeed crucified to a tree. But there was much more to Christ's death than a simple crucifixion. Pilate also permitted the authorities in Jerusalem to kill him according to biblical law. He told them to "take ye him and judge him according to your law" (John 18:31). This was an extraordinary allowance because it subjected Christ to suffer both the Roman method of execution for terrible crimes (the Gentile practice) but it also gave permission to the people of Jerusalem to pelt him with stones in the scriptural (Mosaic) manner. In Leviticus 24:15-18 Moses commanded that all Israelites and aliens in sight of a blasphemer should take up stones and stone the profane and ungodly person to death. The Hebrew actually means that Israel was to "overwhelm" the criminal with countless volleys of stones being thrown at his naked body (Rashi, *Commentary*, vol.II, p.111).

It should be remembered that the crime which the authorities in Jerusalem charged against Christ was that of blasphemy (Mark 16:64). This was the most dastardly crime imaginable to the people of Judaea. And the official judgment against him made him worthy of death in the most despicable fashion (Matt.26:65,66). It is interesting that it was Christ's claim that he was the Son of God that made the

so to "take up cross": follow which also the scorn; stones of the mob. Scary authorities proclaim him a blasphemer. With such a terrible charge against him, the leaders went to Pilate and asked him to allow Jesus to be killed in the manner prescribed by the Law of Moses. "We have a law, and by that law he ought to die, because he has made himself the Son of God" (John 19:7). To the authorities, Christ's appraisal of himself was tantamount to blasphemy. The law that they were referring to was that of Leviticus 24:16.

"And he that blasphemeth the name of the Lord [Yahweh], he shall surely be put to death, and all the congregation shall certainly stone him: as well as the stranger, as he that is born in the land, when he blasphemeth the name of the Lord, shall be put to death."

Thus, all the residents of the land (Jews and Gentiles alike) were required to barrage the blasphemer with volleys of stones. During the time of Christ's ministry, many of the people who did not like his teaching had several times tried to carry out this Mosaic Law against him. "Then they took up stones to cast at him: but Jesus hid himself, and went out of the temple, going throughout the midst of them, and so passed by" (John 8:59). "Then the Jews took up stones again to stone him. Jesus answered them, many good works have I showed you from my Father; for which of those works do you stone me? The Jews answered him, saying, For a good work we stone you not; but for blasphemy; and because you, being a man, make yourself God" (John 10:31-33). The fact is, time and again the authorities were trying to kill him by stoning. "His disciples say unto him, Master, the Jews of late sought to stone you; and go you [to Jerusalem] again?" (John 11:8).

It is made clear in the Gospel record that the people who were hostile to Christ were looking for every opportunity to stone him for his blasphemy (as they considered it). And they finally got their wish when they went to Pilate and said: "We have a law, *and by that law* he ought to die" (John 19:7). And Pilate acquiesced to their wishes. "Take you him *and judge him according to your law*" (John 18:31). [Note that all the references in the previous paragraph about the people desiring him to be *stoned*, are found in the Gospel of

John which records the appeal of the authorities to Pilate to have Christ killed according to the Law of Moses. And this type of capital punishment was, of course, by stoning. There can be no doubt that this is what the authorities in Jerusalem were petitioning Pilate for permission to do. And Pilate gave the allowance.]

It should be realized that when the one being stoned was charged with the most heinous of crimes, such as blasphemy, then it was common for the stoning to be done with as much humiliation upon the person as possible. The main part of the anatomy towards which the stones were hurled was to the face and eyes. Christ himself stated that the stoning of an individual was normally for people to cast the stones at the head. "And again he sent unto them another servant: and at him they cast stones, *and wounded him in the head*" (Mark 12:4). It was to the head and the eyes that the stones were predominantly thrown, at least in the initial stages of the execution. Indeed, in Psalm 38 (one of the Psalms of David which reflects in a typical way what David's son, the Messiah, would have to suffer), it is stated that the person so described *was to be blinded* (see particularly verse 10 and read through verse 14). This was a section of Scripture that even the prophet Isaiah later quoted regarding the Suffering Servant (Isa.53:7). There can hardly be a doubt that sometime during those six hours of being barraged by stones, several of the stones hit his eyes and Christ was blinded by them!

The fact that Christ was stoned to satisfy the prophecy of Isaiah 52:14 that his appearance and form would be *marred* more than any man also helps to explain another New Testament reference that has long puzzled scholars. When Christ instituted the Lord's Supper on the eve of his crucifixion, he took bread and *broke* it and he said this *breaking* was like his body would be *broken* for them (Matt.26:26). He spoke of the *breaking* of his body in the same context as the wine which represented his blood which was shed at his crucifixion for the remission of sins. But it has baffled scholars how *breaking off* pieces of flat and crispy bread (just like the unleavened bread that Jews eat at

Passover today called *matzos*) could in any way represent the body of Christ at his crucifixion? Since the New Testament specifically states that no bones in his body would be broken (John 19:36), many scholars can see no reference whatever to the death of Christ in the *breaking* of the unleavened bread. To many of them they feel that "the breaking of bread" must only refer to a ceremony at fellowship meals without any significance in regard to the crucifixion of Christ. But many early Christians did not view it that way at all. Let us look at what early Christians thought.

There are a number of Greek manuscripts and writings of several Church Fathers which provide a comment of explanation to the text of First Corinthians 11:24 concerning the *breaking* of the bread at the Lord's Supper and they associated it with the *breaking* of Christ's body at his crucifixion. They added their comments that the bread represented Christ's body: "*which is broken for you*" (see *The Greek New Testament*, UBS, p.604). This means that there were early beliefs that the "*broken bread*" in the ceremony of the Lord's Supper did indeed represent the "*broken body*" of Christ at the time of his crucifixion. For one thing, in the prophecy of the Suffering Servant in Isaiah 52:13 to 53:12 there was the statement in Hebrew that the person of the prophecy would be "*broken* for our iniquities" ("*bruised*" King James). There is no question that the Hebrew word *dah-chah* in Isaiah 53:5 means "*broken*" (cf. Isaiah 19:10).

Thus, we have the beliefs of early Christians and the prophecy of Isaiah itself that Christ's body would indeed be *broken* like *breaking off* pieces of unleavened bread. But the scourging of the soldiers before his crucifixion or the simple act of crucifixion itself could not account for such *breaking off* of pieces of his body. But the act of *stoning* would fit the description precisely. The hurling of small and sharp stones at Christ's body would tear away pieces of his flesh ever so slowly until after about six hours of such treatment he would have been hanging on the tree of crucifixion as a person whose visage and form would have been so marred that he would not have resembled a normal human any longer. This is how Isaiah 52:14 describes the Suffering Servant, whom all the New Testament writers identified with Christ Jesus, and I see no reason for not believing it. This is just another evidence that Christ met his death by *stoning* (his body torn to shreds in its frontal areas) and that he did not die by crucifixion alone.

The apostle Paul was fully aware that Christ was not only crucified in the Roman fashion of execution but he knew that the main reason for his death (and punishment) was through the Israelitish method of stoning. In Paul's classic statement that Christ had become a curse for us, he did not mean that it was simply by crucifixion alone that he had become such an "accursed thing." Note what he said in Galatians 3:13.

"Christ has redeemed us from the curse of the law, being made a curse for us: for it is written, Cursed is every one that hangs on a tree."

The apostle Paul was in no way intending his quote, concerning the application of the Mosaic Law in the death of Christ, as pertaining to the Roman method of crucifixion alone. Paul selected the scripture in Deuteronomy 21:23 as describing Christ's death for another reason. Anyone who is acquainted with the Old Testament legislation is well aware that Moses in this reference was in no way speaking about hanging someone on a tree *in order to kill him!* On the contrary. Moses ordered the authorities within Israel to hang the corpse of the "accursed one" on a tree with ropes *AFTER* the person had already been killed *by STONING*. Notice the quote in full that the apostle Paul referred to. It had nothing to do with killing a person by the Roman method of crucifixion, and no such thing was in Moses' mind. Moses meant simply to hang the corpse on a tree *after* the stoning!

"And all the men of his city shall stone him with stones that he die: so shall you put evil away from among you; and all Israel shall hear and fear. And if a man have committed a sin worthy of death, and he be to be put to death, and you hang him on a tree: and his body shall not remain all night on the tree, but you shall certainly bury him that day (for he that hangs is accursed of God), that your land be not defiled, which the Lord your God gives you for an inheritance" (Deut.21:21-23).

Paul realized that though Christ was indeed crucified in the Roman manner (and this contributed to his death), it was actually the stoning by the people of Jerusalem (both by Jews and Gentiles as the Law of Moses required) that caused his death. And while the original Mosaic legislation stated that the Israelites should first stone a blasphemer to death and *then* hang him on a tree until near sunset, in the case of Christ it was Pilate who first nailed him to a tree and then he allowed the people at Jerusalem to stone him! Even using this reversal technique (first hanging on a tree and *then* stoning the criminal) was utilized by the people in Jerusalem within the first century. We now have new discoveries from the Dead Sea area that fully demonstrate this fact with certainty.

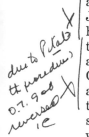

It is now proved that blasphemers and traitors were sometimes *first* hanged on a tree and *then* they were killed. One of the important Dead Sea Scrolls is called "The Temple Scroll." The late Yigael Yadin wrote a major work about the contents of this scroll and we now have available an English version of the full text provided by Johann Maier (edited by Clines and Davies). These scholars were surprised to find a reference in Column 64 of the text that spoke about hanging traitors on a tree *and THEN* they would be killed while they were suspended from the tree. I will quote the section of the scroll concerning this important point.

> "If a man informs against his people, and delivers up his people to a foreign nation, and does harm to his people, *you shall hang him on a tree, and he shall die*.... And if a man has committed a crime punishable by death, and has defected into the midst of the nations, and has cursed his people and the children of Israel, *you shall hang him also on the tree, and he shall die*" (emphases mine).

Both Yadin and Maier considered that these texts in the *Temple Scroll* which spoke about Israelitish executions were referring to crucifixions like the Romans were performing on criminals in the first century. At first glance one might come to that conclusion. But in no way is this what the authors of the *Temple Scroll* had in mind. The text does not say "nail him to a tree and leave him there to die." Had the scroll meant that he was nailed to the tree and then left there without food or water to die, then it would have signified the type of crucifixion that Romans were used to in the first century. But this is not what the *Temple Scroll* meant because it says right in the text itself that "they shall not let *his corpse* hang on the wood, but must bury it on the same day." The *Temple Scroll* itself demands that the criminal which was hanged alive on the tree would be a corpse before sundown of the day he was tied (or nailed) to the tree!

This means that every criminal who was alive and tied (or nailed) to a tree for execution was going to be a dead person (according to the *Temple Scroll*) before sundown of the day the criminal was hoisted up to the tree. But how was such a person to be killed? In the case of the two robbers who were crucified with Christ, the Roman soldiers broke their legs which killed them. But Pilate was surprised that Christ was already dead without his legs being broken to bring on his death. Something had already killed him. Even the *Temple Scroll* informs us how those who had committed abominable crimes were to be killed. In the very context of the *Temple Scroll* of which we are referring it said (in the previous section): "Then all the men of the city *shall stone him, so that he die.*" The only official method of execution in the Mosaic Law (which the *Temple Scroll* was trying to implement) was by stoning. Only by stoning was the blasphemer or traitor executed according to Mosaic Law. And this is the method by which the *Temple Scroll* itself shows that anyone tied (or nailed) to a tree would die before sundown of the day on which the person was hoisted to the tree.

This is clearly what the *Temple Scroll* means, and interestingly, this is the exact method by which Christ Jesus was put to death. Professor Yadin even showed that such an interpretation was understood by the ancients. He pointed out that the Syriac translation of Deuteronomy 21:22 shows a close relationship to what the *Temple Scroll* related. "*He is hanged on a tree AND is put to death*" (p.207). This plainly shows that the criminal was hanged on the tree in order to be put to death. He was certainly not tied (or nailed) to the tree to die a lingering death some days later. The criminal was suspended on a tree in order to be put to death. And what kind of death did the person experience? It was the only one sanctioned in the Mosaic Law and also in the *Temple Scroll* for ultra-criminals. It was by stoning!

And note this point. Not only does the Syriac translation of Deuteronomy 21:22 state that the blasphemer is to be "hanged on a tree AND is put to death" but even in the Christian portion of the *Ascension of Isaiah* the text states that Christ was crucified on a tree (3:13; 9:15; 11:21) but in some manuscripts it shows that Christ was killed *after* he was hanged on the tree. The text states: "he will hang him upon a tree *AND* kill him." This shows that Christ was actually killed *after* having been hanged on the tree of crucifixion. The Slavic Version of the same states: "and they will hang...*AND* he will kill" (Charlesworth, *The Old Testament Pseudepigrapha,* vol.II, p,170 emphases mine). Again, these references show that Christ was hanged on the tree and was later killed. These early opinions agree remarkably with the *Temple Scroll* in the method of executing criminals and blasphemers at the time of Christ. These indications also agree with the teachings of the New Testament regarding Christ's death when all the evidence is brought into play. The truth is, though Christ was certainly crucified to a tree on the Mount of Olives to satisfy the Roman methods of execution, he was also *stoned* by those in Jerusalem to make his death in accordance with Mosaic Law. It was the stoning that actually caused him to die after six hours of enduring the tearing of his flesh away from many of his bones.

The early Jewish people have long known that this was the manner in which Jesus met his death. In *Sanhedrin* 43a of the Talmud we have the following account of the crucifixion of Christ.

"On the eve of the Passover Yeshu the Nazarean [Hebrew for Jesus the Nazarean] *was hanged.* For forty days before the execution took place, a herald went forth and cried, 'He is going forth *TO BE STONED* because he has practised sorcery and enticed Israel to apostacy. Any one who can say anything in his favour, let him come forward and plead on his behalf.' But since nothing was brought forward in his favour *he was hanged* on the eve of Passover."

True enough, Jewish authorities knew that Christ was *hanged*, but they also were aware that he was also stoned to satisfy the Law of Moses. This is what was reserved for blasphemers and those who practiced sorcery. What we find in this Jewish historical reference is the fact that they were knowledgeable that Christ Jesus was actually *stoned* while he was *hanging* on the tree of crucifixion.

This reference in the Talmud shows that the authorities in Jerusalem had been publicly proclaiming (for a period of 40 days before the Passover in A.D.30) that Jesus deserved to be stoned for his statements and teachings. The apostles were well aware of this public pronouncement and they reminded Christ of it. "His disciples say unto him, Master, the Jews of late thought to stone you; and go you [to Jerusalem] again?" (John 11:8). Christ knew that the environment at Jerusalem was hostile to him and his teachings, but he went anyway to the capital. And true enough, the public pronouncements that were being made by the authorities in Jerusalem (starting 40 days before the Passover) were indeed carried out! They were true to their word and had Jesus stoned while he was hanging on the tree of crucifixion in order that the commands of Moses would be fulfilled regarding a person who blasphemed against God.

There is even more Jewish evidence on this matter. Professor Jacob Z. Lauterback in his book "Rabbinic Essays" recalls a Jewish Baraita (a Jewish teaching that was not codified when the first part of the Talmud was devised or that no longer appears in the Talmud) in which it says that Jesus actually met his death *by stoning* and not by crucifixion alone. In a long discourse on this subject, the Baraita recorded: "he [Jesus] is going out *to be stoned*" followed by "they *hanged* him" (pp.494-497). This early Jewish tradition shows that Christ was indeed stoned to death while he was hanging on the tree. This is similar to what the *Temple Scroll* said, but in the case of the *Temple Scroll* the victim was tied (not nailed) to the tree and then he was stoned to death.

Of course, the Gospels make it clear that Christ was truly crucified to a tree in the Roman manner. But once it is recognized that people were also throwing stones at his naked body for almost a six hour period, it can be understood why he died so quickly. The robbers who were crucified with him were not stoned as he was (because they were not judged as being blasphemers). They had to have their legs broken to kill them (as would have happened to Christ under normal circumstances) so that their bodies would not remain on the tree after sundown to accord with the Law of Moses.

It was Christ, however, not the robbers, that Isaiah was talking about when he said that the Suffering Servant of his prophecy would have his visage and form *more marred* than any man (Isa.52:14). And with a barrage of stones being thrown at the front parts of his body (after about six hours of stoning), it can easily be understood how the prophecy of Isaiah was fulfilled precisely. And this is how the apostles (some of whom were eyewitnesses to the death of Christ on the tree of crucifixion) were able to interpret the Old Testament prophecies about Christ's ordeal in paying for the sins of the world. This evidence shows that it was actually the *stoning* that caused Christ's death and not his crucifixion alone.

But this doesn't end the story as far as Christ's punishment was concerned. To complete the humiliation for such an "accursed one," there was one other Old Testament example that had to be accomplished to fulfill the totality of the Old Testament legislation on the punishment of despicable criminals. We find that the tree on which the ultracriminal was hanged had to be consumed by fire as was Achan and all his goods in the time of Joshua. Note what the scriptural example shows for individuals who had been censured as being an "accursed one" as was Jesus.

> "And it shall be, that *he that is taken with the accursed thing SHALL BE BURNT WITH FIRE*, he and all that he has: because he has transgressed the covenant of the Lord [Yahweh], and because he has brought folly in Israel" (Josh.7:15).

And this is exactly what the authorities in Jerusalem were intending to do with Christ. But, as explained in the last chapter, Joseph of Arimathea stepped in hurriedly to prevent this fate happening to the body of Christ. Though it is probable that the tree on which Christ was killed (being considered "accursed") was uprooted and burnt to ashes to keep the land from being contaminated, Christ himself was spared this judicial requirement because Pilate granted Joseph of Arimathea his request to bury Christ in his newly hewn tomb not far away from the crucifixion site.

The fact that Christ's death was brought about by *stoning* and not simply by crucifixion alone is also shown by the example of what happened to the apostle Paul. The first act of persecution against the apostle Paul which the New Testament records is his enduring the punishment of *stoning* (Acts 14:19,20). This occurred to Paul while he was in the area of Galatia about the year A.D.45. Let us now notice an important fact which Paul records about himself when he wrote to the Galatian Christians about four years later. Paul said that he, at that time, *bore in his body* the marks (really, the *SCARS*) which Jesus Christ also had. Notice how he worded it:

> "From henceforth let no man trouble me: for I bear in my body the marks [the *scars*] of the Lord Jesus" (Gal.6:17).

Paul was saying that he had the *scars* of Christ in his body and he was not speaking allegorically. Now, those *scars* were not piercings in his hands, feet and side as a result of being crucified like Christ. No, Paul had never been crucified. But he had been *stoned* and left for dead (Acts 14:19,20). Though the type of stoning Paul endured was an illegal act, it was so severe that the people who stoned him (and then they dragged his body on the ground beyond the city limits) thought he was certainly dead. By a miracle, however, the apostle Paul got up and walked away.

And though Paul was not pelted for almost six hours, as was Christ, he was still greatly tormented by this stoning. It resulted in many scars being on his body. And, as Christ said, the part of the anatomy that persecutors normally injured in stoning was the face or the eyes (Mark 12:4). Is it not remarkable that the apostle Paul about four years after he was stoned told the Galatian Christians that he had at first been teaching them under great physical pain and he indicates that his principal affliction had something to do with his eyes?

"Ye know how through infirmity of the flesh I preached the gospel unto you at the first. And my trial which was in my flesh ye despised not, nor rejected: but received me as an angel of God, even as Christ Jesus. Where is then the blessedness ye spake of? for I bear you record, that, if it had been possible, ye would *have plucked out your own eyes* and have given them to me" (Gal.4:13-15).

Though Paul had survived his stoning in a miraculous way, he was no doubt still suffering from its consequences. Since it was common for hostile people to hurl stones at the face of a person, it can readily be understood why such a stoning could have almost blinded Paul. He wrote with large alphabetic letters (Gal.6:11), and this may well indicate that he had difficulty in seeing clearly. The lacerations had apparently so injured Paul that there was permanent damage to his eyes and face. When he told the Galatians that "my trial in my flesh ye despised not, nor rejected," it strongly implies that his wounds (even four years after his stoning) were ostensibly so bad and unattractive that the common thing for people to do would be to reject him from being in their company. The Galatians, however, did not reject him, but treated him like an angel of God, "even as Christ Jesus" (because they knew that Christ was also stoned and blinded). Since there were no plastic surgeons to improve Paul's outward appearance, this is no doubt why Paul made a special point in telling the Galatians that he bore the *scars* of Jesus in his body (6:17). Those *scars* no doubt came from the wounds he suffered during his stoning.

This reference by Paul to his own *scars* as being the "*scars* of Jesus" is just another proof that Christ himself had been subjected to stoning and not crucifixion alone. So many sharp stones had been thrown toward the front parts of his body that Christ was made to appear like an unrecognizable bloody mass of flesh. It must have drastically altered his appearance. "His visage was so marred more than any man, and his form more than the sons of men" (Isa.52:14). Now I am fully aware that most people will not like this description of Christ's appearance, but this is what the prophet Isaiah said would occur and such a scene would apply precisely to someone pelted with small, sharp stones for almost a six hour period. Many people are simply not able to psychologically accept such a different appraisal of the scene of Christ's crucifixion because they have never heard such a teaching before. That's true, the description of what Isaiah said of the Suffering Servant is so unknown in most religious circles that the teaching that Christ was "an unrecognizable bloody mass of flesh" can hardly be believed by many people. And interestingly, this is exactly what Isaiah said would be the reaction to the very prophecy of which we are speaking.

> "Kings shall shut their mouths at him [keep silent in astonishment]: *for that which HAS NOT BEEN TOLD THEM shall they see; and that which THEY HAD NOT HEARD shall they consider*" (Isa.52:15).

Even the educated leaders of the people, so Isaiah tells us, will be utterly amazed at the real teaching about the Suffering Servant. They will be astonished when they are told the actual meaning of Isaiah's report. Yet, verse 15 shows *they shall see* and *they shall consider* the report that had previously not been told them. But will the leaders believe the report? Isaiah asks a question of those leaders who now have their eyes and ears opened to the truth about the Suffering Servant. His question is put in such a way that Isaiah knows it will take "the arm of the Lord" (the power of God himself) to get them to see the importance of the report.

> "Who hath believed our report? and to whom is the arm of the Lord revealed?"

Isaiah knew that most people (even the kings of the world) would *not* believe his report of the Suffering Servant unless "the arm of the Lord" reveals it to them. How many of us have *truly* believed what it says?. For the first 35 years of my professional life in the fields of history and theology, I failed to see the impact of Isaiah's prophecy entirely! And I dare say that most of my readers have missed it too. Most of us have never heard nor have we read *anything* that would suggest that Isaiah's Suffering Servant (whom the apostles identified with Christ Jesus) was an "unrecognizable bloody mass of flesh" whose outward appearance was so altered by his ordeal that hardly anyone seeing him near the time of his death would have thought him as having a normal human form!

This description of Isaiah about the Suffering Servant is so unknown to most of us (even to Christian people) that even kings will be astonished when they understand it. Even then, however, Isaiah still asks the question: "Who hath believed our report?" Many people find it hard to believe that Christ had the front parts of his body "torn to shreds" in order to fulfill the prophecy of the Suffering Servant (Isa. 52:14). But this is what happened to him if all of the evidence is considered.

The actual description of Isaiah's Suffering Servant may help us to understand other matters in the New Testament that we have wondered about. For example, when Christ was resurrected from the dead, the New Testament states that he appeared quite differently from what he was like before. Even Mary Magdalene and the two disciples on the road to Emmaus were not able to recognize him at first. Surely the apostles understood that his flesh had been restored in a much more glorious way than before (to accord with the prophetic description in Psalm 45:2), but we are told that the scars in his hands (or wrists) and feet, and the scar from the deep sword wound that penetrated his side (where the stones could not easily reach), were allowed to remain on his glorified body as a proof of his identify (John 20:24-31) and probably as a reminder to all of what *He* accomplished for the human race.

In closing this chapter, it should be mentioned that the fact of Christ being killed because of the effects of stoning also helps to show the area in which he was executed. We read in early Jewish writings (written within a century and a half of Christ's death) that there was *only one place* in the Jerusalem area that was designated as "the place of stoning."

We read: "*The Place of Stoning* was outside [far away from] the court [located in the Temple], as it is written, Bring forth him that hath cursed without the camp" (*Sanhedrin* 6:1 and also see sections 2,3 and 4). As explained in chapter four of this book, this place of execution in the time of Christ was located near the summit of the Mount of Olives but slightly downslope towards the Temple so that the criminal could be killed "in the presence of God."

There must have been an area on Olivet that encompassed "Golgotha" (the Place of the Skull) at which executions by stoning (as well as legal crucifixions) could take place. It is interesting that when Stephen the first Christian martyr was stoned, he first gave his witness inside the court of the Sanhedrin (Acts 6:12-15). The Sanhedrin was then located at "the trading station" on the Temple Mount (Cohen, *Everyman's Talmud*, p.302), and even Luke mentioned that the Sanhedrin was *in* "this Holy Place" which was the Temple (Acts 6:13,14). We are then told that Stephen was taken *outside the city* and the people began casting stones until he died. Where did this event take place? It was understood by early Christians to have occurred near the summit of the Mount of Olives. Wilkinson states: "The Martyrium of St. Stephen, built by Melania the Younger, and dedicated in 439, was inside the colonnade of the Imbomon . . . and the Martyrium on the Mount of Olives was probably the principal sanctuary of St. Stephen" (*Egeria's Travels*, p.185, note 1).

We thus find that early Christians built a Martyrium for Stephen inside the colonnade area of what we call the Imbomon today. A Martyrium was originally a place where a martyr suffered martyrdom (Smith, *Dict. of Christian Antiquities*, vol.II, p.1132). As soon as Constantine had the Church of the Holy Sepulchre built in Jerusalem, it became common for ecclesiastics to call it the Martyrium of Christ because they supposed that is where Christ was martyred (*ibid.*). And so it was with Stephen. Since his execution was considered a legal one by the Sanhedrin, it would have been essential for Stephen to have been stoned at *The Place of Stoning*. And, the site of the Imbomon fits precisely.

But where is the Imbomon (the place of Stephen's

Martyrium) situated? It was at the southern summit of the Mount of Olives. And importantly, we have identified the Imbomon area (in chapter six) with "Golgotha" (the place where Christ was also stoned and crucified). This information is just another reason why it is important to know that Christ was *stoned* by the Jerusalem authorities (as was Stephen) and that both executions took place in the legal site for *stoning* called by the Jews "the Place of Stoning."

The information we have given in this chapter provides a reasonable amount of evidence that Jesus met his death by *stoning* and not only by crucifixion. It also helps to show that Christ was executed on the Mount of Olives because that is where "the Place of Stoning" was situated as shown by the Martyrium of Stephen. Once it is understood that Christ died principally from *being stoned*, we can now know just how awful his crucifixion was. This also helps us to realize in a better way why the apostles emphasized that Christians are saved through Christ's blood. It has always been a mystery why so much emphasis is given in the New Testament to the spilling of Christ's blood, while in normal crucifixions little blood ever reached the ground. Only a small amount of blood would ordinarily have issued from Christ's wounds in his hands or feet while he was hanging on the tree (the blood that came forth by use of the spear would not count in a theological sense because that occurred after his death). But with the realization that Christ was also *stoned* with small, sharp stones for almost six hours (and the front parts of his body "torn to shreds") makes it easy to understand why Christ's blood (as a theological symbol for the remission of sins) became an essential feature in Christian theology. Such a condition as described by Isaiah in his Suffering Servant prophecy would account for a great deal of his blood being shed for mankind at the time of his crucifixion.

In the next chapter we will show how important it is to understand the *full* prophecy of Isaiah's Suffering Servant. It will help us to comprehend the fullness of the spiritual meaning of the significant role that Christ Jesus played in the history of the world.

16

The Real Jesus of the Bible

It is amazing that few people today refer to the full prophecy of the Suffering Servant as mentioned by Isaiah when it comes to describing the historical events associated with Christ's life and death. If they did, a new appreciation would emerge of what happened throughout Christ's life and at the time of his crucifixion. But because the information about Christ's body being torn to shreds is primarily based on a prophecy given about 750 years before the event, it has not been seriously considered as having a literal fulfillment. This is a mistake. If it were understood that Christ was indeed stoned while he was nailed to the tree of crucifixion, then more attention would no doubt be given to what Isaiah said. Let us look more closely at the prophecy of Isaiah's Suffering Servant (Isaiah 52:13 through 53:12). It will tell us far more what happened throughout Christ's life as well as the full story of his agony at "Golgotha."

First note a prime misinterpretation that many Christian teachers have insisted on for almost the past 1600 years. It is popular to believe that the last part of Isaiah's prophecy of the Suffering Servant pertains to the final twenty-four hours of Christ's life. As an example of this, note that when the King James Version states "with his stripes we are healed" (Isa.53:5), it is almost consistently interpreted that this refers to the beatings given to him by the Roman soldiers just before his crucifixion. And when Isaiah spoke of his "griefs," "sorrows," "chastisement," "oppression," "affliction," along with the fact that no one would desire him for "beauty, comeliness and form," and that he would be "despised and rejected," it is almost universally believed that *all* these prophetical descriptions of Isaiah must apply *only* to the ordeal of his trial and crucifixion. But a big mistake is made when this is taught.

It is a popular Christian belief today that Jesus never experienced a day of sickness in his life. So certain are most people in this persuasion that even the mention of Jesus having sniffles associated with a cold is held by many to be anathema. The reason for their convictions centers primarily in the New Testament teachings that Christ never sinned at any time during his life on earth. And true enough, this is precisely what the New Testament teaches (I Pet. 2:21,22; II Cor.5:21). Since we read of Christ's sinlessness, it is normally assumed by Christian interpreters that he could never have been ill at any time during his life. This is because there is biblical teaching that sickness can certainly be a result of sin (John 5:14), but this is not *always* the case and Christ himself made this point quite plainly (John 9:13).

Indeed, common sense ought to show anyone that sicknesses are not always caused by sins (that is, the transgression of divine or human law). For example, animals get ill but they are quite incapable of sinning as we humans know it. Also, when bubonic plague swept through Europe in the Middle Ages, it infected the righteous as well as the wayward. And remember, a child might be accidently bitten by a rabid animal, and the disease of rabies would set in, but it could not be imagined that the resultant sickness was because of some sinful act done by the child.

Still, it is a prevalent belief among many Christians that sickness is more often than not a punishment for sin. Since we are assured that Christ never sinned once in the entirety of his life, and because he is symbolically compared to the *unblemished* Passover Lamb, it is felt by many that these factors exempt Jesus from even having a sniffle!

All of this may seem to be a reasonable proposition on the surface, but there are some major difficulties with this interpretation. The problem comes from the New Testament itself. It shows that Jesus was put under trial in *all things* as are other humans, and this of necessity must include the experience of sickness. And certainly, the Book of Hebrews states assuredly that Christ was subjected to sicknesses while he was in the flesh.

"For we have not an high priest that cannot be touched with the feeling of our *infirmities* [translated *sicknesses* in several contexts]; but one that has been in *ALL POINTS* tempted [put under trial] like as we are, *yet without sin*" (Heb.4:15).

There was not a major type of trial that all of us humans ordinarily go through that did not afflict Jesus! And that includes the common trials associated with *sicknesses* that are very much a part of our human experience. However, one must admit that it is difficult to understand how a sinless person (as the New Testament insists that Christ was) could ever be sick. But the author of the Book of Hebrews said *he was sick*, and he came under the same type of trials that all humans go through. And though Jesus was indeed *sick* in a variety of ways, yet the Book of Hebrews states he was "*without sin*" (Heb.4:15). The reason the phrase "*yet without sin*" was tacked on to the teaching given above is because most people were then under the impression (as most people still are today) that experiencing *infirmities* [sicknesses] was very much a consequence of sinning! The writer of Hebrews, knowing the inclination of humans to make this assertion, emphatically stated that Jesus (though he underwent many sicknesses as other humans) was still "*without sin*."

This explanation in the Book of Hebrews would not have satisfied many of Jesus' hometown people who thought him to be a sinner. They chided him because they were told that he could heal others, yet he was unable to heal himself. Christ said they would say of him: "*Physician, heal yourself*" (Luke 4:23). When they observed how Jesus appeared, they could tell that he needed *healing!* This reference of Christ concerning the opinion of his hometown people of Nazareth was not some well-known proverb or philosophical statement that they were applying to Jesus. They were simply observing the facts in front of their eyes. It was quite obvious to them that Jesus had been subjected to *sicknesses* in the past and that he was presently *sickly* in appearance.

It is important to note that it was his own hometown people who were ridiculing him by saying "*heal yourself*." They had grown up with him, and they were well aware that he had been frequently *sick*. To them, this meant that he was being subjected to the consequences of sin in his body. It appeared certain to them that he could not be a sinless person since he experienced sickness just as all humans. And, this opinion is the common one that is believed by most Christians today. They find it difficult to believe that Christ even had a sniffle, let alone experience real sicknesses as do most humans. But it was very different with the author of the Book of Hebrews. Though he admitted that Jesus was indeed subjected to *sicknesses*, he still insisted that he was "*without sin*." And so did the rest of the apostles (I Pet. 2:21,22; II Cor.5:21).

The truth is, Jesus was not free of sicknesses while he was growing up in Nazareth, nor was he a person showing forth a vibrant and healthy constitution while he was preaching the Gospel. Indeed, he appeared just the opposite of what most people imagine today. Christ himself made reference to the fact that people looking on his physical frame would have wanted to reject him, because he did not look "perfect" as most people would think the Son of God should. This is shown by a reference that Christ himself made. Recall his statement that the stone which the builders *rejected* had become the head of the corner (Psa.118:22; Matt.21:42; Eph.2:20 and I Peter 2:4-7). The masterbuilders of the early Temple could observe, without doubt, that the external condition of "that particular stone" was in an "imperfect state." This appraisal was so positive to them that they disqualified that stone (and rightly so) from being a part of the Temple which had been ordained of God to contain only "perfect" stones. But who was that "imperfect stone" that the masterbuilders rejected as imperfect? Christ said it applied to him. Most people looking on the outward fleshly condition of Jesus would have considered him "quite imperfect" (if one relied on physical appearance alone). He was one that most people would have rejected had he not been a great miracle-worker and people followed him for that primary reason (John 6:2) or that they wanted to be fed with the free food he provided for them (John 6:26).

This illustration of the "stone rejected of men" was given by Christ to show that when people of his time looked upon him they all saw him as an "imperfect" specimen of humanity. This made them wonder how he could be God's Son. How could a person who was obviously "imperfect" in his outward flesh be the prophesied Messiah to redeem mankind to God? But they were not paying close attention to the description of the prophet Isaiah about the Suffering Servant. Had they done so, they would have realized that Jesus was precisely fulfilling the prophecy. And we today also need to pay close attention to what Isaiah said because he reveals a Jesus that many people have never been introduced to in the flesh. Let us now look at what the Suffering Servant would be like from his birth to his death.

> "For he shall grow up before him [Yahweh] as a tender plant, and as a root out of a dry ground: *he has no form or comeliness; and when we see him, there is no beauty that we should desire him.* He is despised and rejected of men; a man of sorrows, and acquainted with *grief* [rendered *sickness* in the King James 12 times]; and we hid as it were our faces from him; *he was despised, and we esteemed him not*" (Isa.53:2,3).

The first point that one should recognize is Isaiah's statement that the prophecy gives a historical description of the Suffering Servant from the time *of his birth to that of his manhood and finally his death*. "For he shall grow up before him as *a tender plant*" (Isa.53:2). His physical appearance throughout the time of his growing years would be like a *tender plant*, not a strong, robust and hearty one! He was also to be like "a *root* out of a *dry ground*." This shows that he would be like a parched and undernourished plant, not full-fleshed, abundantly healthy or handsome! In fact, Isaiah (in the kindness of language that he could use yet remain truthful) said that he would actually be *ugly* as far as human opinion was concerned. "He has no form nor comeliness; and when we shall see him, there is no beauty that we should desire him" (Isa.53:2). In no way was he like the handsome Anglo-Saxon or Italian gentlemen as he is so often depicted today. Indeed, he was just the opposite. To describe him in practical language today, he was frail in physique, homely in appearance and was subject to many infirmities and sicknesses of the flesh! This is precisely what the prophet Isaiah said the Suffering Servant would be like and it fits Jesus Christ perfectly as shown by the narratives about his person given in the New Testament.

In fact, when one understands what the actual Hebrew means in regard to the Suffering Servant, we find that he was "*knowing sickness*" [translated "acquainted with grief" in the King James]. That he was "*bearing sicknesses*" in his body [King James: "borne our griefs" though in the New Testament quote of this verse they correctly translate the phrase as "*bare our sicknesses*" (Matt.8:17)]. And while the King James Version translates verse 10 as: "he hath put him to grief," the actual intent of the original is: "he has made him *to be sick*." And though the King James says: "for the transgression of my people was he stricken," the actual intent is: "for the transgression of my people *was he plagued*." The truth is, Jesus was bearing sicknesses and infirmities in his body. He was being plagued with illnesses. And all of these things were happening to him *not simply when he was on the tree of crucifixion, but throughout his life!* This can easily be shown if a person will pay close attention to the fulfillment of these prophecies about the Suffering Servant as understood by the apostles.

The apostles recorded that Isaiah's prophecy was being fulfilled by Christ long before his crucifixion. They saw him *bearing* sicknesses even during the height of his ministry. His personal experience with sickness gave him knowledgeable power over spirits and the sicknesses of others.

"When the even was come, they brought unto him many that were possessed with demons: and he cast out the spirits with his word, and healed all that were sick: *That it might be fulfilled which was spoken by Isaiah the prophet, saying, Himself took our infirmities, and bare our sicknesses*" (Matt.8:16,17).

Christ even learned to be obedient to God because of *bearing* those infirmities and sicknesses which he suffered (Heb.5:8).

His sufferings led to continual obedience, and that obedience gave him power and authority over evil spirits and the sicknesses of others. By *bearing* sicknesses he learned how bad they can be. He was even *bearing* the evidence of sin in his body at the start of his ministry. When John the Baptist proclaimed Christ's Messiahship at the first he said: "Behold the Lamb of God which *takes away* [present tense] the sin of the world" (John 1:29). The verb can mean either "*takes upon him*" (that is, *he bears* in the present tense) or "*takes away*" (meaning, *carries away*). What did John mean?

There can be little doubt that John the Baptist had reference to Isaiah's prophecy which said "he hath *borne* our sicknesses, and *carried* our sorrows" and "the Lord has *laid on him* the iniquity of us all" (Isa.53:4,6). Thus, Jesus was then *bearing* [present tense] the sin of the world on his shoulders and in his body (as John the Baptist said). Or, as Matthew put it, "he *carried* our diseases" (Matt.8:17), and this *carrying* of those sicknesses in his body was long before his passion. Since Isaiah commenced the prophecy of the Suffering Servant with his birth, we can see why the New Testament writers show that Christ was *bearing* the sins of the world (not his own, because he had none) throughout his life in the flesh.

But now for an important question. What kind of sicknesses did Christ bear throughout his lifetime? Actually, the prophecy of the Suffering Servant is most important to inform us of this matter. If one will pay close attention to what the prophecy actually relates we can gain a great deal of information to illumine this subject for us. I now wish to refer to a book published in 1969 of an out-of-print volume first printed in 1877 which gives a rundown of Jewish interpretation over the past twenty-two centuries on the meaning of Isaiah 52 and 53 in regard to the Suffering Servant. It is titled *The Fifty-Third Chapter of Isaiah* by S.R.Driver and A. Neubauer (printed by Ktav Publishing, NY). The work is in two volumes. The first gives the original Hebrew, Aramaic, Greek, etc. of the ancient documents which were consulted. The second volume gives the English translations. It is a remarkable work and is indispensable in gaining the Jewish understanding of Isaiah's prophecy about the Suffering Servant from the historical viewpoint.

What is significant is the fact that the majority of about 60 Jewish sources (which the authors referred to) claim that the prophecy *COULD NOT* refer to Jesus because, among other things, Isaiah said that the man of the prophecy would be *sickly*, while the Jewish scholars had been told over the centuries by their Christian counterparts that Jesus had never been sick a day in his life! And true enough, that is what most Christians erroneously have taught about Christ. This has been one of the main reasons why Jewish scholars (who adhere to the simple teachings of Isaiah's prophecy about the Suffering Servant) fail to see Jesus in it. They have taken Christian professors at their word that this was what the New Testament taught.

But in no way does the New Testament teach what most Christian interpreters have been stating over the centuries. If one will read carefully what the apostles wrote, it can be recognized that they were well aware that Jesus had been *sickly* during his life (*bearing* the sicknesses and sins of mankind in his body), though he never sinned once. This is exactly what the author of the Book of Hebrews stated (Heb.4:15). The apostles (many of whom were eyewitnesses of Christ's ministry) thought that he was precisely fulfilling Isaiah's prophecy of the Suffering Servant. The hometown people of Jesus were not uttering some kind of proverb when they said of him: "*Physician, heal yourself*" (Luke 4:23). They knew that he needed *healing* himself!

Let us now look at the catalog of Jewish references about the Suffering Servant from the book cited above. They are given in chronological order from the third century before Christ onward.

The first citation is that from the Septuagint Version. This is a Greek translation of the Old Testament began in the third century before Christ. We will concentrate on the first five verses of Isaiah 53 since that is the primary section that shows the Suffering Servant as being frail and sickly. This Version is important to the issue because the apostles were familiar with it and it was a pre-Christian translation.

"O Lord, who has believed our report? and to whom has the arm of the Lord been revealed? We brought a report as of a child before him: he is as a root *in a thirsty land*: he has no form or comeliness; and we saw him but he had no form or beauty. But his form was *ignoble*, and *inferior* to that of the children of men; he was a man in suffering, and acquainted with *the bearing of sickness*.... But he was wounded for our sins, and was *made sick* because of our transgressions" (emphases mine).

The Septuagint Version shows that the Suffering Servant would certainly be sickly (but, as the text says, not because of his own sins). Let us now go on to other references. There are three second century A.D. translators who indicate the same thing. Aquila said: "a man of pains and known to illness." Symmachus: "a man of pains and known to sickness." Symmachus went on to say: "Surely he took up our sins, and endured our labors: but it thought him to be under the touch [of disease], plagued by God and humiliated." Theodotion said: "a man of pains and known to sickness."

It is certain from the above translators that they understood the Hebrew of Isaiah to mean that the Suffering Servant was prophesied to be sickly, even that he was subject to what was called "the plague." But they were not the only ones who understood Isaiah in this fashion. The Targum of Jonathan (an early paraphrase from the Hebrew into the Aramaic) rendered the verse: "like a man of pains and like one destined to sickness."

References in the Jewish Talmud are even more specific. Mentioning the verse: "Surely he hath borne our sicknesses," the Talmud states that this verse does not refer to Jesus, but to their prophesied Messianic redeemer. They said: "The Messiah, what is his name? The Rabbis say, *The Leprous One* [or] *The Sick One*" (*Sanh.*98b). Also: "The Lord was pleased to bruise him, *he made him to be sick*" (*Ber.*5a).

Certainly, Jesus was not leprous because he was not isolated from the people in all his preaching experiences like a leper was required to be. But the strong language of Isaiah 53 is so similar to that which describes a leper in other contexts that it became a common teaching among some Jewish scholars to think that Isaiah's Suffering Servant would be so sickly that only a leprous condition could properly describe him. And this opinion is reflected in what later Jewish scholars after the time of the Talmud understood Isaiah to be saying. We will now look at several of their remarks as recorded in our book under discussion.

Yepheth Ben Ali (10th century) gave the following comment: "By the words, 'surely he hath carried our sicknesses,' they mean that the pains and sickness which he fell into were merited by Israel, but that he bore them instead: the next words 'yet we did esteem him, etc.' intimate that they [the common people] thought him afflicted by God for his own sins, as they distinctly say, 'smitten of God and afflicted.' And here I think it necessary to pause a moment [said Yepheth] in order to explain why God caused these *sicknesses* to attach themselves to the Messiah for the sake of Israel."

Rabbi Shelomoh Yizhaqi (Rashi, 11th century) said that Isaiah 53 spoke of the person of the prophecy "like a person stricken with leprosy...and that the sickness which ought to have fallen on us was carried by him."

Rabbi Yoseph Qara (12th century) thought that the Suffering Servant carried "sicknesses and pains which for our iniquities should have been borne by us."

Rabbi Abraham Ibn Ezra (12th century) said the verses suggest that people "thought that he had been stricken with the stroke or plague of leprosy.... It was God who smote him and afflicted him because the sickness ought to have come on us."

Rabbi Jacob Ben Reuben (The Rabbanite, 12th century) is even more specific. He wrote: "The prophet declares that he was 'despised and forlorn of men,' a 'man of pains and known to sickness.' It seems to me [said Jacob Ben Reuben] that no one would be called 'known to sickness' or a 'man of pains' except a man who suffered from *severe sickness continually*" [emphasis mine].

Rabbi Jacob Ben Reuben went on to censure Christian interpreters who were saying that Jesus was the Suffering Servant of Isaiah though they taught that he was always free of sickness because of his sinlessness. He continued: "I know in fact that Christians will not find either in their New

Testament, or in the words of the wise men of their own religion who tell them about the Messiah and his deeds, or, in fact, in any book in the world, that he [Jesus] ever had a pain, even a headache, up to the day of his death when he was delivered into the hands of those who smote him: we see then that the very terms themselves which are employed, 'pain' and 'sickness,' were not realized in his person, and consequently cannot apply to him."

Rabbi Jacob could probably be excused for his error in stating that the New Testament did not state that Jesus was ever sick. This is because he would not have studied it carefully. But the New Testament has Christ even saying of himself that he was "the stone that the builders rejected," and that the people said "Physician, heal yourself," and the Book of Hebrews said he had infirmities and was subjected to all the things that humans are commonly afflicted with. While Rabbi Jacob can be excused, the Christian scholars of his own time have no excuse because many of them could read what the Hebrew of Isaiah 53 actually said, *and they failed to apply it to Jesus even when the New Testament did!*

Let us now go on with early Jewish interpretation of what Isaiah 53 said the Suffering Servant would undergo. Rabbi Jacob Ben Reuben (the Karaite, 12th century), a different person from the Rabbi of the previous paragraph, said that Isaiah stated the Suffering Servant would be "continually sick: he was like a leper from whom all hid their faces.... He became as one who was sick."

Rabbi Eliezer of Beaugenci (12th century): "It was our sicknesses, those which for our sins we ought to have endured, he carried, sighing and groaning, and afflicting himself with sickness.... and by his stripes and sickness, which we ought to have laid to heart and made our own, we were healed."

Rabbi Yoseph Ben Nathan (13th century): "He was a man of pains, and broken by sickness...but he carried our sickness, which ought to have come on us, came upon him."

Rabbi Yeshaeyah Ben Mali (13th century): "The Lord was pleased to bruise him and sicken him, and therefore delivered him into the hands of the Gentiles."

Rabbi Mosheh Ben Nahman (13th century): "He was pained for the iniquities of Israel, which occasion his tarrying, holding him back from becoming king over his people; and known to sickness, because a man who is sick is continually distressed with pain. Yet he carried our sicknesses, being himself sick and distressed for the transgressions which should have caused sickness and distress in us, and bearing the pains we ought to have experienced."

Rabbi Aaron Ben Yoseph (the Elder, 14th century) said Isaiah 53 showed the prophesied atonement-bearer was "to be made sick...but the Lord was pleased to bruise him in order to increase his reward, and to make him sick with long-continued sicknesses."

Rabbi Mosheh Kohen Ibn Crispin (14th century): "Despised, and forlorn of men: despised, namely, in the eyes of the world *because of his loathsome appearance* [emphasis mine]. A man of pains and destined to sicknesses: as all that see him will say of him." And, of course, this is exactly what those of Jesus' hometown of Nazareth said of him: "Physician, heal yourself" (Luke 4:23).

Rabbi Shelomon Astruc (14th century) is even more to the point: "He was despised and forlorn of men, that is, he was not permitted to enter the society of men, because he was a man of pains, and broken by sickness. Perhaps the world denotes that he was so well known generally for the sicknesses which he endured, that in oaths made by men people would say 'May such an one be like him'."

Rabbi Abraham Farissol (16th century): "He was in truth despised and forlorn of men, exposed to accidents and sickness...but he was made sick and punished in our stead. He carried our sicknesses."

Rabbi Mosheh El-Sheikh (16th century) has a most interesting recognition of what Isaiah intended: "In spite of his holiness, he was a man of pains and broken by sicknesses: now there are two species of sickness, one when a man is in pain but is still able to move about, the other when he is attacked by some such disease as consumption of fever, when he is prostrated upon his bed but is free from pain; in the latter case he is said to be 'broken by sickness.' The prophet

Isaiah says that both descriptions unite against the man spoken of."

All these early Jewish scholars which we have just mentioned were simply endeavoring to show what the Hebrew of Isaiah actually was stating about what would happen to the Suffering Servant. Many of them felt that the *Jesus* of the Christians could in no way fulfill what Isaiah was saying because the majority of Christian theologians were united in their belief that Jesus had never been sick a day in his life. According to Christian authorities, Jesus never once had a sniffle! If this were the case, then the *Jesus* of the Christians could in no way be the Suffering Servant prophesied by Isaiah. This is one of the main reasons that Jewish interpreters (who could easily read the Hebrew of Isaiah 53) simply dismissed the *Jesus* of the Christians, and they focused their eyes on a future Suffering Servant who would fulfill what the prophet Isaiah said would one day occur. And one could hardly blame them.

The truth is, a great disservice has been done to people in the world who have been wanting to hear the Christian message from theologians of the Christian faith for the past 1000 years. People (including the Jews) have been told just the opposite of what the New Testament (and Isaiah the prophet) said happened in the person of Christ Jesus. Though he was indeed faultless, he was nevertheless burdened with many pains, humiliations and sicknesses all his life. He was *bearing* the sins of the world long before he went to the tree of crucifixion.

It is interesting, however, that non-Gnostic Christian teachers *before* the time of Constantine (A.D.325) were consistent in showing forth the *real* Jesus of history. They truly portrayed him as one who was under continual suffering and that he was repulsive to look at, just as the prophet Isaiah stated he would be. Note what Keil and Delitzsch said in their commentary on Isaiah 53 (vol.II, p.307 note 1).

"The Church before the time of Constantine pictured to itself the Lord, as He walked on earth, as repulsive in His appearance; whereas the Church after Constantine pictured Him as having quite an ideal beauty."

Smith's *Dictionary of Christian Antiquities* provides a number of historical references to show that the early fathers of the Church (before the time of Constantine) were well aware (*and believed*) that Jesus was repulsive in appearance (vol.I, p.875). But from the time of Constantine the description of Jesus in the flesh changed drastically. After Constantine he was portrayed by many Christians as the most handsome of men (the same article in Smith's *Dictionary* quotes these later references too).

With the fourth and fifth centuries, a *new* Jesus comes on the scene that was far different from the Suffering Servant of Isaiah or from what the New Testament and the early fathers had to relate. It became common to quote sections of Scripture which described God as a king and that he was fair in his divine appearance (Psa.45:3). And true enough, the apostles believed that Christ was a person of beauty *before* he came to earth and also *after* his resurrection. But while he was on the earth, and in the flesh, they understood him to have appeared very differently. The apostle Paul said that Christ gave up the glory that he had before his birth and became *Jesus*, the one who no longer had any kingly glory or fair appearance. When Christ came to earth, he became the lowly *Jesus* who manifested himself among mankind as a servant. He was then lacking in beauty. He was even poor and forlorn. Paul said: "For you know the grace of the Lord Jesus Christ, that though he was rich he became poor for your sakes, that you might become rich through his poverty" (II Cor.8:9). Paul went on to say:

> "Let this mind be in you, which was also in Christ Jesus: who, *being in the form of God*, thought it not robbery to be equal with God: *but made himself of NO REPUTATION*, and took upon him the form of a servant, and was made in the likeness of men: and being found in the fashion of a man, he humbled himself and became obedient unto death" (Phil.2:5-7).

But in the fourth century, theologians began to abandon the teachings of Isaiah concerning the Suffering Servant and the indications within the New Testament about Jesus' fleshly existence and they imagined him as maintaining his God-like characteristics (even in his physical appearance). The Constantine (and the post-Constantine) theologians emphasized the teaching that Jesus was like the *unblemished* Passover Lamb and they applied this to his outward appearance as well as to his character. But anyone who understands the scriptural records knows that this evaluation can only refer to his character, not to his outward, physical frame. Actually, even the "*unblemish*ness" of the sacrificial lamb only meant that it was not to be deformed at the time of sacrifice, not that it could never have been sick in its life. Certainly, Jesus was not deformed in his outward physique, but he was nonetheless reckoned as the "stone" that the builders rejected (Psa.118:22; Matt.21:42; Eph.2:20 and I Peter 2:4-7). It was his character that resembled the *unblemished* lamb and not his outward appearance. The New Testament writers were well aware of this. They knew that Jesus did not retain his form and glory that he possessed before his incarnation. He emptied himself and became the *Jesus* who fulfilled the prophecy of Isaiah's Suffering Servant.

But people in the fourth century began to portray Jesus very differently from what earlier Christians believed. Not only did they begin to make him *handsome*, they put *long hair* on him that closely resembled pagan gods and early philosophers. Eusebius, bishop of Caesarea, whom we have mentioned in earlier chapters, was not pleased with Constantia Augusta (the daughter of Constantine and wife of Caesar Gallus) when she wanted Eusebius to provide her with a portrait of Jesus. Indignantly, he wrote:

"Since you have written about some image, it seems of Christ, wishing the said image to be sent to you by us, what, and of what kind, is this image which you call that of Christ?.... Has this scripture alone escaped you, in which God by law forbids to make the likeness of anything in heaven, or on earth beneath? Have you ever seen such a thing in a church yourself or heard it from another? Have not such things been banished throughout the whole world, and driven off out of the churches; and has it been proclaimed to us alone among all men that it is not lawful to do such a thing' (quoted in Smith's, *Dictionary of Christian Antiquities*, vol.I, p.814).

Eusebius then proceeded to say he had taken from a woman

two pictures of persons dressed like philosophers, which the woman thought to be portraits of Christ and Paul (*ibid.*). What was a normal outward dress and type of grooming for philosophers? Dio Chrysostom, the practical philosopher who lived in the first century, told his readers that he and other philosophers wore their hair long (*Oration Thirty-Five*, vol.III.pp..391,401 Loeb ed.). Another common characteristic of philosophers was to have beards (see Hatch, *The Influence of Greek Ideas on Christianity*, p.151). Having long hair and a beard were marks of Gentile philosophers and also pagan gods, but this is how people in post-Constantine times began to imagine Jesus to have groomed himself.

The *Dictionary of Christian Antiquities* (vol.I,p.875) provides evidence that it was during the fourth century that the depictation of the *Jesus* we are accustomed to today had its invention. This is when the *handsome*, bearded, long-haired *Jesus* came into existence. Earlier portraits showed him to be beardless and short-haired which answered more closely to what was his true appearance. But whether shown as beardless and short-haired (as in pre-Constantine times) or with a beard and long haired (after Constantine), theologians even in the fourth/fifth centuries knew that the Holy Scriptures forbad any such depictations of deity. Augustine in the early fifth century showed how unlawful this was.

> "It is not to be thought that God the Father is circumscribed by human form.... It is unlawful to set up such an image to God in a Christian temple. Much more is it wicked to set it up in the heart where the temple of God truly is" (quoted in the *Dictionary of Christian Antiquities*, vol.I, p.875).

Actually, it is easy to show that Christ did not have the long hair that many in the fourth century began to imagine he had. The apostle Paul said the male was head of the wife as Christ is head of the Church (I Cor.11:3) and that the human male resembles God in shape and form (verse 7). He then stated that it was a shame for any male person to have long hair since he was in the image of God (verse 14). He noted that it was custom in all the Churches of God (whether in Judaea or in Gentile lands) for men to have short hair and

With the time of Constantine a new type of JESUS began to be portrayed among the Christian population of the Roman Empire. They took the style of grooming which was typical of the pagan gods and adopted it as their "JESUS." The above drawing is from a bust in the British Museum of Sarapis, the Egyptian version of Zeus (the chief of the Gentile gods). See reference Harper's "Dictionary of Classical Literature and Antiquities," article "Coma."

Though Eusebius said that making any depictation of Christ was contrary to the Second Commandment, in the pre-Constantine period we find people in some quarters making Jesus to appear as the Good Shepherd, youthful, beardless and with short hair. From Didron's "Christian Iconography," vol.I, p.339.

women to have their hair long (verse 16). In the Book of Revelation women's hair in the first century is shown to have been quite distinct from men's (Rev.9:8).

If Jesus himself would have had long hair, Judas (at the time of his arrest) would only have needed to point out "the man with the long hair" rather than singling him out with a kiss (Luke 22:48) because it was quite out of the ordinary for normal Jewish men to have long hair. True, those under a Nazarite Vow let their hair grow long for a season, but Christ was not a Nazarite because he drank wine which Nazarites were prohibited from doing (Matt.11:19). (The term "Nazarite" had nothing to do with the town called "Nazareth" where Jesus was reared and the two words should not be confused.) Josephus records an incident which shows that Jewish men let their hair grow long if they were pleading for mercy in front of the Judges of the Sanhedrin (the Supreme Court). This grooming of their hair was reckoned a gesture of sorrow for having committed their crimes (*Antiq*.XIV.172). But this sign of contrition by criminals clearly shows that males who were ordinary law-abiding citizens were accustomed to having short hair.

The simple truth is, the *real* Jesus of the Bible did not have long hair. Nor was he handsome in his outward form. According to the writers of the New Testament he came into the world to fulfill Isaiah's prophecy of the Suffering Servant and they believed that Jesus performed the role perfectly. This means that the *real* Jesus who was crucified (and stoned to death) at Golgotha on the Mount of Olives was in actual fact continually frail and sickly in body and was bordering on *ugliness* in appearance.

17

The Temple and the Trial of Jesus

The New Testament contains geographical information that provides us with a fascinating account of what *really* happened on the day of Christ's crucifixion. This is especially true when we combine it with Jewish records concerning the Temple in the first century. They provide us with a *new* understanding of the history of that day that is truly eye-opening. The actual historical scenario has been obscured because most observers have followed the commonly accepted account of Christ's crucifixion that has prevailed since the time of Constantine. What needs to be done is to re-think the historical and geographical evidences that are given to us in the early documents. We especially need to know *where* the House of Caiaphus was located in which Jesus underwent his preliminary examination and *where* the Sanhedrin (the Jewish Supreme Court) was situated in which he was condemned. Also we should know *where* Pilate finally pronounced his judgment to have him crucified. When these points are properly understood, the events as shown by the New Testament give a profound historical and doctrinal significance to the role of Jesus Christ in fulfilling the prophecy of Isaiah's Suffering Servant. It also shows even more poignantly how he became the *literal* (as well as the *symbolic*) sin-bearer for Israel and the world as reckoned by the apostles and early Christians.

Let us look at the geographical evidences that can help us locate these significant sites. Our quest should start with his arrest in the Garden of Gethsemane and proceed until he was hanged (and stoned) on the tree at Golgotha. The first thing we should realize is that Jesus was arrested about midnight by both Roman and Jewish soldiers (and both groups are distinguished in John 18:12). He was led first to Annas who is designated a chief priest and no doubt the deputy (or *sagan* in Hebrew) to the actual High Priest who was Caiaphus. Edersheim in his *Life and Times* (vol.II,p.547) notes that there is no further mention of Roman troops (or police) after Jesus was placed in the hands of Annas. Not until Jesus was handed over to Pilate for final judgment do we again meet with Romans. There is a significant reason why Roman Gentiles had nothing to do with any affairs involving Annas, Caiaphus and the Sanhedrin. The fact is, the place where their homes and chamber hall were located did not permit Gentiles to be within its precincts (and the Roman authorities upheld the restriction). We will soon understand why Romans could not be in those areas.

Annas and Caiaphus lived at the time in different sections of the same house as most commentators have believed because a single courtyard served them both (compare John 18:15-18 which deals with Annas and Matthew 26:69 which mentions Caiaphus in association with the same courtyard). This gives credence to the belief that both priests were then in some kind of official capacity that required them to be near each other. Indeed, it was then the Passover season and both the High Priest and his deputy would have needed to be in residence close to one another.

Jesus along with John were then led into the courtyard (Greek: *aule*) of the residence of Annas and Caiaphus. This is also called the *house* or *home* (Greek: *oikos*) of the High Priest (Luke 22:54). Peter, however, was only able to stand near the door (and later in the vestibule) of the courtyard where he warmed himself with others because it was cold. After a preliminary examination, Annas handed Jesus over to Caiaphus (John 18:15-18).

At this juncture a large number of members of the Sanhedrin (the Supreme Court of the nation) began to arrive at the residence of Caiaphus (Matt.26:59; Mark 14:55) and there they began to question Jesus about what they considered to be his unlawful activities. But when it became daylight, Luke said that the whole group then went to the building in which the Sanhedrin normally held their official trials and judgments (Luke 22:66). Luke makes a special point of informing his readers that this removal of the High Priest, the chief priests, the scribes and elders from the house (*oikos*) and courtyard (*aule*) of the High Priest into the official Chamber of the Sanhedrin *was after daylight* because the law required that trials and judgments involving capital crimes had to take place within the Chamber of the Sanhedrin itself, and within the hours of daylight (*Sanh.*4:1).

Interestingly (and most importantly), Caiaphus and the members of the Sanhedrin only had to walk fewer than 50 yards from the High Priest's house (*oikos* and/or *aule*), which would have taken no more than two or three minutes, in order for them to enter the official Chamber of the Sanhedrin. There is no doubt that this was the case, because (in the time of Christ) the Chamber of the Sanhedrin was situated directly inside the Temple itself. It was located at what was known as the Chamber of Hewn Stone which was about 40 yards southeast of the entrance to the Holy Place where the curtain was hanging that tore in two at the time of Christ's death. We are told that half of the Sanhedrin Hall was in the Court of the Israelites and half in the Court of the Priests (*Mid.*5:1; *Sanh.*11:2; *Yoma* 25a).

The particular *house* (*oikos*) and *courtyard* (*aule*) of the High Priest were also located in the Temple complex and adjacent to the Chamber of Hewn Stone as one would expect for the High Priest (who was the President of the Sanhedrin and the political and religious head of the nation underneath the Romans). In the Mishnah (the earliest part of the Talmud), it states that the residence of the High Priest was at or near the "Wood Chamber" located west of the Chamber of Hewn Stone (*Mid.*5:4) and next to the House of Abtinas (sometimes spelled Avtinas) where the incense was prepared for the Temple services. It was in the Upper Chamber of this "Temple House" that it is believed the House of the High Priest was located when he lived in his official residence upon the Temple Mount (*Ency.Judaica*, vol.III.991). These "Houses" of the priests abutting to the Chamber of Hewn Stone (the Sanhedrin) were constructed on the second storey around and above a columned courtyard below. Remarkably, the New Testament states specifically that Jesus was taken into the Upper Chamber of the High Priest's house while Peter had to stay below near the vestibule of the courtyard (Mark 14:66). This answers precisely to the description of the second storey residences for the High Priest (and other priestly dignitaries) which the Mishnah shows were supported by columns over a courtyard. These "Houses" were located just to the west and abutting to the Chamber of Hewn Stone (*Tam.*1:1). Since these quarters of the High Priests were within the Temple, this explains why the Roman soldiers are no longer mentioned until Christ met Pilate. Such soldiers, being Gentiles, were forbidden entry into the Temple enclosure itself where the High Priest lived during the festival periods.

The High Priest actually had more than one residence in Jerusalem. While it can be reasonably reckoned that he had a sumptuous home in the aristocratic region of Jerusalem on the southwest hill, he also had at least two other residences within the Temple itself in which he had to live at certain times of the year or when special sacrifices were offered. For example, when the High Priest was required to offer the Red Heifer, he had to precede the sacrifice by a stay of seven days in what was called the "House of Stone" at the northeastern corner of the Temple building (*Parah* 3:1). And also before the Day of Atonement, he had to reside seven days in his "Temple House" near the Chamber of the Hewn Stones (of which we have been speaking above) (*Yoma* 1:1). Look what the Mishnah says about this particular event.

> "Seven days before the Day of Atonement the High Priest was taken apart *from his own house* [that is, his regular home on the southwest hill] unto the Counsellor's Chamber and another priest was made ready in his stead lest aught should befall him to render him ineligible."

This is very revealing information for our subject at hand. Note that it was customary at special times to have a *second* priest ready in case the High Priest was in someway unable to perform the ceremonies. And at the time of Christ's trial, there was both Annas and Caiaphus being called "High Priests" and they were housed in the same residential area in the *house* (*oikos*) of the High Priest. This was not his regular *house* (or palace) on the southwest hill, but Caiaphus had retired from that *house* into his special *house* on the Temple Mount. The Mishnah called this *house* the Counsellor's Chamber. It was designated with this title because the "Counsellor" was the President of the Sanhedrin (who was the High Priest). This is why his Chamber (or *house*) was directly adjacent to the Chamber of Hewn Stones, the official building for sessions of the Sanhedrin. Would it not appear normal for the Chief Justice (President) of the Sanhedrin to have an official residence abutting to the Sanhedrin itself? Of course! And this was the case in the time of Christ.

In addition to his normal *house* (or palace) on the southwest hill, it was necessary for the High Priest to have this *home* or official *house* within the Temple enclosure in order to perform certain ceremonies demanded in the Mosaic law. Such a separate residence was required when each High Priest was consecrated. It was demanded in the Law that he stay seven days within the Temple and near the Holy Place (Lev.8:33). There were other times when this was necessary. Josephus (who himself was a priest) stated that the High Priest presided in the Temple over the ceremonies of the Sabbath, the new moons, "and on any national festival or annual assemblage of all the people" (*War* V.230). Since the trial of Jesus took place at the time of Passover, there can be no doubt that Caiaphus (along with his deputy Annas) were then away from their ordinary homes (or *houses*) and they were then resident in the Upper Chambers adjacent to the Chamber of Hewn Stones where the Sanhedrin met. As a matter of fact, we have New Testament evidence that the "House of Caiaphus" at the time of Christ's trial was his "Temple House" and *not* his regular one on the southwest hill. Note that when false witnesses accused Christ at Caiaphus' House they said: "We heard him say *I will throw down THIS Temple* that was made with hands and in three days I will build another not made with hands" (Mark 14:58). It is important to realize that they did not say "*the* Temple,"

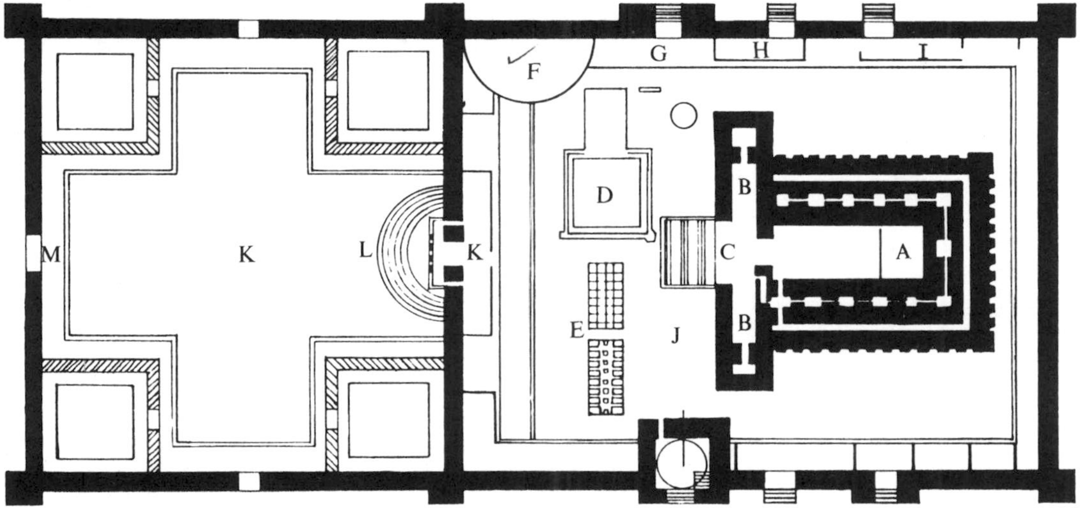

The Temple at the time of Christ. A) Holy of Holies, B) Outer Holy Place, C) Outer Curtain, D) Altar of Burnt Offering, E) Slaughter Areas, F) Chamber of Hewn Stone (Sanhedrin Hall), G) Counsellor's Chamber, H) House of Abtinas, I) Chamber of Wood, J) Court of Priests, K) Court of Israel, L) Steps to Nicanor Gate, M) Eastern Gate. Diagram by Norman Tenedora.

as though it was situated at a distance from them. They referred to it as "*this* Temple," which means they were then situated within the Temple complex itself.

This is New Testament evidence that the "House of Caiaphus" at the time of Christ's trial was not his ordinary residence, but it was his "House" within the Temple enclosure. It is important to realize that the *universal* testimony of early Jewish historical sources (from the start of the second to the end of the fifth centuries) shows that the Chamber of Hewn Stones in the year A.D.30 was the official seat of the Sanhedrin, and that it was located in the Temple about 40 yards southeast of the entrance to the Holy Place.

We are told, however, that in the year that Christ was crucified (A.D.30), the Sanhedrin ceased holding its sessions in the official Chamber of Hewn Stones. They were banished to an insignificant section of the Temple a little farther to the east called "the Trading Place." It is not recorded in the early Jewish records why the Sanhedrin had to move from their palatial quarters in the Chamber of Hewn Stones (which must have been most beautiful and majestic) into a part of the Temple with much lesser esteem. Indeed, for some reason they did not remain long even at "the Trading Place," because Josephus tells us that just before the Jewish/Roman War of A.D.66 to 70, the Sanhedrin was then meeting outside the Temple area and within a common part of the city of Jerusalem. This was at a gymnasium inside the city of Jerusalem just to the west of the Temple next to a building called the Xystus (*War* V.144; comp.*War* II.344). And then, after Jerusalem and the Temple were destroyed in A.D.70, the Sanhedrin moved to a city called Jamnia (or Jabneh) about 30 miles west of Jerusalem.

These three moves of the Sanhedrin from the Chamber of Hewn Stones near the Holy Place in the Temple, to "the Trading Place," and then to near the Xystus in the city of Jerusalem are mentioned in the Jewish Talmud (they also record seven additional moves of the Sanhedrin up to about A.D.425 when the Sanhedrin was abolished by the Romans). Note first a reference in *Shabbath* 15a followed by another in *Rosh ha-Shanah* 31a,b.

"Forty years before the destruction of the Temple [in A.D.30], the Sanhedrin was banished (from the Chamber of Hewn Stone) and sat in the trading-station (on the Temple Mount)." "The Sanhedrin suffered ten removals: from the Chamber of Hewn Stone to the trading-station, from the trading station to (the city of) Jerusalem [next to the Xystus on the western side of the Temple], from Jerusalem to Jabneh [after the destruction of Jerusalem], from Jabneh to Usha [in Galilee], from Usha back to Jabneh, then back to Usha, after that to Shaphraam, from Shaphraam to Beth Shearim, from Beth Shearim to Sepphoris, from Sepphoris to Tiberias" (the comments in brackets are mine).

This is very important historical information because it indicates that at the time of the trial of Jesus the Sanhedrin was meeting in the Chamber of Hewn Stones on the Temple Mount. This must be the case because the New Testament tells us that the courtyard (*aule*) and house (*oikos*) of the High Priest were not far away from the Sanhedrin and Jewish documents show that the High Priest would have been in his *house* on the Temple mount next to the Chamber of Hewn Stones at that time of Passover. The festival seasons required the High Priest to be in his "Temple House."

Something, however, caused the Sanhedrin to be banished (as the Talmud tells us) from the Chamber of Hewn Stones to "the Trading Place." This happened in A.D.30. We are not told in what day or month that this "banishment" took place. Whatever the case, when Stephen (the first Christian martyr) was brought before the Sanhedrin for trial, we find that they were still meeting in a building that was part of the Temple. The Book of Acts tells us that Stephen was led "into the Sanhedrin" (Acts 6:12). While there, false witnesses were brought in who said: "This man does not stop speaking against *THIS Holy Place* and against the law. For example, we have heard him say that this Jesus the Nazarene will throw down *THIS Place* and change the customs that Moses handed down to us" (Acts 6:13,14). Clearly, these statements show that the accusers of Stephen, who were then within the official chambers of the Sanhedrin, were still located in *THIS Holy Place* [the Temple complex itself]. They did not say, simply, "*the* Temple," as one would expect if they were then situated somewhere away from the

Temple. They were still meeting within the Temple complex when Stephen was tried before the Sanhedrin.

What we now need to ask is: What would have caused the Sanhedrin to abandon the official (and quite palatial) Chamber of Hewn Stones very near the Holy Place itself to meet in an insignificant area on the Temple Mount called "the Trading Place"? The Talmud relates it was because of a "banishment." But who would have "banished" them from their normal place for meeting in A.D.30? There would have been no reason for the Romans to have demanded such a move because they cared little for what the Jews did in a religious sense as long as they remained obedient to Rome and paid their taxes. It could hardly have been the Roman government that made them transfer their Sanhedrin a few yards east of the Chamber of Hewn Stones.

It may be explained by something else that happened in the same year. There is a Jewish record that the doors in back of the huge curtain in front of the Holy Place *opened of their own accord* sometime during the year A.D.30. Note what the account relates:

> "Forty years before the Temple was destroyed [in A.D.30]...the gates of the *Hekel* [the Holy Place] opened by themselves, until Rabbi Yohanan B. Zakkai rebuked them [the gates] saying: *Hekel, Hekel,* why alarmist thou us? We know that thou art destined to be destroyed. For of thee hath prophesied Zechariah ben Iddo [Zech.11:1]: Open thy doors, O Lebanon, and the fire shall eat thy cedars" (*Yoma* 39b).

Some two days before Christ was crucified, he told his disciples that Jerusalem and the Temple would soon be destroyed. And in the very year that Christ said this, Rabbi Yohanan B. Zakkai was commenting on the mysterious opening of the doors behind the curtain of the Holy Place. Edersheim (in his *Life and Times of Jesus the Messiah*) was of the opinion that the opening of these Temple doors was in some way associated with the tearing of the curtain which happened at the precise time of Christ's death (vol.II, pp.610,611). This would be a logical conclusion because the doors were positioned directly in back of the curtain itself! For the tearing of the curtain to be a symbolic gesture that

God the Father had now "destroyed" the barrier into the Holy of Holies itself, then the symbol would have been meaningless had the doors behind the curtain remained closed. In fact, for the intended symbol to have had any relevance whatever, the two events would have had to occur simultaneously.

So spectacular would both events have been (the tearing of the curtain and the opening of the doors) that it would have been most unusual for such circumstances to have happened at different times in the same year. Only a simultaneous occurrence makes any sense at all (as Edersheim observed).

But how did the doors of the Holy Place open? As explained in chapter one of this book, a Jewish Christian work of the early second century called "The Gospel of the Nazaraeans" said that the large stone lintel which supported the curtain (which no doubt had the inner doors attached to it for stability) split in two at the same time as the curtain (cf. Hennecke-Schneemelcher, *The New Testament Apocrypha*, vol. I, pp.150,153). There is no reason to deny the possibility that the collapse of this lintel (which was an enormous stone at least 30 feet long and weighing around 30 tons) was the "natural cause" of the curtain rending in two. The fact that the curtain was severed from the top to the bottom also suggests that it was the force of the falling lintel (which happened at the exact time of a great earthquake) that caused the curtain of the Holy Place to tear in two.

But what has this to do with the Sanhedrin having to abandon the Chamber of Hewn Stones in which they normally met? It has very much to do with it. If an earthquake of the magnitude capable of breaking the stone lintel at the top of the entrance to the Holy Place was occurring at the exact time of Christ's death, then what would such an earthquake have done to the Chamber of Hewn Stones (a vaulted and columned structure) no more than 40 yards away from where the stone lintel fell and the curtain tore in two?

There is every reason to believe, though the evidence is circumstantial, that the Chamber of Hewn Stones was so damaged in the same earthquake that it became structurally unsafe from that time forward. Something like this had to have happened because the Sanhedrin would not have left this majestic chamber (to take up residence in the insignificant "Trading Place") unless something approaching this explanation took place.

If this is actually what happened (and I have no doubt that it did), we then have a most remarkable witness that God the Father engineered every action happening on the day of Christ's trial and crucifixion. It means that the judgment made by the official Sanhedrin against Jesus within the Chamber of Hewn Stones *was THE LAST JUDGMENT* ever given by the official Sanhedrin in their majestic chambers within the Temple! It would show that God the Father demonstrated by the earthquake at Christ's death that the *sentence* of the Sanhedrin against Jesus *would be the last judgment* it would ever make in that authorized place!

It should be remembered, that in normal circumstances it was felt proper that *all* judgments of God in the Jerusalem area had to take place "in the presence of God." This concept was explained in chapter four of this book. That is one of the main reasons why the Sanhedrin was placed in the Temple directly east (and slightly south) of the entrance to the Holy Place. Since the entrances to the Holy Place and the inner Holy of Holies were on the *east*, it was reasoned that God faced *eastward* to see all events which were happening in "His House" (the Temple itself).

This is why the sacrifices were performed at the *eastern* entrance to the Holy Place, and even the remote Red Heifer sacrifice also was killed *east* (and in "sight" of God) at the summit of the Mount of Olives. This is the reason capital judgments made in the Sanhedrin were rendered (ideally) on the *east* side of the Temple, and why criminals condemned to die were executed near the top of the Mount of Olives in order for them to be a "sacrifice of atonement" for themselves "in the presence of God." Thus, Jesus was judged and executed "in the presence of God" that the Old Testament requirements could be satisfied. In both his judgment and his execution, the action was carried out by the Sanhedrin *east* of the Holy Place in the Temple.

But the sentence of the Sanhedrin did not end the matter. There was still the Roman authorities that had to be consulted. It was then necessary to take Jesus to Pilate, the Roman procurator, for his approval of the judgment. In what region of Jerusalem was Pilate at the time? Was he then in Herod's Palace on the southwestern hill or was he among the majority of his troops which would have been at the fortress called the Antonia situated just outside the northwestern angle of the Temple enclosure? The Fortress of Antonia (named after Mark Antony by Herod) has by far the best credentials. There are good reasons to believe that it was to *this* Praetorium that Christ was brought to be finally judged by Pilate.

This can be shown in several ways. It would have been unwise for any Roman commander to be anywhere else but the Antonia next to the Temple itself when there were thousands upon thousands of Jews assembling in the Temple for their national holy periods. While it was normal for Roman procurators to live in Herod's Palace on the southwest hill (as shown by Josephus in *War* II.325-329), at the times of the Jewish annual festivals it was customary for the Roman commander to take up residence with his main body of troops at the Antonia adjacent to the Temple. This is what Cumanus, the procurator of Judaea who ruled in the middle of the first century, did at the time of Passover (*War* II.223-227).

There can hardly be a doubt that Pilate (at the time of Christ) had done the same thing. It should be noted that Pilate's wife sent him a message about a dream she had. This would have been unnecessary had Pilate been with his wife that night (Matt.27:19). Pilate was away from his ordinary living quarters at the time. At that Passover season he was where "the whole army" was stationed (Matt.27:27). This is a description that favors the Antonia. Note also that the Jews did not want to enter into the Praetorium where Pilate was in fear of becoming impure and unfit to take the Passover (John 18:28). This fear of impurity would fit the Antonia far more than Herod's Palace. The truth is, the Antonia was really a "city" in itself and it was *a Gentile one* located right in the midst of Jerusalem. The only restriction against taking the Passover for Jews was to come in contact with a dead body (Num.9:6-12). Unless there was someone who had recently died (and was lying in state) in Herod's Palace, there would have been no restriction whatever to prevent the Jews from eating the Passover that they could not have overcome by simply washing themselves before sundown (Edersheim, *Life and Times*, vol.II, pp.556, 557). But the Antonia, however, was a very different place. It was virtually a large "Gentile town." Such places would ordinarily have had some dead bodies within them who were either waiting to be buried or cremated. There would also have been chambers for retaining the remains of dead soldiers (who died in line of duty) awaiting transport back to their home areas for interment. For any Jew to enter the central area of this "Gentile city" called the Antonia would have rendered the person unclean for at least a seven day period. Thus, again, the region of the Antonia fits far better the description of the Praetorium in which Jesus was brought before Pilate rather than the Palace of Herod located on the southwest hill.

This belief is further strengthened by the information provided in this chapter, because all of the events of Christ's interrogation and trial at the House of Annas and Caiaphus and in the Chambers of the Sanhedrin took place on the Temple Mount about 300 yards from the Antonia. For Pilate to have been at his ordinary residence on the southwestern hill would have involved a great deal of extended walking (and back-tracking) on the part of Christ and the Sanhedrin members. But going the short distance from the Temple to the Antonia makes perfectly good sense. See the excellent account by Finegan, *The Archeology of the Old Testament*, pp.156,157 which shows that Pilate was then at the Antonia and VanElderen's comprehensive article in the new *International Standard Bible Encyclopedia* (vol.III, p.929).

When it is realized that the proceedings against Christ by the Sanhedrin occurred on the Temple Mount and that Pilate judged him at the adjacent area called the Antonia, it gives a great deal of credence to the belief that all of the deliberations that took place that day were within the Law of

Moses. Some commentators have thought the inquisition and trial of Christ were illegal because they believe that the "House of Caiaphus" in which Jesus was interrogated was on the southwestern hill. True enough, had this been the case, then the proceedings against Jesus would have to be reckoned illegal. But this is not what happened. Since it was the Passover, the gates of the Temple were opened at midnight (Josephus *Antiq.*XVIII.29; Mishnah *Yoma* 1:8) and it was proper for people to enter the Temple after that time. And with the sentence of Jesus *being after sunrise* (a definite requirement for legality and it occurred within the official Chamber of the Sanhedrin), then it can be shown that everything that happened to Christ that day was within the Law of Moses. The fact that some witnesses perjured themselves is of no consequence to the issue because even in legal trials (that result in false convictions because of perjury) it cannot be said that the trials themselves were illegal.

There is little doubt that people will continue to look at the details of Christ's interrogation, his formal trial and sentence and find some fault (in their own minds) here and there. But such nit-picking can be eliminated if one will simply look at the actions of Pilate. The apostle John makes it clear that Pilate tried his best to prevent the execution of Jesus (at least at the time the Sanhedrin brought Jesus to him). Had Pilate found the slightest illegality in the manner of his trial even from the Jewish point of view (and it is only reasonable that Pilate had a bevy of lawyers around him trained in Jewish jurisprudence), he would have dismissed their charges against Jesus or demanded that they hold another trial under *legal* circumstances.

The accounts in the Gospels, however, make it clear that no such illegality was found by Pilate or his advisors. He then washed his hands of the whole affair and let them kill him according to the Jewish laws (John 18:31). The truth is, Jesus was not tried or executed to satisfy Roman laws because even Rome allowed a formal court hearing (and one scheduled on the court calendar) in which the defendant would be given time to produce witnesses for his defence. No such trial under the authority of Rome was given to Jesus.

All Pilate did (as the Roman procurator) was to give permission to the Sanhedrin to carry out *their* judgments upon Jesus because they did not have the power to execute criminals at the time (John 18:31).

But what about the fact that Christ was crucified? Was that not a Roman means of execution? Yes, but not exclusively. Recall that the Gospels show that it was the inhabitants of Jerusalem that demanded of Pilate that he "crucify him" (John 19:6,15). The crucifixion (and his death by stoning) were to satisfy Jewish laws (in Pilate's opinion), not those of Rome. As explained in chapter four of this book, the *Temple Scroll* (found among the Dead Sea Scrolls) shows that it was then a Jewish practice to hang (or nail) a person to a tree and then have him stoned to death. The truth is, Pilate (and the Empire of Rome that he represented) washed their hands of the whole affair (Matt.27:24). The trial, sentence and execution of Jesus was by Jewish laws (the Law of Moses). The only thing involving Pilate (and Rome) was to allow them to do it. As Pilate said: "Take you him, and judge him according to *your* law" (John 18:31).

It was absolutely essential that Jesus was tried and convicted in a legal manner in order to fulfill all the laws and types of the Old Testament. This is a matter of profound theological importance. Look at it for a moment. Had Christ's death not been legal, then what he did for Christians and the world by dying for their sins (as the New Testament attests that he did) would have to be put aside as not legally proper. In no way would Peter or Paul have accepted such a proposition. If his death was not legal, then his atoning sacrifice for the sins of the world would also not be legal! But when Christ died on the tree of crucifixion, *all legal requirements* of the Law of Moses had been met.

In the next chapter we will observe some fascinating spiritual teachings regarding the fulfillment of the ceremonial system of sacrifices by the *legal* condemnation of Jesus. This evidence from the Gospels provides us with a much better understanding of how the apostles (and early Christians) viewed the atoning sacrifice of Christ as it pertained to Israel and the world.

18

Temple Rituals and the Crucifixion of Christ

We now arrive at one of the most important aspects of this new research. When it is realized that the crucifixion and resurrection of Christ took place near the southern summit of the Mount of Olives, the spiritual significance behind many historical, prophetical and doctrinal teachings of the Old and New Testaments becomes much more intelligible. Sections of scripture that may have been difficult to comprehend in a practical way can now make perfectly good sense. In this chapter we wish to discuss some of the interesting teachings that are able to emerge once the true site of Golgotha is recognized.

We have noticed in the last chapter that Christ was actually sentenced to death by the Sanhedrin practically on the doorstep of the entrance to the Holy Place in the Temple. He was taken from there to Pilate at the Antonia and then he was forced to carry the crosspiece on which he was to be crucified up to the summit of the Mount of Olives (Simon of Cyrene helping the last part of the way). It is important to understand that Christ was judged *legally* in the Temple. The sacrifice he paid for the sins of the world had to be *legal* in every way, and of course it was!

But what kind of sin offering was Christ supposed to represent in the eyes of the people and of God? To recognize this, we must recall that the Temple was symbolically reckoned to be the residence of God on earth. It was consistently called the "House of God." This "House" (or *Bethel*) had three compartments to it. The first was the inner sanctum where only the High Priest could enter on the Day of Atonement. It was considered the throne room of God and it was designated the "Holy of Holies." The Mercy Seat within this holiest spot was symbolically acknowledged as the royal seat from whence God governed the world. The next compartment *eastward* was called the Holy Place. Into this only priests were permitted to enter. They could do so daily in the ordained ceremonial occasions which demanded it. The third section was a large *eastern* courtyard (with several divisions in the time of Christ) into which the ordinary Israelites could congregate to worship God and to bring their various offerings. Outside this Court of Israel was the "Gentile world" and it was considered as common or secular territory. The only exception was the Miphkad Altar region located just outside the camp of Israel (and in the time of Christ it was near the summit of the Mount of Olives directly *east* of the entrances to the Court of Israel, the Holy Place and the Holy of Holies).

Let us now note a most important point regarding the Temple and its three general compartments. Since it was understood to be the "House of God," it was thought to be an earthly replica (or pattern) of God's palace in heaven (Heb. 9:23). The abode of God in heaven was called *Paradise* and it is referred to in the New Testament (Luke 23:43; II Cor.12:4; Rev.2:7). This heavenly *Paradise* was reflective of the physical *Paradise* (Garden or Park) that God once had on earth at the time of Adam and Eve. It was called the Garden of Eden and the earthly Garden of Eden was a type of the heavenly *Paradise*. For a comprehensive treatment about this heavenly *Paradise* from the Jewish point of view, see Cohen, *Everyman's Talmud*, chapter XI, section VI.

The heavenly *Paradise* of God had another symbol besides the Garden of Eden. As stated before, this was the Temple and its various compartments. Since the Temple was an exact physical replica of the heavenly "House of God" (Heb.9:23), it follows that the Temple was also a reflection of the "Garden of Eden." Each of the three compartments to the Temple represented the three main divisions that comprised the "Garden" and the general area of "Eden" within which our first parents were placed soon after their creation. Notice the parallel. The Holy Place of the Temple into which only the priests could enter to perform their administrations was acknowledged as "the Garden" section of the Land of Eden. This was where Adam and Eve lived at first before they sinned. Further inside "the Garden" was an inner part to which God would appear at specified times. This was like the Holy of Holies. This agreement was also made a hundred and fifty years before Christ. The Book of Jubilees stated that the inner "Garden" was analogous to the sanctuary in the Temple (*Jubilees* 8:19 and compare *Jubilees* 3:10-12).

These matters are good evidence to show that this "Garden" area was represented by the Holy Place in the Temple of Solomon. The Bible records that Solomon "carved all the walls of the house [the Holy Place] round about with carved figures of cherubim and palm trees and open flowers within and without" [that is, the carvings were on the inside walls of the Holy Place as well as on its outside walls] (I Kings 6:29; see also Ezekiel 41:18 where the prophet also decorated his future, prophetic Temple in the same way). When observers would enter Solomon's Temple (or the projected one of Ezekiel) and look westwards to the outside of the Holy Place, they were expected to imagine that they were looking at the replica of a Garden. True enough. The Holy Place of the Temple was designed to be a pattern of the "Garden" in "Eden" and both the Temple and the "Garden of Eden" also represented the *Paradise* (Garden) of God in heaven.

Let us now recall in detail what happened to Adam and Eve in their association with the "Garden." After they sinned, they were cast out and cherubim were placed at the entrance of "the Garden" to keep them from re-entering the enclosure. This is why Solomon and Ezekiel placed carved cherubim around the Holy Place (I Kings 6:29; Ezek.41:18). They wanted the worshippers to recognize that they were depicting *the* "Garden." And though Adam and Eve were not permitted to return to the "Garden" (and the cherubim guarded it carefully), they were still able to reside in the Land of Eden. It was only in the "Garden" section of Eden that they could no longer enter. And then, sometime later their two sons Cain and Abel built an altar. This was positioned before the entrance to "the Garden" (in which God was supposed to dwell). Concerning the sacred furniture in the Tabernacle and Temple this altar was analogous to the Altar of Burnt Offering which was positioned just *east* of the entrance to the Holy Place [or "the Garden"]. But Cain killed Abel. This forced Cain to move *east* of Eden (Gen.4:16). This signalled that Cain and his descendants could no longer live in the Land of Eden. They had to remain *eastward* of "Eden" in the Land of Nod (Wandering).

Now note this next point carefully. While *east* of Eden and in the Land of Nod, God promised Cain a sacrifice for sin if he ever did wrong. God said to Cain: "if you do not well, sin [a *sin offering*] couches at the door" (Gen.4:7). The couching of this sin offering for Cain meant (in the usage of the word in other contexts of the Bible) that it would be so weighted down with "sin" that it would have to couch at the door because of the heavy weight. Before what door was this sin offering placed? Since all sin offerings had to be presented "in the presence" of God for acceptance (and since God dwelt in the inner sanctum of "the Garden" in the Land of Eden), Cain's sin offering was prophesied to couch before the door which represented the *eastern* gate to the Land of Eden.

In Tabernacle and Temple times, this Land of Eden came to represent the outer courts of the sanctuary. Cain, because he was prevented from entering the Land of Eden, was analogous to the Gentiles who were not allowed entrance into the courts of the Temple. But Cain and his descendants were still provided by God with a sin offering that would be couching under a heavy burden of sin at the *eastern* door (entrance) to the Land of Eden. In Tabernacle and Temple times *this* altar on which Cain's sin offering would be placed was represented by the *Miphkad Altar* located on the Mount of Olives and outside the Temple (even *outside the camp* of Israel) (Ezek.43:21). It was on this altar that the major sin offerings for the priesthood and the congregation of Israel were burnt to ashes. And it was also on this same altar that the sin offerings on the Day of Atonement were burnt to ashes. This was the identical altar at which the sin offering of the Red Heifer was killed and burnt to ashes. But it doesn't end there. This altar was also the one that the Book of Hebrews associated with the crucifixion of Christ. This was an altar located without the courtyard area of the Temple, even "*outside the camp*" of Israel which the Land of Eden symbolized. In effect, the sin offering for Cain and his descendants which was prophesied to be sacrificed *east* of Eden (or *east* of the Temple) was the one that best suited Christ. This is clearly the case because we now know that Christ was crucified not far south of the *Miphkad Altar* (the altar for the sin offerings) on the summit of the Mount of Olives. This Miphkad Altar was reckoned symbolically as being in the Land of Nod (Wandering). It was "in the midst of the world."

This point has profound symbolic teaching associated with it when understood properly. As for me, it was this recognition that the compartments of the Tabernacle and the later Temples represented the "Garden" and "Eden" (and that the Miphkad Altar answered to that of Cain in the Land of Nod) that first led me to think (in August, 1983) that Christ must have been crucified *east* of the Temple and near the summit of the Mount of Olives. Since it was clear from Jewish symbolic teaching that "the Garden" represented the Holy Place of the sanctuary and that the Altar of Burnt Offering in the Tabernacle and Temples answered to the altar on which Cain and Abel offered their sacrifices, it also meant that the sin offering which was prophesied to couch at a door *east* of the entrance to the Land of Eden must refer to the crucifixion of Christ. It began to appear reasonable to me in August, 1983 that Christ had to have been crucified *east* of Eden (that is, *east* of the Temple Mount) in order to fulfil this prophetic type. And, that is exactly where the greatest sin offering of all time was sacrificed for the world. [For more detailed information explaining this important subject, read my paper titled "Temple Symbolism in the Book of Genesis" which is obtainable from A.S.K.]

We must recall again the historical evidence which this book provides in chapter four that the Jews reckoned that all "unclean" things and those bearing abject "sin" had to be dealt with in an *easterly* direction from the sacred areas of the Temple and Jerusalem. This was to prevent "uncleanness" being carried by the winds over the city of Jerusalem (which was considered an area of purity and holiness). When Christ was crucified, he was certainly considered "unclean" and a "sinner" by the Sanhedrin (indeed, they reckoned him a *blasphemer*) and they sentenced him to death. In the symbolic teaching of the Bible as understood by first century Christians, Christ became that prophesied sin offering mentioned in Genesis 4:7 who was destined to couch under the heaviest burden of sin known to mankind. This was the one sacrifice that would not only cover the sins of Cain and his descendants, but it would also apply to all Israelites and everyone in the world.

Now all of this makes sense *only if* Christ were sacrificed *east* of the Temple (which signified being *east* of "Eden") and that his death took place near the Miphkad Altar which was the principal altar for the major sin offerings. Remarkably, Jesus fulfilled these requirements perfectly. This is why it is so important (and significant) to recognize that Christ was crucified (and stoned to death according to the Law of Moses) near the southern summit of the Mount of Olives just a short distance south of the Miphkad Altar. The apostles must have recognized the profound theological importance of these symbolic and spiritual agreements with the sacrificial ceremonies associated with the Law of Moses. There were simply too many similarities for the apostles (and early Christians) to conclude that the occurrences were mere coincidences.

This same conviction was also expressed by many Jews about 50 days after the crucifixion of Jesus because 3000 men responded favorably and were converted to what the apostles related about Christ and his resurrection from the dead (Acts 2:41). So certain did many Jews become (in the very region of Jerusalem where the events happened), that within 25 years after Christ's crucifixion *tens of thousands* of them were believing that Jesus was indeed the Christ -- the one who fulfilled the ritualistic symbols of the Law of Moses (Acts 21:20 Greek).

The symbolic teachings concerning the rituals of the Temple which pertain to Christ and his role as the one who fulfilled *all* aspects of the Mosaic Law are further illustrated by what happened at the time Abraham attempted to sacrifice his son Isaac as a burnt offering to God (Gen.22). The Jews in the time of Christ (and throughout the later period of the Talmud) considered that the altar that Abraham built on Mount Moriah for the sacrifice of Isaac was located at the identical spot where the Altar of Burnt Offering was erected in the time of Solomon and in the latter Temples. This identification is specifically stated in the Old Testament itself (II Chron.3:1) and Josephus shows it was common opinion in the time of Christ that this was so (*Antiq*.I.222,226).

Since the type of offering that Abraham was preparing Isaac to be was a Burnt Offering (Gen.22:3,8,13), it was reckoned as the same type of offering that was consumed on the Altar of Burnt Offering in the Tabernacle and later Temples located just *east* of the entrance to the Holy Place. A ram was finally substituted for Isaac and it was sacrificed as a Burnt Offering (Gen.22:13). This would have been the same type of offering that Cain and Abel were supposed to have brought to the entrance to the "Garden" (which is analogous to the "Holy Place" in the Temple). This means that the offerings of Abel and Abraham were not intended to be sin offerings. They were simply offerings of thanksgiving which were burnt to ashes on an Altar of Burnt Offering.

But what has this to do with Christ and the sacrifice he made for the world at the time of his trial and crucifixion? The apostle Paul and early Christians thought there was very much symbolic teaching in the incident on Mount Moriah that involved Abraham, Isaac and the ram caught in the thicket. It should be noticed that Abraham told the two men who attended the animal and baggage at the bottom of the mountain "Abide you here with the ass; and I and the lad will go yonder and worship, *and WILL COME again to you*" (Gen.22:5). But how was it possible for both Abraham and Isaac to return to them if Isaac was to be killed? The fact is, God had already told Abraham that Isaac would have children (and multitudes of descendants) (e.g. Gen.21:12), but Isaac was not yet married and had no offspring at that time. For God to keep his promise about Isaac, Abraham believed that if he killed Isaac, that God would have to resurrect him from the dead in order to keep his previous promises (Gen.18:18). And that is why Abraham told the two men at the bottom of the mount to wait for them, because Abraham believed both he and Isaac would return. To Abraham, this would happen even if Isaac had to be resurrected from the dead.

This is precisely what the author of the Book of Hebrews stated was Abraham's belief. He said that Abraham accounted "that God was able to raise him up, *even from the dead*; from whence also he received him in a figure" (Heb.11:19). This is an important piece of teaching on what first century Christians thought about this event. In a figurative sense, Isaac was resurrected from the dead. And to Christians, the second "Isaac" (Christ Jesus) was the true "seed" of Abraham (Gal.3:16) who was *actually* raised from the dead. This shows that early Christians recognized that the burnt offerings (like that of the ram caught in the thicket as well as the animals burnt on the Altar of Burnt Offering in the Temple) were *typical* of Christ and his atoning sacrifice.

But there was much more agreement between Isaac and Christ in the eyes of first century Christians than simply recognizing that Christ was the *real* Burnt Offering that the ram prefigured. The history of Isaac was in many ways *typical* of the life of Jesus himself. There are seven points that need to be mentioned. 1) The birth of Isaac was miraculous (Gen.18), and so was Christ's (Matt.1:18). 2) In Abraham's attempt to sacrifice Isaac, Isaac even assisted Abraham in carrying the wood to the Altar of Burnt Offering (Gen.22:6). In like manner Christ also carried his own crosspiece to his crucifixion. 3) Isaac did not dispute Abraham's will in the matter of his own sacrifice, nor did Christ with God the Father: "not as I will, but as you will" and "your will be done" (Matt.26:39,42). 4) Christ and Isaac were both "offered" within the place which became the Temple in latter times.

Christ was condemned to die by the Sanhedrin about 30 yards from the Altar of Burnt Offering, and Isaac was "killed" (in a figurative way) at the same place. 5) Isaac was also willing to lay down his life of his own free will, just as Christ did. Note that Isaac was younger and stronger than his father Abraham. No one knows the age of Isaac when the attempted "offering" took place, but Isaac was not an infant as the translation of the King James Versions suggests (note that it says "lad" in verse 5). The truth is, the word translated "lad" (Hebrew: *nahgar*) was the same one that described the two young men Abraham left at the bottom of the mount and telling them to mind the animal and baggage until he and Isaac would return. These men were really young adults (that is, they were *"young"* relative to Abraham), because Joshua the son of Nun was also called a *nahgar* when he was forty years of age (Exo.33:11). Josephus in the time of the apostles thought that Isaac was twenty-five years of age at the time (*Antiq.*I.227). As far as Bible chronology is concerned, Isaac could have been any age of young manhood less than thirty-six, because the next event recorded as having happened was the death of Isaac's mother Sarah who died when Isaac was thirty-six (see Genesis 23 for details). As a matter of fact, nothing in the biblical record would have prevented Isaac from being *the same age as Jesus* when he was crucified. And since early Christians saw such *typical* agreements between Isaac and Jesus, this may very well have been the case! 6) Abraham also was willing to sacrifice his only son (that is, his only legal or legitimate son) while God the Father did in fact give up his only begotten son. 7) Abraham was presented with a substitute sacrifice for Isaac and Isaac was *typically* "killed" by the offering of an animal. But the author of the Book of Hebrews said this sparing of Isaac was tantamount to Isaac having been resurrected (Heb.11:17-19). Isaac had a three day journey to be "offered" and *figuratively* to be resurrected from the dead, while Christ himself was *actually* resurrected three days after he was sacrificed. While Isaac had a ram to take his place, Jesus had no substitute.

So, regarding this *typical* teaching of the burnt offerings, Christ was offered up to the Father as a sacrifice for the people by the Sanhedrin (as Caiaphus the High Priest had said as recorded in John 11:50 and 18:14). And interestingly, Christ's death sentence (his "offering up") was pronounced upon him in the Temple not 30 yards south and a little east of the Altar of Burnt Offering. This was a highly significant feature which *typically* (in the person of Christ) had a great bearing in Christian theology. It meant that Christ was also being offered as a sweet smelling savor [a burnt offering] to the Father. Note how the apostle Paul made this precise comparison: "Walk in love, as Christ also has loved us, and has given himself *for us* an offering and a sacrifice to God for a sweetsmelling savour" (Eph.5:2).

This *typical* teaching of the apostles makes perfectly good sense *if* it is realized that Christ was indeed sentenced to die by the Sanhedrin and the High Priest *right in the Temple itself!* But with the beliefs of most theologians today that Christ was tried *illegally* at Caiaphus' House on the southwestern hill and that the Sanhedrin were then outside their official chambers, it means that Christ was not in the interior of his Father's House (the Temple) when he became that burnt offering (or the sin offerings). But those sacrifices *had to be* legally associated with the Altar of Burnt Offering in the Temple or at the Miphkad Altar on Olivet. This is why it is so important to realize the *actual* locations of Christ's trial and sentence (as recorded in the New Testament and Jewish records) in order to understand why the apostles made the *typical* agreements that they did regarding Christ and how he precisely fulfilled the ritualistic requirements of the Mosaic Law.

Let us now rehearse some of those important Temple rituals involving the sacrifices that *typified* Christ and his role in human salvation. Christians in the first century believed that Christ fulfilled *all* of the sacrificial rituals performed in and around the Temple. For example, every animal which was considered a Burnt Offering (Leviticus 1) had to be killed at the slaughter area just to the north of the Altar of Burnt Offering. *All* the peace offerings (Leviticus 2) and the sin and trespass offerings (Leviticus 4 and 5) also had to be killed at the same place. The single exception to this was the Red Heifer which was killed and burnt to ashes at the Miphkad Altar at the top of the Mount of Olives (Numbers 19). Even the bullock and the goat which were sacrificed on the Day of Atonement (Leviticus 16) had to be killed near the Altar of Burnt Offering within the Temple and then their carcases were required to be taken out the eastern gate to the Miphkad Altar at the Mount of Olives and there they were burnt to ashes (Leviticus 4). Besides that, *all of the ashes* of the animals killed and burnt in the Temple had to be taken to the area of the Miphkad Altar on Olivet and poured out at the base of the Altar (Leviticus 4:12,21; 6:11) (where the ashes could descend through a conduit system into the Valley of the Kidron below).

With these ritualistic facts in mind, look at what happened to Christ. Since we now know that he was officially condemned and sentenced to die by the High Priest and the Sanhedrin at the Chamber of Hewn Stones *on the Temple Mount*, then (for symbolic purposes) Christ himself was reckoned "killed" (like Isaac was *typically* "killed") *in the very heart of the Temple* (and in the *same place* as Isaac). But there is more. Let us look at the sin offerings associated with the Day of Atonement. Since it was necessary for those sin offerings on that most holy day to be taken eastwards from the Temple, out the eastern gate, over the two-tiered arched bridge crossing the Valley of the Kidron, and then up to the summit of the Mount of Olives to be burnt to ashes, so Jesus was also taken from the same Temple, out the eastern gate (Heb.13:10-13), also over the two-tiered bridge, and up to the summit of Olivet just south of the Miphkad Altar and there crucified (and stoned to death). The similarity must have struck early Christians as highly significant. Even the ashes of *all* the animals sacrificed and burnt to ashes in the Temple had to be taken out the same eastern gate, over the two-tiered bridge, and up to the summit of Olivet to be poured out at the base of the Miphkad Altar.

This means that Christ Jesus, with the events that happened to him on the day of his trial and crucifixion, followed the <u>same</u> path of *all* the animal sacrifices (or their ashes) in the ritualistic ceremonies of the Temple. With an understanding of these geographical and ritualistic indications associated with the passion of Christ, we are provided with even more symbolic and theological teaching that Jesus Christ did in fact fulfill the role of the sin-bearer, and that he was the prophesied one to offer a pure and complete sacrifice to God for all people in the world.

As a final point, let us look at a ritual which also *typically* prefigured Christ in his role as the sin-bearer. Notice the most mysterious of the sin offerings (as the Jewish authorities have seen it over the centuries). This was the burning of the Red Heifer at the Miphkad Altar on the summit of Olivet. There is hardly any offering that figuratively represents Christ more precisely than that of the Red Heifer. Let us notice the parallel.

When it was time to offer a new Red Heifer (and only *nine* had been burnt since the time of Moses, see *Parah* 3:5), it was essential for a priest (traditionally the High Priest) to leave his own residence in Jerusalem and spend seven days being purified at what was called the House of Stone at the northeast corner of the Temple building (*Parah* 3:1). After this seven days' stay on the Temple Mount in one of the priests' residence, the Red Heifer was then escorted out of the Temple area via the *eastern* gate, over the two-tiered arched bridge over the Valley of the Kidron, and up to the Miphkad Altar where it was killed and burnt to ashes. The Miphkad Altar was not the normal type of altar which was made of stones with a ramp to an elevated square area. It was in the form of a pit (*Parah* 4:2). The transport of the Red Heifer to this spot was a very solemn procession from the Temple Mount to the summit of the Mount of Olives. Not only did priests ascend the mountain, but it was led by all of the elders of the land (*Parah* 3:6,7). And once at the designated place, the Red Heifer was placed with its head facing the Temple and it was then killed and burnt to ashes. These ashes were then mixed with pure spring water and they served for all matters of purification dealing with the holiest affairs associated with the Temple.

Now note how this *typically* prefigured what happened to Jesus. He was judged to be killed by the High Priest and the Sanhedrin in the Temple itself. After Pilate gave his permission for them to carry out the sentence according to *their* Law, he was led from the Antonia past the Temple on his right, out the *eastern* gate of the Temple, over the two-tiered arched bridge, up to the summit of the Mount of Olives. But instead of being killed at the Miphkad Altar, he was taken a short distance south (to where criminals could be executed "in the presence of God," that is, in sight of the Temple) and there he was crucified (and stoned to death). And what is interesting, just as the Red Heifer was preceded by all of the top officials of the nation, the apostle John said that it was the chief priests themselves who led Jesus up to the place of crucifixion and it was they who had him put to death (John 19:15,16). There could hardly be any closer agreement!

Of course, these *typical* parallels between the Red Heifer sacrifice (and the other sin and burnt offerings) are only possible if we recognize that Christ was judged in the Temple (his own Father's House) and taken up to the Mount of Olives for his execution. But with the new information in this book showing the *real* geographical locations where these important events took place, then we are granted a marvelous historical scenario of the figurative agreements of Christ's sacrifice for the sins of the world with the sin and burnt offerings that Moses gave to ancient Israel.

There is one other point, however, that needs to be mentioned. Since the Red Heifer was taken to the summit of Olivet and *burnt to ashes*, why was not Jesus also *burnt* in order for the figure to be precise? This is a good question. And even here it is possible to see a major parallel. What needs to be recognized is the fact that the example of the Old Testament regarding the disposition of a dead body of a *blasphemer* (or one who was considered "*accursed of God*") was that of Achan in the time of Joshua. What happened to the body of Achan after he was killed by stoning? He and his possessions were grouped together into a pile and they were then *burnt to ashes* (Josh.7:15,25,26).

This was the example of dealing with an "*accursed one*," as the apostle Paul said Jesus was reckoned (Gal.3:13), and this meant that his corpse had to be treated like that of Achan who was also reckoned as "*accursed*" (Josh.7:15). There can hardly be a doubt that the authorities in Jerusalem were in the very process of placing Christ's body on a pile of wood (along with the tree on which he was nailed) and they were getting ready to *burn up the accursed thing* with all the items that had come in contact with him. Only his garment was going to be spared which the Roman soldiers (being Gentiles) secured for themselves.

Since there is no doubt what the authorities were preparing to do, it is no wonder that Joseph of Arimathea rushed quickly to Pilate to crave for the body of Jesus to be given to him, and the Greek wording shows his boldness was because of utmost urgency (Mark 15:43). Pilate then gave Joseph his request and the body of Jesus was placed in his charge. Had this not happened, there is every reason to believe that the body of Jesus would have been *burnt to ashes* (thus fulfilling the sacrifice of the Red Heifer to a tee). The reason the authorities were wanting his body burnt up was to prevent his disciples from stealing the body and making out later that he was resurrected from the dead as he had been telling people would happen (Matt.27:63-66).

But note this point. Though Jesus' body was not actually *burnt up* (as the authorities in Jerusalem no doubt wanted), it could be said that he was "*burnt up*" in a typical sense (just as the author of the Book of Hebrews taught that Isaac was figuratively resurrected from the dead when a ram became a substitute for him). However, though the body of Jesus was spared from being *burnt up*, this fate could hardly have escaped the tree on which he was crucified. Since *everything* that touched an "*accursed one*" was itself considered "*accursed*" (even the land around the place of execution "was defiled") (Deut.21:22,23), then it can hardly be imagined that the tree (or even if one considers the instrument of his execution to have been a Roman cross) would have survived their judgment. That instrument of execution had to be *burnt to ashes!* And it no doubt was. This would mean that the three crosses found under the Temple of Venus in the time of Constantine (that the people of the fourth century thought were those associated with the crucifixion of Christ) could in no way have been genuine. One of the greatest hoaxes in history was accomplished (and it has proved so successful over the past sixteen hundred years) by Judas Quiriacus when he showed those false crosses to Helen the mother of Constantine.

Be this as it may, there is still more New Testament teaching to survey about the significance of the Red Heifer. There are several analogies from the apostle Paul that seem to be directly associated with the ritual of the Red Heifer and it is important that we consider them. Let us once again turn our attention to this most holy of sin offerings -- the Red Heifer sacrifice.

The first point to consider is that the sin offering of the Red Heifer had to be a perfect female with red colored hair, never yoked (Num.19:2) and the rabbis understood that it should never have been mounted by a male (Mishnah, *Parah* 2:4). This Red Heifer was burnt to ashes and the ashes were mixed with clean spring water. It was with these purification waters that not only Israelites were purified from ceremonial defilements, but even the priests and the Temple itself were cleansed in certain ways with these holy waters.

Thus, the Red Heifer was a most important sin offering. But what did it represent to first century Christians? The fact is, the animal was a *female* and how could this relate to Christ Jesus who was a man? This is an interesting point, and we may find that the apostle Paul gave the proper interpretation of how this *female* sin offering (the holiest of all) represented Christ in a figurative way though he was a male.

Let us look at one central teaching of Paul in which he reckoned Christ to be "female" in a figurative (or mystical) way. This was in regard to his "Body," the Church! The apostle Paul consistently called the corporate body of Christians (both males and females) by the word *ecclesia* (which we in English translate as *church*). Interestingly, the word is feminine! This was not simply a grammatical formality of Paul but it had profound *typical* significance. This is because Paul called "the Church" the "Body of Christ" (I Cor.12:12-

27). In this case, the "Body" is feminine, not the actual masculine body of Christ. This feminine "Body" was certainly the Body of Christ because it represented "his flesh" (his *one flesh*). This "one flesh" relationship is what Paul called the marriage union that Christ has with his Church. In Paul's teaching the husband and wife represented *one flesh*. To Paul, one was masculine (the husband) and the Church was feminine (the wife). Notice how Paul explained his teaching.

"Husbands, love your wives, even as Christ also loved the Church, and gave himself for it.... So ought men to love their wives as their own bodies. He that loves his wife loves himself. For no man ever yet hated his own flesh; but nourishes and cherishes it, even as the Lord the Church: *for we are members of his body, of his flesh, and of his bones*. For this cause shall a man leave his father and mother, and shall be joined unto his wife, *and they two shall be one flesh*. This is a great mystery, but *I speak concerning Christ and the Church*" (Eph.5:25-32).

In a *typical* sense the Church is the "wife" of Christ. To Paul, the Church was "his body, his flesh, and his bones." Since this figurative teaching of Paul was a central part of his theological understanding of what Christianity was all about, we may find that it explains (from Paul's point of view) how the Red Heifer could be feminine and yet denote Christ as well. Note that the Red Heifer was an animal that was required to be *free, unblemished, and to be a female virgin*. So holy were the ashes of this sin offering that even the most sacred items were purified by the waters mixed with its ashes. In a word, the Red Heifer had to be *holy, without blemish and not having spot.* Also, its purification waters were able *to sanctify people, to cleanse them, and to wash them clean from all impurities.*

Remarkably, these identical factors are the ones the apostle Paul associated with the Church (the "wife" of Christ), because he thought that the Church was also a *free* woman and one *without a yoke* as the Red Heifer (see Galatians 4:22-31). He told the Galatians to "stand fast therefore in the liberty wherewith Christ has made us free" (Gal. 5:1).

But Paul was even more specific. In the section of

Ephesians quoted above, there is one portion I deliberately left out of the context at the time, but it needs to be re-inserted and emphasized. Paul's description of the Church as being Christ's wife is typical of the requirements associated with the ritual of the Red Heifer. Here is the quote.

"Husbands, love your wives, even as Christ also loved the Church, and gave himself for it; that he might *sanctify it and cleanse it with the washing of the word, that he might present it a glorious Church, not having spot or wrinkle, or any such thing; but that it should be holy and without blemish*" (Eph.5:25-27).

Everything that Paul was saying in this scripture fits the ritualistic qualifications of the Red Heifer. But the apostle Paul's analogy doesn't stop here, because the Church, like the Red Heifer, was considered by Paul a chaste virgin.

"For I am jealous over you with godly jealousy: for I have espoused you to one husband, that I may present you *as a chaste virgin* to Christ" (II Cor.11:2).

This figurative analogy is even carried further by the apostle John in the Book of Revelation when he spoke of the hundred and forty four thousand.

"These are they which were not defiled with women; for they are virgins. These are they which follow the Lamb whithersoever he goes. These were redeemed from among men, being the firstfruits unto God and to the Lamb. And in their mouth was found no guile: for they are without fault before the throne of God" (Rev.14:4,5).

These figurative descriptions make good sense when one recognizes that the apostles Paul and John were applying familiar and *typical* teachings of the ritualistic ceremonies of the Law of Moses. The apostles saw Christ Jesus as fulfilling the rituals precisely. But in the case of the Red Heifer (being *feminine*), it no doubt represented Christ as being his virgin wife (the Church). The Church was (and is) Christ's feminine Body, but it is reckoned as being as much a part of his body as his own flesh. "For we are members of his body, of his flesh, and of his bones" (Eph.5:30).

Thus, the Red Heifer sacrifice can also be applied to Christ, but to his *feminine* part -- the Church. In a mystical way, Paul identified the Church as also "dying" with Christ when he met his death on the Mount of Olives (Col.2:20). And when Christ was raised from the dead, so were the members of the Church (in a *typical* sense) (Col.3:1). Also the Church is figuratively seated (in Christ) on the very throne of God in heaven (Eph.2:6). Of course, all of this is symbolic teaching, but so was every ritualistic act associated with the Red Heifer and the other animal sacrifices. This could mean, in a mystical way, that the Church (as Christ's "wife" and being "one flesh" with him) also died *with him* as shown by the sacrifice of the Red Heifer. Paul's mystical language and his knowledge of the Temple ceremonies (and his penchant for explaining their significance) would certainly allow this interpretation.

If it be true that the early Christians saw the symbolism of the Red Heifer as fulfilled in Christ through his *feminine* body, the Church, then this is just another reason why the Jewish Christians right after they returned to Jerusalem subsequent to its destruction by the Romans in A.D.70, built the Mother Church of all Christendom at the summit of the Mount of Olives as Eusebius said they did (see chapter eight of this book). But more important than anything, the southern summit of Olivet was where Christ was crucified (and stoned to death) and where he was buried and resurrected from the dead. It was at Olivet where the greatest purification for sin ever took place. That place was also analogous to the altar where the sin offering promised to Cain and his descendants was to be sacrificed for them.

When the proper geographical locations for Christ's trial, his sentence by the Sanhedrin, and the actual place of his crucifixion (on the southern summit of the Mount of Olives) are recognized, then we are provided with a much better understanding of what the New Testament teachings are all about. In the next chapter we will see just how important these historical and geographical evidences really are in comprehending spiritual principles.

19

The Spiritual Significance of Golgotha

When it is recognized that Christ was crucified on the Mount of Olives east of the main Temple, a whole new perspective awaits us than what is normally believed today. This necessitates looking at the biblical accounts in a far different way. Once the proper geographical locations are realized events which have not been understood for their symbolic value can now take on substantial significance. In this chapter we will look at some of these important points associated with the crucifixion of Christ at Golgotha.

First, look at the crucifixion scene itself. Realizing that it occurred near the southern summit of Olivet but facing the Temple and Jerusalem, we are provided with quite a dramatic spectacle. Imagine people walking down the roadway called "The Descent of the Mount of Olives" (Luke 19:37) with their Passover lambs in their arms going into the Temple to have them killed (the worshippers would afterwards take the animals to their homes for roasting). On the way to the Temple these people would have seen the building of the Miphkad Altar (called the *Beth haDeshen*) on their right and at the summit itself (on their left) they would have seen three men crucified to a tree. It would have been an extraordinary scene for the Passover season. This would have been especially so *if* Christ were looking westward towards his Father's House. This would mean that one robber was nailed to the same tree with his back to Christ and facing northeastwards, while the other would be in a similar position but facing southeastwards. There would have been six arms extended upwards suspended from each of their *patibulums* (crosspieces) while in the center of this scene would have been the trunk of the tree with its upper part exposed above them all. There may be much symbolic teaching in this view of the crucifixion and it will pay us to give attention to it. But first, we need to ask ourselves if symbolism is important in understanding biblical themes?

The truth is, the Bible is filled with symbolic teaching. Since the people of Palestine in the first century were dominated by the teachings of Scripture (and their whole lives were governed by scriptural application), what we are suggesting in this chapter could have had a definite relevance to them. In the study of history, it is important that we do not read back into the historical accounts what we are accustomed to believe or to appreciate. The proper interpretation of history is to account for what the people *at the time* believed no matter if we consider their opinions irrelevant and even absurd. So, in this chapter we will show some of the significant symbolic themes that were commonplace among the Jews in the first century.

Let us look at the symbolism of the seven branched lampstand. First of all, it represented the Tree of Life which was once located in the Garden of Eden. In a fascinating book titled *The Tree of Light*, written by Leon Yarden of Jerusalem, we have a penetrating study into the meaning of the Menorah. He concluded his investigation with the recognition that the Menorah figuratively depicted an *almond tree*, and not just any *almond tree*, but the one that represented the Tree of Life. There is every reason to believe that Yarden is correct in his research. The Old Testament description of the Menorah constructed in the time of Moses showed that it was intimately connected with the *almond tree* motif. Note that the flowers and the bowls for the oil on each of the seven branches of the Menorah were designed to be like those of the *almond tree* (Exo.37:17-24).

This almond tree type of lampstand was placed by Moses in the Holy Place of the Tabernacle just outside the Holy of Holies. But inside the inner sanctum itself was deposited the rod of Aaron that budded. It too had the symbol of the *almond tree* associated with it. The rod brought forth almond flowers and even almonds themselves in a supernatural manner (Num.17:1-13). Because Moses placed this *almond* rod of Aaron inside the Holy of Holies, this goes a long way in showing that the rod (with its *almond tree* genre) was the symbolic Tree of Life which had been in the Garden of Eden.

Philo, in the time of Christ, said the almond tree was "the emblem of the priesthood" (*Life of Moses*, III.22) because it was the first to bloom in the springtime and the last to lose its leaves. This tree showed the greatest longevity of life each year and it was a fit symbol for the Tree of Life.

We should recall that the Tabernacle and the Temple at Jerusalem were built to be a pattern of God's heavenly abode (Heb.8:5; 9:23,24), but they also represented the Garden of Eden in which our first parents were placed. When one reads the early chapters of Genesis carefully, it will be noticed that there is a distinct "Temple imagery" associated with almost every event or item of interest. For example, we are told that God appeared in the Garden "at the cool of the day" (Gen.3:8). This time of day answers to the period of the evening sacrifice in the Temple (I Kings 18:36; Dan.9:21). While Adam and Eve were talking to God, they were considered in the *presence* of God (Gen.3:8), just as one who was in the Temple was also in the *presence* of God (II Chron.20:19). And where was the Tree of Life in the Garden of Eden? It was in the midst (Gen.2:9). Significantly, in the Holy of Holies in the Tabernacle there was the rod of Aaron which represented the Tree of Life. The rest of the Garden area of Eden (other than where God talked to Adam and Eve) was analogous to the outer Holy Place of the Temple where only the priests could enter. And in this Holy Place in the Tabernacle (and later Temples) was the seven branched lampstand which was a replica of the Tree of Life.

But Adam and Eve sinned by eating the forbidden fruit from the Tree of the Knowledge of Good and Evil (Bad). They were then expelled *eastward* from the Garden (note that the entrance to the Garden was from the *east*) (Gen. 3:22-24). Cherubim were positioned at this eastern portal to prevent re-entry to the Garden. This was to keep Adam and Eve from the Tree of Life. The rest of the story of what happened to Cain and Abel is recorded in chapter seventeen of this book.

What we need to recognize, however, is that the Tree of Life was reckoned by the early Jews to have been the *almond tree.* And early Christians considered the tree on which Christ was crucified as being the Tree of Life. Since Christ was crucified on a literal tree, could it have been an *almond?*

"Early Christian art indicates a close relationship between *the tree of life* and the cross. The cross of Christ, the wood of suffering and death, is for Christians a *tree of life.* In the tomb paintings of the 2nd century it is thus depicted for the first time as the symbol of victory over death. It then recurs again and again. The idea that the *living* trunk of the cross bears *twigs* and *leaves* is a common motif in Christian antiquity" (Kittel, *Theological Dictionary,* V, pp.49,41 italics mine).

If the Tree of Life motif is to be followed in detail, then the most logical tree would have been "the tree of the priesthood" -- the almond. There are presently a number of almond trees growing on the slopes of Olivet and it is feasible for three men to be impaled on the larger ones.

Some have thought that the tree of crucifixion might be the olive. While the olive has a great deal of symbolic significance in the Scriptures, it is unlikely to be the Tree of Life. As is well known, olives cannot be eaten directly from the tree because of the extreme bitter taste of uncured olives. But in all symbolic contexts of the Bible which concern the Tree of Life, not only can its fruit be eaten from the tree but even its leaves are useful (cf. Rev.22:2). In Christian symbolism, the real "fruit" of the Tree of Life is symbolically represented as the "flesh of Christ" (John 6:51-58). He was the actual "edible part" that all people must consume in order to inherit everlasting life. The life-giving fruit hanging on that symbolic Tree of Life (represented by the almond tree?) was reckoned by early Christians as the spiritual "fruit" of immortality (John 6:51ff).

If the almond tree was figuratively associated with the

Tree of Life, what was the other significant tree in the Garden of Eden -- the Tree of the Knowledge of Good and Evil? While many different types of trees have been guessed (the pomegranate, date, grape and even the apple), the only tree mentioned in the context of Genesis describing the "fall" is the *fig.* It is to be noted that as soon as Adam and Eve knew they had sinned, they sewed fig leaves together to hide their shame. It is well documented among the Jews that this was the Tree of the Knowledge of Good and Evil.

"What was the tree of which Adam and Eve ate? Rabbi Yosi says: It was the fig tree. . .the fig whereof he ate the fruit opened its doors and took him in" (Midrash, *Bereshith Raba*, 15,7).

"The fig leaf which brought remorse to the world" (*ibid.*, 19,11).

"The tree of which the first man ate. . .Rabbi Nehemiah says: It was the fig, the thing wherewith they were spoilt, yet were they redressed by it. As it is said: And they stitched a fig-leaf" (*Berahot* 40a, and see *Sanhedrin* 70a).

In the non-canonical Book of Adam and Eve (20:5) it says:

"I sought a leaf to cover up my nakedness and found none, for, when I ate, the leaves withered off every tree in my plot except for the fig, and from it I took leaves and it made me a girdle, *even from the tree of which I ate.*"

Thus the fig tree was believed to represent the Tree of the Knowledge of Good and Evil. Some might ask at this juncture: What difference does it make? Granted, it may seem like an exercise in futility and unnecessary speculation. But this would be a mistake. The fact is, the symbol of the fig tree as being the "evil" tree in the Garden of Eden, figures in a prominent episode that occurred during the week just before Christ was crucified. Once the symbolic meaning of the fig tree is recognized, then this special event can make a great deal of doctrinal sense in regard to the role that Christ played in expelling "sin" from the world. I am talking about the time when he saw a fig tree on the Mount of Olives as he was approaching Jerusalem, and he cursed it. Before that day was over that particular fig tree was withered up and completely dead. This has a remarkable figurative meaning to it.

What happened to that fig tree four days before Christ's crucifixion has a real bearing on the symbolism of the crucifixion itself. This can be shown because we now know that Christ was executed on the Mount of Olives. The interesting thing is, the cursing of the fig tree and the impaling of Christ to another tree (not a short distance away) has a remarkable parallel theme to events that occurred in the Garden of Eden with our first parents. Let us see how this is shown.

Four days before his crucifixion, Christ left Bethany and started walking towards Jerusalem. When he was near the summit of the Mount of Olives, he noticed on the side of the road a *fig tree*. He went over to it and finding no figs on its branches (but the tree was covered with leaves), he cursed *that* fig tree and said: "Let no man eat fruit from you henceforth forever. And his disciples heard it" (Mark 11:14). The *cursing* of that particular fig tree has baffled men ever since. The truth is, even Mark said that "it was not the season of figs" (verse 13). Indeed, it went further than that. *It was not even the time for fig trees to have leaves!* It has puzzled people for generations why Christ was so upset with a fig tree that by nature should not have had figs or leaves!

It is certain that the whole event was a miracle from start to finish. To produce a sign of this nature must have involved a great deal of symbolic importance. If it were not of major significance then the event makes little sense and certainly there would be little relevance for its occurrence. But it does have symbolic meaning.

The fact that the fig tree had leaves was in itself a miracle because leaves would not have naturally been on the fig tree for at least a month later. Also, there should not have been any figs on the tree. Since the tree was located on a main thoroughfare into Jerusalem and with the heavy population around the city at that Passover season, it is not to be imagined that Christ expected to find a few dried figs of last year's crop on the branches. The tree would surely have been stripped clean of its fruit. Christ must have known that he would not find any figs on this unusual fig tree. The truth is, however, the lack of figs and the abundance of leaves were important factors in a miraculous occurrence. In this scene we are provided with a most important symbolic teaching by Christ with his actions.

Note that the next day after Christ's cursing, the disciples found it *withered* (Mark 11: 20,22; Matt.19:19,20). What was significant about this? It meant that the type of tree that Adam and Eve first ate which brought sin and death to them (and in an extended sense to all humanity) was now *withered* and *dead*.

Tradition had it that the only tree under Adam's care in the Garden of Eden that did not shed its leaves after our first parents took of the fruit was the fig tree. It was the Tree of the Knowledge of Good and Evil. But with Christ's miracle on the Mount of Olives, it meant *that* symbolic tree was now withered and dead. It signified that no longer would that symbolic tree be in the midst of humanity to encourage mankind to sin in the manner of our first parents. But there is even more teaching. It meant that when Christ went to that miraculous tree looking for some figs to eat (like Eve did), Christ could not find any whatsoever! This signified that there was not going to be a repitition of what Eve (and later Adam) did in regard to the fig tree that they partook of. One fig tree was the instrument to bring "sin" into the world, but the Son of God could not find any figs on his fig tree (the miraculous tree on the Mount of Olives that was typical of the Tree of the Knowledge of Good and Evil). Christ cursed *that* symbolic tree at the top of Olivet so that no man would eat of it again. And to complete his victory over sin, four days later Christ was going to be sacrificed for the sins of the world just a few yards away from this *withered* and *dead* tree.

What Christ was doing in the last week of his life on earth was acting out a symbolic victory over all the factors in the Garden of Eden around which our first parents failed. The Tree of the Knowledge of Good and Evil was now *withered* and *dead* and the Tree of Life a short distance away (probably an *almond* for the symbol to be carried out fully) became the very tree on which Christ was crucified. This did not take place within the former area of the Garden of Eden located hundreds of miles northeast of Jerusalem, nor did it occur inside the Temple which typified the Garden and Eden. The miracle of these two trees happened "in the midst of the world" (near the outside Miphkad Altar which represented the altar promised to Cain and his descendants at the top of the Mount of Olives). The two trees on Olivet symbolized those two principal trees in the Garden of Eden.

Of course, all these matters we have been discussing are *symbols*. They must be understood in the allegorical and mystical sense. But even those scholars who demand actual historical data as the only criteria for belief still recognize that Christians in the first century were thoroughly convinced in the spiritual messages embedded within the figurative teachings of the Bible. As a matter of fact, it can be stated without fear of contradiction that every major doctrine of Christianity is in some way dependent upon symbolic teachings, including all facets on interpretation concerning the crucifixion of Christ. One cannot begin to grasp what the principles of Christianity really entail without the use of symbolic illustrations. It makes no difference if we of modern times approve or disapprove the application of such teachings, no one will find any meaning to Christianity without the recognition and understanding of biblical symbols.

This certainly applies to the spiritual significance surrounding the purpose of Christ's crucifixion. Every ritualistic, geographical and chronological detail associated with the crucifixion is symbolically full of meaning. It is not possible to comprehend the New Testament teachings concerning this matter without taking into consideration the figurative meanings. In reality, the physical details are always given in the Bible to support the symbolic teachings. With this in mind let us carry the symbolic teaching of Christ's crucifixion a little farther.

Mention has been made in chapter fourteen of this book that Christ was crucified on a tree with two robbers also affixed to the same tree. This would have meant that there were six arms extending upwards around the tree itself. This scene could provide a symbolic spectacle of a living Menorah (the seven branched lampstand). The Menorah did in fact represent the Tree of Life and the Light of the World. And notice the irony of the crucifixion scene. Here was Christ east of the Holy of Holies and looking westwards towards the curtain of his Father's House. Beyond that curtain were supposed to be a mercy seat (denoting the Throne of God) with the wings of two cherubim outstretched over that throne. Both cherubim were made to face one another and to face the One who symbolically sat on the mercy seat. These were found in the original Temple within the inner curtain of the Holy Place.

Now look at the scene of the crucifixion "outside the camp." It was a significant reversal to what was originally designed by God to be within the Holy of Holies. Here was the real Lord being crucified on a tree having two robbers as his "cherubim" with their arms stretched upwards and their faces turned away from him in the opposite direction. And if the tree of crucifixion were an almond, we have Christ and the two robbers being sacrificed on the tree that Philo called "the tree of the priesthood." It represented the Tree of Life.

Their six arms extending upwards around a central trunk of a tree (the trunk being the seventh "arm") could be reckoned a symbol of a *living Menorah.* Christ was pictured after his resurrection as standing in the midst of the seven branched lampstand (Rev.1:3) in a glorious and living existence with all the power of the universe at his beck and call. Was his crucifixion intended to show an opposite signification on a "Menorah" of degradation and shame? Whereas he should have been sitting on the mercy seat in the Holy of Holies, he was in a diametrically contrary situation as a sin offering being crucified near the *outside* altar of the Sanctuary. The scene, from the Christian point of view, would have been totally opposite from what should have been.

If there is anything to this symbolism, then the national symbol of the modern State of Israel (the seven branched lampstand) represents Christ being crucified between two robbers (his "cherubim") for the sins of the world. This would mean that the Menorah is the symbolic crucifix of Christ, not the kind that is normally seen in Christian society today. The representation of the cross (and its various forms) that most Christians look to today (atop churches, around peoples' necks, and even embossed on Bibles) is made of two pieces of dry (not *living*) wood which could have no connection to the *living* Tree of Life.

And further, the people who were carrying their Passover lambs to be killed in the Temple at the time of Christ's crucifixion were turning their backs on the individual to whom they were intending to present those Passover lambs. This is because the roadway that led to the eastern gate of the Temple was descending from the top of the Mount of Olives. The people would have passed directly by Christ hanging on a tree of crucifixion. And while worshippers were entering the Temple to pay tribute to the One sitting within the Holy of Holies (originally enthroned between two cherubim), the crowds were actually turning their backs on the real Christ from heaven and his two "cherubim" (the robbers nailed to the same tree with their backs to him as well). And when Christ finally died on the tree (while all had their backs to him), he cried out: "My God, My God, why have you forsaken me?" This means that God the Father himself (momentarily) also turned his face away from him. Christ Jesus truly died *rejected* -- rejected by all including the Father himself! This is because in symbol he was carrying all the sins of the world on his back when he found himself in that final sacrificial position.

But this doesn't end it. There is another symbolic parallel to the events of the crucifixion that should be mentioned. It was then the custom in Jerusalem of releasing a notable prisoner during the season of Passover. Pilate wanted to restore Jesus to the people, but they demanded that he release a man called Barabbas. This person was a prominent prisoner (Matt.27:16) who had been charged with the crimes of sedition and murder (Mark 15:7; Luke 23:18,19). This could well mean that he was some kind of revolutionary hero to the Jews -- one who endeavored to overthrow the Roman yoke and bring in the expected Jewish domination over the Middle East and the world. Whatever the reason, the authorities in Jerusalem requested and received the release of Barabbas.

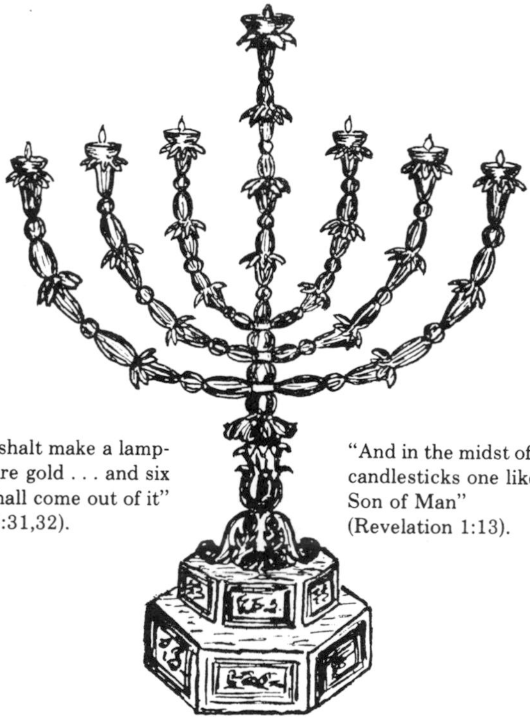

"And thou shalt make a lampstand of pure gold . . . and six branches shall come out of it" (Exodus 25:31,32).

"And in the midst of the seven candlesticks one like unto the Son of Man" (Revelation 1:13).

It is not usually understood by the general public but the Menorah (the seven branched lampstand which was deposited in the Holy Place of the Tabernacle) actually denotes a living tree — a Tree of Light. Indeed, its prime significance is its relation to the Tree of Life which was found not only in the Garden of Eden but is talked about in the concluding book of the Bible, the Book of Revelation. The symbolic motif of the lampstand was that of an almond tree. Just as Aaron's rod that budded and brought forth fruit was an almond, so likewise (as we have shown in this book) the Menorah denotes an allegorical almond tree. It may well be that Christ and the two robbers were actually crucified on such an almond tree. If so, then Christ ironically died on the tree that represented the Tree of Life.

Now to an interesting point in regard to this Barabbas. In some important manuscripts of Matthew 27:16,17 Barabbas is given a first name. Ironically, it was *Jesus!* The fact that there were biblical texts that called *Barabbas* by his first name *Jesus* was noted by Origen (early third century). It was Origen's opinion that it was not proper to call him *Jesus* because he was not aware of any sinner in Scripture who had ever been called by such an august name. The truth is, however, the majority of scholars who comprised the United Bible Societies' committee to judge the genuineness of New Testament texts believed that *Jesus Barabbas* was the original reading (Metzger, *Textual Commentary*, pp.67,68).

This information provides us with more ironical comparisons. The name "Barabbas" was a title and meant: "The Son of the Father." In this case, the name signified "The Son of the High Father" (like that which Paul used in Romans 8:15 and Galatians 4:6 where he referred to God as "Abba, Father"). It was also used by Christ on the eve of his crucifixion: "Abba, Father, all things are possible unto you; take away this cup from me: nevertheless not what I will, but what you will" (Mark 14:36). The word "Abba" in these usages signified *the Exalted Father*, and meant none other than God the Father. Thus, the name and title of Barabbas, by interpretation, meant: "Jesus, the Son of the High Father."

What a paradox! Here were two men. One was a seditionist and murderer and the other the sinless Son of God -- and *both* with the same name and title. And who did the authorities choose to be released? They selected the criminal, while the Jesus who was the actual "Son of the High Father" was led out to be crucified between two robbers.

The recording of this unique situation may have been intended by the writers of the New Testament to show the fulfillment of a most unusual ritual that occurred on the Day of Atonement. On that day two identical goats were selected. There was not the slightest difference between them as far as appearance was concerned. They were brought into the Temple and lots were drawn over them. One became a goat designated as "the Lord's" and the other was "the Azazel" (the goat of the evil one). The goat selected to be "the Lord's" was killed, its blood sprinkled in the Holy of Holies and its carcase was taken to the Miphkad Altar on the Mount of Olives and burnt to ashes (Lev.16:27). The other goat was led away into the wilderness by the hand of a fit man and let go alive in that desolate area as commanded in the original Law of Moses (Lev.16:20-22).

Now look at the remarkable similarity between these two identical goats and the two men standing before Pilate. Both had the same first name and title. Strangely, the people picked *Jesus Barabbas* the seditionist and murderer (and they let him go free), but the real *Jesus Barabbas* (the actual Son of God the Father in heaven) they led out the eastern gate of the Temple (the easiest way to reach the two-tiered bridge over the Kidron Valley from the Antonia) and up to the summit of the Mount of Olives where they executed him. The parallel of Jesus to the sin offering of the "Lord's goat" on the Day of Atonement is too close to be coincidental. But this symbol can only be understood if it is realized that Christ was crucified on the Mount of Olives.

But there is yet another incident that happened on the day of Christ's crucifixion that has ritualistic significance to it. It is the fulfillment of a major part of the sacrificial services that were performed in the Temple. It concerns the role that Judas Iscariot played in the drama of that day. Let us notice this matter carefully.

We are told by Christ that Judas was selected to be one of the apostles even though it was known by Christ that he was an adversary (a *devil*). "Jesus answered them, Have not I chosen you twelve, and one of you is a devil?" (John 6:70). This recognition by Christ was stated a full year before he was betrayed by Judas. The New Testament writers show that it was Satan who inspired Judas to perform his deed at that Passover season. "And supper being ended, the devil *having now put into the heart* of Judas Iscariot, Simon's son, to betray him" (John 13:2).

Be this as it may, why was Judas picked by Christ for the role that he played? If one will look closely at the text of the New Testament it shows that Judas was not a common person such as a fisherman or a tax collector. Judas was actually a high ranking ecclesiastical official. He *was a priest of the line of Aaron*! This can be proved by paying close attention to what the New Testament says of him.

Note that after Judas betrayed Christ to the chief priests, they gave him thirty pieces of silver to hand Jesus over to them when there were no crowds around that might prevent his arrest (Luke 22:6). Later, when Judas had realized what he had done (and became remorseful for it), he took those coins to the Temple and threw them over the floor of the *naos* (a Greek word meaning the *holy place* into which only Aaronic priests could enter) (Matt.27:5). *But note this!* The original Greek of a large number of New Testament manuscripts on Matthew 27:5 says that Judas scattered the coins while *in* the holy place (see *The Greek New Testament*, UBS, p.108). This verse shows that Judas was *inside* a part of the Temple which was reserved only for priests. It means that Judas was in fact *a priest.* But that is not all.

The best reading of Mark 14:10 shows that Judas was more than an ordinary apostle. He was "*the one of the twelve*." This expression gave Judas a preeminence among the apostles. Prof. Wright (*Synopsis of the Gospels in Greek*, p.31) was of the belief that Mark makes Judas "the chief of the apostles." Field, the New Testament scholar in his *Notes on the Translation of the New Testament*, said Mark meant that Judas was "the *first* (that is number one) of the apostles." This may be going a little too far, but even the *Dictionary of Christ and the Gospels* (vol.I.p.908) states that Mark's definition gave Judas some kind of priority.

This makes sense if Judas was an Aaronic priest. The authorities among the Israelites of the first century, as far as spiritual offices were concerned, were *first*, priests, *second*, Levites, and *third* were the ordinary Israelites (see Christ's Good Samaritan parable of Luke 10:30-37 for a use of this type of ranking). This fact concerning the preeminence of priests can explain the puzzle of who sat on Christ's left side and right side at the Last Supper. We know that John sat on one side because he was able to hear Christ whisper a statement to Judas Iscariot that the other apostles did not hear, and we are told he was reclining in Christ's bosom

(John 13:26) -- compare John 13:26-28 where it shows how John was the only one who heard distinctly what Christ said to Judas. This indicates that Judas sat *next to Christ* on the opposite side of John. And since it was customary for priests to have top positions at festivals or other functions, this shows that Judas (as a priest) was no doubt on Christ's right side! This makes his crime even more heinous. One of the persons ordained in the Old Testament to be an official representative for God was the very person to betray Christ! Many are familiar with a common epithet that signifies the ecclesiastical rank of Judas. It is: "*Judas Priest.*" These historical evidences show that Judas was in fact a priest.

But what has this to do with the rituals of the Temple and the crucifixion of Christ? Very much indeed. In the primary sin offering for the sins of a priest, a bullock was killed at the Altar of Burnt Offering at the entrance to the Holy Place and some of its blood was taken *into the Holy Place and sprinkled before the inner curtain of the Temple* (Lev.4:6). A similar sin offering was that for the whole congregation of Israel (verse 17). The carcases of these sin offerings were then taken up to the Miphkad Altar at the summit of Olivet and there they were burnt to ashes (Lev.4:12,21).

With this in mind, we need to ask how the blood of those two sin offerings could represent the blood of Christ in his atoning sacrifice for sin because Christ's literal blood was not taken into the Holy Place and sprinkled before the inner curtain? No, but the thirty shekels that Judas obtained (no doubt from monies deposited in the Temple treasury) were reckoned by the chief priests to be "blood money" (Matt.27:6-8). Importantly, we have seen in Matthew 27:5 that Judas the priest scattered the thirty shekels (representing the blood of Christ) while he was *within* the very Holy Place where the priests sprinkled the blood of the sin offerings which we have just mentioned (Lev.4:1-21). This would have been, in a symbolic sense, an official sprinkling of the blood of Christ by an ordained priest (Judas) within the very place ordained by Moses. Again, the symbolic parallel is too close for these circumstances to be coincidental. At least the apostles must have understood that this was a priestly requirement of the Law of Moses that was being carried out by Judas the priest. The author of the Book of Hebrews in his account of Christ's crucifixion mentioned the typical significance of the "blood brought within the sanctuary" (Heb.13:11). And, as a priest, Judas would have had the authority to bring the blood of the sin offerings into that Holy Place (Lev.4:5,6).

One more thing should be mentioned. There is one parallel between the Temple sacrifices and Christ's trial and crucifixion in one important ritual that took place on the Day of Atonement that *was not* fulfilled in a figurative sense by the High Priest or by other priests at the time of Christ's ordeal. That was taking the blood of the sin offerings on the Day of Atonement into the Holy of Holies (Lev.16). But even this type was fulfilled by Christ. This important figurative teaching was not accomplished by a surrogate priest on behalf of Christ or on behalf of the nation of Israel. It was done by Christ himself. The author of the Book of Hebrews says that this single most important ritual was reserved to be fulfilled by Christ himself. Instead of going with his own blood into the Holy of Holies located in the Temple on earth, we are told that after his resurrection Christ took a portion of his own blood and went into heaven and sprinkled the celestial Holy of Holies with his own purifying blood right at the place where God the Father was seated on his throne of glory and that the Father accepted it as valid (Heb.9: 12,23,24). With this final act of Christ, *all* the sacrificial rituals associated with the Tabernacle and Temple were fulfilled precisely by the ordained Son of God as far as the New Testament writers were concerned.

What is important for us to realize is that all of these remarkable symbolic parallels (which were no doubt very impressive to the apostles and early Christians) can only be understood as fulfilled precisely if it is realized that Christ was judged on the Temple Mount and that he was crucified on the Mount of Olives.

20

"What Difference Does It Make?"

What difference does it make *where* Christ was judged by the Sanhedrin and *where* he was crucified? It is sometimes thought (even by people who love the biblical revelation) that as long as Christ was in fact judged, crucified and resurrected from the dead then it is non-essential to determine *where* those events took place. But for all of you who have read this book up to this chapter, I would hope that you can now realize that it makes all the difference in the world! One of the most important subjects in biblical study is to know the exact geographical areas where Christ's passion occurred. Once these true sites are recognized, then whole sections of doctrinal material in the Old and New Testaments (hitherto unrealized) as well as historical accounts of the early Christian Church (which have not been referred to by most historians) become much more understandable. By solving these "Secrets of Golgotha," we find that many mysteries of the biblical revelation become plain.

It makes a great deal of difference to know the true geographical sites associated with Christ's trial and crucifixion. For one thing it shows that the many wars over the centuries that have been fought between Christians and Christians, Christians and Moslems, and squabbles between Moslems and Jews over many of the holy sites in Jerusalem were fought for *the wrong places!* Even to this very hour we find open hostility among the above groups, and still for the most part they are fighting for *the wrong places!* Perhaps, if nothing more, the information in this book might cause people of today to sit back and survey the futility of those wars of the past and the fighting that is presently going on for control of the religious sites in the city of Jerusalem.

There is one great advantage that the information in this book can afford to Christians. If this evidence is taken seriously, then the present arguments over who controls various parts of the Church of the Holy Sepulchre could cease. The fact is, it is the *wrong* place! The best credentials for the site of Christ's burial and resurrection is the *cave/tomb* under the ruins of the Eleona Church which is presently in the control of the Carmelite Convent at the Pater Noster Church. This fact has some interesting ramifications associated with it. It signifies that the Roman Catholic Church has full control of what most Christians reckon as the holiest spot in all Christendom. It could be interpreted that God has placed in their hands the care of Christ's tomb. It is remarkable that it is the Carmelite Order that is allowed to have this privilege. That Order traditionally has its origin with Elijah the prophet and such eminent personalities as Elisha and John the Baptist (so the Carmelites believe) have been members of that Order. It may be looked on as significant in some circles that the "Elijahan Order" of the Roman Church has been given full control of the holiest of Christian shrines! There are prophecies in the Bible that Elijah, or the spirit of Elijah, would be in operation just prior to the Second Advent of Christ to restore all things (Matt.17:10,11) and that John the Baptist was a similar precursor for Christ's first advent (verse 12). The apostle Peter made the definitive prophecy that such a restoration of essential knowledge would occur before Christ's return from heaven (Acts 3:19-21). The prophecy of Malachi in the Old Testament stated the same thing (Mal.4:4-6).

Whatever the case, it is interesting that the Carmelite Order of the Roman Catholic Church has sole proprietorship of the *real* Holy Sepulchre which has been hidden from the knowledge of the world over the centuries. And who better to have control of this significant site (as Catholics would no doubt view it) than the very Order which traditionally has its origin with Elijah himself and having as one of its members a person of no less esteem than John the Baptist? It could well be that some ecclesiastical leaders may see more importance to these matters than I do. As for me, my profession is that of a historian and I have no religious interest in holy places on earth. Such things are only of archaeological and historical relevance to me. Though I take pleasure in visiting them (and even honoring them because others do), they are only of academic interest to me. Still, the sites contain a great deal of spiritual symbolism associated with them. In my view it is important to determine the true locations since such symbolism can give us of modern times a better comprehension of the messages in the Gospel. For that reason I am happy to present this historical research to the general public.

But now that it is shown that the present Church of the Holy Sepulchre and the Garden Tomb area are *not* authentic as the "Golgotha" of Christ, what should one do in regard to these sites? They are revered by millions upon millions of people. All I can do, for what it's worth, is to give my personal opinion. From my point of view I see no reason why these two sites cannot be honored and respected as memorials for Christ's burial and resurrection. There may be biblical evidence to allow this. In the time of Christ even the Tomb of Rachel was located just outside Bethlehem (where it is still situated to this day), but the Old Testament makes it clear that her actual tomb was at least ten miles north of Bethlehem. I have explained this in detail in a research paper titled *The Tomb of Rachel* (available from A.S.K.). The present tomb of Rachel is thus a cenotaph (a memorial to a dead person buried elsewhere) and the Church of the Holy Sepulchre or the Garden Tomb sites could be equally honored. It would only be right, however, that those who might continue to honor those places should tell Christians that they are only cenotaphs and that Christ was actually buried and resurrected from the dead at the *cave/tomb* underneath the ruins of the Eleona Church on the Mount of Olives.

And indeed, what about the *real* Holy Sepulchre on Olivet? Will it be preserved by God for all time as a memorial of the true site of the holiest occurrence ever to happen on earth? The truth is, even that place itself will be utterly destroyed into insignificance when Christ returns from heaven. "And his feet shall stand in that day upon the Mount of Olives, which is before Jerusalem on the east, and the Mount of Olives shall cleave in the midst thereof toward the east and toward the west, and there shall be a very great valley; and half of the mountain shall remove toward the north, and half of it toward the south" (Zech.14:4). It seems that God himself is not interested in the preservation of "holy places" on earth -- even though they be the holiest! In the final analysis, physical things on earth appear to be of relative unimportance in the eyes of God when compared to spiritual matters dealing with the heart.

As a final point, let me say that the research in this book is not intended to change the religious thinking of people. I am simply endeavoring to show the historical and biblical evidences that identify the exact spot of Calvary (which was located at the site of the Imbomon at the southern summit of Olivet and now under control of the Moslem authorities) and also the actual place of Christ's burial and resurrection (which the Roman Catholic Church controls at the Eleona church). But what people do with these matters in regard to their personal religious lives is their business, not mine or anyone else's. I do feel, however, that a reasonable case has been made that Christ's passion took place near the southern summit of the Mount of Olives. And I have not the slightest doubt that this is correct! But if readers of this book can show me where I am wrong, I will honor their criticisms and thank them for their help.

In closing, I wish to make a last comment. It is my opinion that finding the true locations for the trial, crucifixion and resurrection of Christ *makes all the difference in the world* in recognizing what the real teaching of the Gospel of Christ is all about! And when the "Secrets of Golgotha" are revealed to everyone's knowledge a new dimension in New Testament understanding will emerge on the scene.

Epilogue

Why is it that many of the significant points of evidence to show that Christ was crucified on the Mount of Olives have not been realized before? This is a good question. Before August, 1983 I did not recognize a single one of the major factors shown in this book which identifies Olivet as the crucifixion site. About two years before, I noticed that the apostle John used the word *stauros* in the singular number to describe the instrument on which Christ and the two robbers were executed (John 19:31), but because it seemed absurd to imagine that three men could have been crucified together on one Latin cross (which it is), I dismissed the matter as a grammatical oddity without any significance. Indeed, about three weeks before discovering that the phrase "the Place of the City" (near where Christ was crucified) meant the Temple, I had a rather intense discussion with a friend (J.M.Gray) who was insistent that the New Testament said Christ was crucified on a literal *tree* and not two pieces of dead wood nailed together in the form of a Latin or Greek cross. At the time I was adamant that the Greek word for "tree" (*xylon*) (used in the crucifixion contexts) only meant some dry pieces of wood (and in some contexts within Greek literature it does have that meaning). Though Ms. Gray was unable to convince me at the time, it wasn't long until I found out she was right. After all, Christ used the word *xylon* for a living tree at the very time of his crucifixion (Luke 23:32) and the "Tree of Life" in the Book of Revelation was certainly a *living* tree. Thus, it finally became simple to see that Christ and the two robbers were nailed to a single tree -- the singular *stauros* that the apostle John referred to (John 19:31).

Within a matter of two days of understanding that "the Place of the City" was the Temple, I was able to piece together the essential teachings which are now found in this book to identify the Mount of Olives with the crucifixion site. Mr. Ken Fischer, my executive assistant at the time, wrote an editorial explaining how this biblical matter was finally understood. He wrote: "The key to the new discovery came to his [Dr. Martin's] attention while writing a chapter on the crucifixion for his new book, *The Original Bible Restored*. He decided to make a final analysis of all the scriptures pertaining to Christ's death. All appeared in order until he read John 19:20. It was a footnote regarding this verse that aroused his interest. The Greek actually said that Christ was crucified near *the Place of the City*. By checking other sources, he came to the realization that *the Place of the City* was the Temple! This meant Christ was crucified near the holy Temple! The importance of this indication had not been realized before. With this new clue, the doors began to really open up. It took only a short time to realize that to be near the Temple but outside Jerusalem could only be on the city's east side. And, for the Roman centurion to see the Temple curtain tear in two at the exact time of Christ's death meant that those at the crucifixion scene had to be standing on an elevated site looking westward into the Holy Place. This placed the crucifixion on the Mount of Olives -- the only place outside the city where the Temple curtain could be observed! He explained his findings to other staff members and friends of FBR [the organization of which I was then president]. They then pitched in to supply many corroborative evidences. Mr. Gary Arvidson supplied much typical teaching. Leona McNair connected *Golgotha* with a numbering of Israel (Numbers 1) along with the Miphkad altar of Ezekiel 43:21 which must have been connected with the Miphkad Gate of Nehemiah 3:31. Dr. Martin thought it was now time to show that Christ's crucifixion was on a living tree" (comments in brackets are mine).

Since that time many people (scholars and lay persons alike) have read the basic material in this book and have given further suggestions to make the historical research much clearer and understandable. One of these who has been of constant help with his constructive criticisms and comments has been David Sielaff on the staff of Fuller Theological Seminary here in Pasadena. He pointed out to me that Professor Glenn F. Chesnut in his informative work

"The First Christian Histories" recounted that "Constantine was a man who saw visions with considerable regularity--not just occasionally, *but thousands of them*" (p.172, second edition, emphases mine). This indication by Chesnut made me examine in detail the history surrounding Constantine and Eusebius the Bishop of Caesarea. This was of inestimable value. It showed that the Temple of Venus was selected as the spot of Christ's crucifixion because of visions, dreams and signs, *not* because of sound historical or archaeological evidence.

Most people realize that one of the biggest problems in discovering any truth is our resistance to change the traditionalism adopted by our societies. This is something that none of us can avoid. Our minds from youth have become so wedded to what society around us believes to be correct (whether academic or not). All of us by nature are reluctant to "rock the boat" in most things we have grown up with. It is truly unpleasant (and in some cases quite devastating) to discover that some of our traditional beliefs are not what we thought them to be. Many of us, including myself, have endeavored to maintain the traditions which are common to us all. It is a most difficult thing having to admit that our forefathers whom we love could possibly be wrong. More important than that, it is the opinions of our present colleagues and our desire to maintain an economic security within the academic or religious society with which we are attached that impedes a free and unhampered attitude of research. I have personally been worried in the past what my academic friends would say of me if I publish new historical teachings which go contrary to accepted belief. Really, the whole thing is scary because not only is one's prestige in jeopardy of being eroded away by critical colleagues, but even the economic security of maintaining a job (whether it be in a university, seminary or within a church administration) is a definite factor in trying to maintain the concepts which society accepts. The change of one's cherished beliefs is at best a disquieting experience and at worst it can be a traumatic event if one loses friends, loved ones and the security of a job over it. However, is presenting the truth (or what one believes to be the truth) worth the risk? That is a question each of us individually must ask.

It is my belief, however, that the biblical and historical information in this book should be seriously considered, whether we are mainline or evangelical Protestants, Catholics of various persuasions, charismatics and/or members of various ethnic churches. The curse against any new research (and the greatest enemy of truth) is mankind's utter devotion to, and their love for, the cult of *traditionalism*.

As a note of gratitude, I must mention that this book could not have been produced without the support and encouragement of a wonderful group of people who are associated with the Academy for Scriptural Knowledge of which I am the director. No one could ask for finer individuals to be friends and supporters. I also wish to thank my son, Samuel, for his constant efforts in helping to make the contents of this book readable and comprehensive, and also a deep appreciation goes to my wife, Ramona Jean, for her encouragement, wise criticisms and patience with me while this book was in preparation.

As a closing comment, I wish to say that I have not tried, in a deliberate manner, to create new interpretations for the sake of shocking people or to overthrow any belief which Christians have accepted over the centuries. My intent is simply to publish what appears to me to be right. My quest has been to make the "Secrets of Golgotha" understandable and appreciated by people today. True scholarship involves the sincere wish to weed out the errors that we are all plagued with and to accept new understandings with a humility of thankfulness. In this spirit I am submitting this research to those who are interested. My best critics will be those who show me, and the rest of the world, just where the truth lies. I close with a quote from a man I admire very much for his academic excellence and his friendly criticisms.

"...we must bear in mind that the cause of learning has often been promoted by scholars who are prepared to take a risk and expose their brain-waves to the pitiless criticisms of others" (F.F.Bruce, "Modern Studies on the Judean Scrolls," *CT*,1 (11):5).

This is a photograph of the small Moslem Shrine situated at the very top of the southern summit of the Mount of Olives. Somewhere within twenty or thirty yards of this building is where Christ Jesus was crucified. It is most interesting that it is the Moslem authorities who have been graced with the preservation of this spot. Because of this there are no icons or pictures of deity anywhere on the grounds. It is a beautiful and significant site which is a pleasure to visit. Certainly, all who go to Jerusalem should see this area for its historic value. (Photo: Professor William S. LaSor)

Select Bibliography

Barnes, T., *Constantine and Eusebius*, (Harvard: University Press) 1981

Bruce, F.F., *New Testament History* (London: Oliphants) 1971

Chesnut, G.F., *The First Christian Histories* (Macon: Mercer University Press) 1986

Cohen, A., *Everyman's Talmud* (New York: Dutton) 1949

Cornfeld, G. (Mazar, B., Maier, P.L.), *The Jewish War* (Grand Rapids: Zondervan) 1982

Danby, H., *The Mishnah* (Oxford: University Press) 1958

Edersheim, A., *Life and Times of Jesus the Messiah* (New York: Longmans) 1896

Eusebius, *Ecclesiastical History* (Minneapolis: Augsburg) 1965

Eusebius, *Preparation of the Gospel* and *Proof of the Gospel* (Grand Rapids: Baker) 1981

Finegan, J., *The Archeology of the New Testament* (Princeton: University Press) 1969

Frend, W.H.C., *Martyrdom and Persecution in the Early Church* (Grand Rapids: Baker) 1981

Hunt, E.D., *Holy Land Pilgrimage in the Late Roman Empire* (Oxford: Clarendon) 1982

Maier, J., *The Temple Scroll* (Editors: Clines, J.A. and Davis, P.R.) (Sheffield: University Press) 1985

Mazar, B., *The Mountain of the Lord* (New York: Doubleday) 1975

McBirnie, W.S., *The Search for the Authentic Tomb of Jesus* (Montrose: Acclaimed Books) 1975

Schurer, E., (New English Version: *History of the Jewish People in the Age of Jesus Christ,* Vermes, Millar, Black) (Edinburgh: T. & T. Clark) 1979

Thompson, J.A., *The Bible and Archaeology* (Grand Rapids: Eerdmans) 1982

Wilkinson, J., *The Jerusalem Jesus Knew* (Nahsville: Nelson) 1978

Wilkinson, J., *Egeria's Travels* (Jerusalem: Ariel) 1981

Yadin, Y., *The Temple Scroll* (New York: Random) 1985

Yarden, L., *The Tree of Light* (London: East & West Lib.) c.1975